OECD PROCEEDINGS

INDUSTRIAL COMPETITIVENESS IN THE KNOWLEDGE-BASED ECONOMY

The New Role of Governments

ORGANISATION FOR ECONOMIC CO-OPERATION AND DEVELOPMENT

ORGANISATION FOR ECONOMIC CO-OPERATION AND DEVELOPMENT

Pursuant to Article 1 of the Convention signed in Paris on 14th December 1960, and which came into force on 30th September 1961, the Organisation for Economic Co-operation and Development (OECD) shall promote policies designed:

- to achieve the highest sustainable economic growth and employment and a rising standard of living in Member countries, while maintaining financial stability, and thus to contribute to the development of the world economy;
- to contribute to sound economic expansion in Member as well as non-member countries in the process of economic development; and
- to contribute to the expansion of world trade on a multilateral, non-discriminatory basis in accordance with international obligations.

The original Member countries of the OECD are Austria, Belgium, Canada, Denmark, France, Germany, Greece, Iceland, Ireland, Italy, Luxembourg, the Netherlands, Norway, Portugal, Spain, Sweden, Switzerland, Turkey, the United Kingdom and the United States. The following countries became Members subsequently through accession at the dates indicated hereafter: Japan (28th April 1964), Finland (28th January 1969), Australia (7th June 1971), New Zealand (29th May 1973), Mexico (18th May 1994), the Czech Republic (21st December 1995), Hungary (7th May 1996), Poland (22nd November 1996) and the Republic of Korea (12th December 1996). The Commission of the European Communities takes part in the work of the OECD (Article 13 of the OECD Convention).

FOREWORD

This book has its origin in the Conference on "Industrial Competitiveness in the Knowledge-based Economy – The New Role of Government", which was held in Stockholm on 19-21 February 1997 and was jointly organised by the OECD's Directorate for Science, Technology and Industry and the Swedish Ministry of Industry and Trade. The Conference was attended by some 180 delegates, with strong participation from business as well as government officials and academia.

The Stockholm Conference was the fourth in a series of conferences organised in the context of the OECD project on Technology, Productivity and Job Creation. It followed and built upon the October 1993 Helsinki Conference on "Technology, Innovation Policy and Employment", the November 1994 Copenhagen Conference on "Employment and Growth in the Knowledge-based Economy", and the January 1996 Oslo Conference on "Creativity, Innovation and Job Creation". It has been an important contribution to the final report on this project which will be submitted to the April 1998 meeting of the Council at Ministerial level and to the preparation of the February 1998 meeting of the Industry Committee at Ministerial level.

Previous OECD work in this area, and in particular the above-mentioned conferences, point to two far-reaching trends:

◊ Increased globalisation, including greater international competition, increasing international trade in goods and services, and increasing international flows of investment and technology.

◊ A shift towards the so-called knowledge-based economy, with development and exploitation of knowledge becoming more important in all economic activities.

The central purpose of the Conference was to provide a high-level policy forum to discuss the implications of these trends for the role of governments with regard to industrial competitiveness.

In such an environment, firms are seeking more flexible and innovative strategies and forms of work organisation and production in order to improve quality of output as well as their capacity to respond to changing consumer preferences. There does, in general, appear to be a move towards a type of organisation that focuses more on core activities, has a more decentralised management structure, distributes responsibility more widely and demands greater flexibility and skills from its workforce. As a consequence of their focus on core activities, firms increasingly have recourse to outsourcing and various types of industrial networks. The Conference therefore included a Seminar on the Changing Nature of the Firm (Part I of this report) aimed at a better understanding of the changes taking place and their implications for policy.

As a result of globalisation (Part II), the room to manoeuvre is diminishing in national macroeconomic and budgetary policies, and structural microeconomic policies which affect the framework conditions that determine the competitiveness of firms are assuming increasing importance. There is thus an increasing need for interaction between macroeconomic and structural policy (Part III). In the knowledge-based economy, a number of issues require particular policy attention: intangible assets (Part IV); knowledge infrastructure and flows (Part V); intellectual property rights (Part VI).

In the new context, there is also a need to reconsider the policy approaches to the private sector's role in producing what have traditionally been considered public goods, and more generally to the social responsibility of enterprises (Part VII). Finally, all these ingredients which assume considerable importance in framing the conditions for industrial competitiveness raise the delicate question of policy co-ordination and the related adaptation of government structures and practices (Part VII);

This report brings together most of the contributions to the Conference, including the general introduction by the Swedish Minister of Industry, Anders Sundström, the opening address of the Deputy Secretary-General of the OECD, Joanna Shelton, and a summary of the Conference debate by Keith Drake.

TABLE OF CONTENTS

Part I
The Changing Nature of the Firm

Part II
Are We Moving Towards a Borderless Economy?

Part III
The National Agenda – Increasing Interaction Between Macroeconomic and Structural Policy

Part IV
Intangible Assets

Part V
Knowledge Infrastructures and Flows

Part VI
Enterprises and Social Responsibility

Part VII
Intellectual Property Rights

Part VII
Final Session

Chapter 1

WELCOME AND OPENING REMARKS

by

Anders Sundström
Swedish Minister of Industry

Ladies and Gentlemen,

It is an honour and a pleasure for me to welcome you to this Conference on Industrial Competitiveness – The New Role of Government. I would like to express my thanks to the OECD for joining us in organising this conference. I extend a special welcome to those of you who have come to Sweden from overseas.

The Swedish Government has formulated the objective of halving unemployment by the turn of the century. This is a very ambitious objective; reaching it will require a good business climate. The new jobs will be created mainly in the private sector and, in order to achieve its objective, Sweden will have to maintain its competitive position on the world market.

Over the 1991-95 period, relative unit labour costs in Sweden fell by 27 per cent. One reason for this was the devaluation of the Swedish krona. In the first half of the 1990s, Swedish industry raised productivity levels faster than any other OECD country. This increase in productivity has enabled a number of industries to progress from being merely good performers to becoming productivity leaders in the OECD area. Sweden is very dependent on multinational companies, which account for more than 80 per cent of all Swedish exports and close to 100 per cent of all industrial R&D. The development of the Swedish economy is thus closely linked to the "well-being" of our large corporations. Meeting this enormous challenge will require the renewal of industry and trade in order to make better use of human skills and to improve the climate for innovation.

This leads me to the policy issues. In October 1995, the Swedish Government presented a Bill to Parliament outlining the guidelines for policy for growth and competitiveness for the next three years. These guidelines cover fiscal and monetary policy, energy, business, education, research, communications and employment. The Bill was followed up by detailed proposals for specific areas.

The aim is for Sweden to compete through high skills, rather than through low wages. The transformation from an industrial society to one in which the production of goods and services is characterised by high knowledge intensity should be stimulated through:

◊ promoting entrepreneurship;

◊ improving human skills; and

◊ increasing competition on domestic and international markets to create pressure to promote efficiency of production and structural transformation.

Competitiveness policy can use different kinds of measures to achieve these objectives. The first method is to change institutions; institutions are, of course, laws and regulations decided by politicians. However, institutions are also determined by the social partners, such as through the wage bargaining system. Institutions are also attitudes and habits. Start-ups of new firms are more frequent in some parts of the country because there is a local culture that works in that direction.

The second method is to invest in infrastructure. Infrastructure cover not only roads and railroads, even though they are very important. Today, it is especially important to compete through high-quality telecommunication systems.

The third strategy is to give financial aid to firms in the case of market failure. However, financial support or incentives work well only if the right institutions are in place.

We have, of course, made use of all three types of measures. Tax systems have been changed, as have social security systems, in order to improve the conditions for small firms. And further steps will be taken in the future. As far as infrastructure is concerned, the telecommunication sector has been regulated. We are also developing a system whereby different knowledge providers will be linked up in a national system which is easily accessible by small firms. In addition to these measures, the Swedish Government has also formally made it clear that universities have an obligation to work with industry.

Another area where a combination of institutional changes and incentives are used is in increasing the involvement of local and regional actors in growth policy.

Finally, let me say a few words about what I hope will come out of this conference and the challenges ahead for industrial policy. I hope that this conference will lead to further insights into what kinds of policies are required by the knowledge-based economy and how these policies should be delivered. This is important because in the political debate we are faced with two options.

The first option is based on developing towards an economy based on low pay and a low-value currency. Quite simply, labour is made cheaper. The other implies basing production on highly skilled labour, continuous development of new technologies, product renewal and high value added. Labour can then be better paid because of increased value added. These are the options – there is no third way.

The Swedish Government will make an effort to implement a more active industrial policy. In the development of this policy we can learn from other countries' experiences. The OECD is a forum where such advice might be found. I see two main areas where we see room for learning:

◊ How can we design better rules of the game for the knowledge-based economy?

◊ How can we develop our policies so that local and regional players are more involved?

Let me illustrate the first of these questions through an example. Paper and pulp and other forestry products are very important to the Swedish economy and have been so for a long time. We have recently presented a development programme for this sector. The paper and pulp industry is dominated by large firms with highly scale-intensive production systems. On the other hand, we in Sweden would like to see growth in the multimedia industry. This is a new industry, with many small firms. The cost structure is totally different from that of the paper and pulp industry.

The rules of the game that are important to the multimedia industry are, of course, very different from those that are important to the pulp and paper industry. So, we must have rules of the game that work for both types of industries. We have, of course, a similar problem concerning large companies *vs.* small firms.

Now, to the second question on local and regional players. Here in Sweden we have made local participation a major issue of our growth policy. Government has requested growth programmes from all of our counties. Recently a group was formed to develop this dialogue with the regions. We believe that there are analytical as well as democratic grounds for these actions. I hope that the OECD can help us in developing this approach to growth policy: it is crucial to implement better policies in these fields because the present labour-market situation is unacceptable both to the unemployed and to society as a whole.

With these words I conclude, and wish you all two fruitful days of knowledge-intensive work.

Chapter 2

OPENING ADDRESS

by

Joanna R. Shelton
Deputy Secretary-General, OECD

Ladies and Gentlemen,

This is the fourth in a series of conferences organised jointly by the Nordic countries and the OECD's Directorate for Science, Technology and Industry, to address key challenges of the knowledge-based economy for today and the future. I would like to thank Minister Sundström and his staff for organising this important event, which I'm sure will make a major contribution to the work of the OECD in addressing the issues of technology and jobs.

This conference, and the three that preceded it – in Helsinki, Copenhagen, and Oslo – are aimed at answering some of the most pressing questions confronting our policy makers and societies. Among these questions are: How do we respond to the ever-accelerating change in technology and the global economy? How must the role of government adapt to this rapid change?

The current situation

We are living in a time of rapid and far-reaching innovation and organisational change in our economies. The internal operations of, and links between, firms are changing fundamentally. Much of this process is driven by firms' recognition of the need to adapt more readily to change, as well as the need for workers to learn more and to become more creative in identifying and exploiting the new opportunities that change offers. These changes and the challenges they entail transcend borders between sectors, nations and cultures.

The speed of technological progress and organisational change is greater than any policy maker or social planner could have predicted. The process is not being led by government. On the contrary, in an increasingly globalised world, change is being driven by the aspirations of individuals seeking to identify new approaches to the problems and opportunities facing us. Due to advancements in information and communication technology, new knowledge can be built upon by others at an increasingly rapid pace, thus bringing about yet another generation of discoveries. In our efforts to exploit this information revolution, we can be compared to *dwarfs standing upon the shoulders of giants,* to borrow a phrase from Sir Isaac Newton.

At the same time, governments and societies around the world are struggling to understand and respond to the new rules of the game. Many perceive greater risks than opportunities. The world seems to have become more threatening and unstable. For many people, the greatest concern is that of job security, and of widening gaps in income, as the skills needed in the workplace become increasingly demanding. This pressure for change comes on top of already high unemployment rates and widening income gaps in many OECD countries.

Given these trends and social concerns, how should we react? Trying to slow down technological progress is certainly not the answer. Impeding labour or capital mobility would represent just as much a dead end: innovation and technological progress are essential for raising productivity and economic growth rates which in turn will bring new, well-paid jobs. Still, it is becoming increasingly obvious that we cannot simply hope for automatic gains from economic growth to meet the challenges we are facing. Instead, we must pave the way for more broad-based innovation and economic growth, and prepare our workforces of today to handle the jobs of tomorrow.

Government responses

What can governments do? How can they help our societies respond to change, adapt to it, manage it? For most OECD countries, there is no longer much room for manoeuvre in fiscal, monetary or exchange rate policy. The provision of subsidies to individual firms and industries is increasingly circumscribed and in any event is not likely to result in general economic expansion. Nor is protection against foreign competition the answer.

But this does *not* mean that governments are powerless to help their firms and workers in the face of a changing world landscape. Some priority areas for government action include:

◊ strengthening education and training programmes to raise learning, creativity, and to promote the development of new knowledge;

◊ facilitating the diffusion of technology, for example by improving the access of small and medium-sized firms to technology and to the managerial and organisational know-how for absorbing technology;

◊ embarking on regulatory reform to improve the functioning of markets;

◊ adopting policies which permit the growth of venture capital markets capable of supporting potentially successful new firms – particularly small and medium-sized enterprises;

◊ and, finally, setting guidelines for improved corporate governance, to ensure that corporations respond to the interests of shareholders and other interested parties.

Taken together, these policies are all part of the so-called framework conditions for industry, which allow firms to thrive and adapt to changing circumstances.

Governments need to keep in mind other policy considerations as well. Because the behaviour of firms and individuals is influenced by a wide range of government policies pursued in a wide variety of different areas, there is a need for greater consistency in policy making across these areas. Of special concern are expectations about future policy. The knowledge-based economy requires not only flexibility but also sufficient stability to encourage investments with long-term payoff, in such fields as basic science, telecommunications, aviation and energy. Of course, this is not to say that there should be no changes in policy. The point is that the direction and timetable for policy change should be clear: change should not be too frequent; and it should be based on a rationale that can be readily understood by firms and individuals. Policy change should not be carried out for the sake of change itself.

Looking ahead, the question for us at the OECD is: How can we help Member governments meet these new challenges? Our multi-country, multi-disciplinary approach to issues is, I believe, particularly well-suited for responding to the broad range of issues facing governments. Through shared experience, in-depth analysis, and policy co-ordination, we can help Member countries understand national and global trends and develop responses together. Let me cite just a few of the areas in which we have developed policy recommendations:

◊ ageing populations;

◊ bribery and corruption;

◊ cryptography and electronic commerce;

◊ employment – where we have elaborated a *Jobs Strategy* adapted to each country;

◊ negotiations on a Multilateral Agreement on Investment;

◊ regulatory reform, with a major report to Ministers due in May 1997;

◊ taxation;

◊ trade – including the so-called new issues of trade and competition, trade and labour, and trade and environment.

Against this background, the OECD's Directorate for Science, Technology and Industry has undertaken important activities of its own.

First, it has embarked upon the Framework Conditions programme, examining how more consistent rules, institutions and policies for industrial development can be elaborated. The programme has been strongly supported by Sweden. In fact, both Chairmen of the working party on this activity have been Swedish.

Second, this Conference will address the issues raised in a new project on Globalisation and the Changing Nature of the Firm.

Third, the project on Technology, Productivity and Job Creation which grew out of the *Jobs Strategy*, has entered its second phase, which is to identify, among other things, best policy practice in innovation and the diffusion of technology.

The road ahead

The task facing all of us – in government, industry, labour and at the OECD – is to evaluate what governments are doing well, and what not so well, with respect to the key challenges of the knowledge-based economy. From that, we can draw lessons and make recommendations. This conference, and those that preceded it, are designed to help us find answers in these important areas.

I am sure that this Fourth Nordic Conference will prove to be at least as productive and useful as the previous three, and I look forward to this morning's discussions.

Chapter 3

INDUSTRIAL COMPETITIVENESS IN THE KNOWLEDGE-BASED ECONOMY: THE NEW ROLE OF GOVERNMENT

by

Keith Drake
University of Manchester, United Kingdom

For two days participants from 24 OECD countries and the European Commission debated the new role of government which is emerging as technological change and globalisation alter the way firms organise their operations within and across the boundaries of nation states. On the previous day, many of these participants attended a seminar on the implications for public policy of shifts in firms' strategies for work organisation, production and marketing. Insights and conclusions about the changing nature of the firm were an important input to the conference. They provide an essential foreword to the conference report proper.

The changing nature of the firm

The seminar on 19 February 1997, like the subsequent conference, formed part of a four-year OECD project on technology, productivity and job creation. Seminar and conference enabled policy makers to explore new directions for policy with contributions from business executives and academia.

In most OECD countries, an increasing number of firms appear to be refocusing their structures in response to greater international competition, greater international flows of investment and technology, and a shift towards a more knowledge-based economy (on which see Andreasen *et al.*, 1995; Nonaka and Takeuchi, 1995; Capelli *et al.*, 1997). Familiar signs of this are management decentralisation, which distributes responsibility widely and requires greater workforce flexibility and skill, more outsourcing and increased networking inside and outside the firm the better to leverage knowledge into business value.

There was a widespread view that national macroeconomic and budgetary policies are tending to converge, and in some blocs, for example the European Union, are almost paralysed. Attention is switching towards structural microeconomic policies. These frame the conditions which can hinder firms or help them to improve their competitiveness. The objective of the seminar was the identification of the best structural policy options against an all-too-common background of low economic growth, high unemployment, weak public finances and growing income differences.

The seminar could be seen as a development from the Ottawa conference, in December 1996, organised by Human Resources Development Canada and the OECD, on "Changing Workplace

Strategies, Achieving Better Outcomes for Enterprises, Workers and Society". Stockholm focused the wide-ranging Ottawa agenda right down onto the views of:

◊ prominent industrialists on the main ways in which firms are coping with increased competition, technological advances and the move to a knowledge-based economy; and

◊ leading researchers in industrial economics on the main issues to be addressed by governments in their industry, technology and business policies.

The host country

Opening the seminar, Per Tegnér, Director of the Division for Structural and Ownership Policy in the host country's Ministry of Industry and Trade, reminded participants of the OECD estimate that approximately eight out of every ten new jobs in Member countries are for knowledge workers. Sweden is famous for its (mostly manufacturing) multinationals and has the highest value of multinationals per head of population of all OECD countries. But Tegnér emphasized the extent to which the value of such businesses now depends on customer loyalty, management capability and employee know-how, *i.e.* on intangibles rather than on tangibles. Tegnér mentioned the estimate that firms use only 20 per cent of their intellectual capacity on a day-to-day basis. This may not be a very accurate figure, but it is nevertheless likely that firms could greatly increase the return on their intellectual capital.

In one of its publications, Skandia (no date, pp. 5-11) has highlighted a few features of the Swedish economy which may be less well-known internationally than its great manufacturing companies:

◊ in 1993 Sweden ran one of the world's largest trade surpluses in intellectual property, after the United States and the United Kingdom;

◊ in 1995 tourism was Sweden's third largest export industry and Sweden was the world's third largest exporter of music, after the United States and the United Kingdom;

◊ largely due to speedy internationalisation, Sweden's per capita spending on R&D relative to GDP is the highest in the world;

◊ the majority of newly established businesses in Sweden produce services, where, like manufacturing, the key to increased productivity is increased quality, and the key to that is "a continuous increase in the level of knowledge".

In other words, far from being a museum of the machine age, Sweden fairly represents the modern OECD economy in combining a strong manufacturing inheritance with a fast growth in internationally traded services and in increasingly knowledge-intensive production of both goods and services.

Business perspectives

The first of five presentations from business people was from **Leif Edvinson**, Director of Intellectual Capital at Skandia Insurance Company, Sweden. Using the image of the tree of knowledge, Edvinson made the case for altering the emphasis of reward systems from rewarding those who harvest the fruits to those who nurture the roots, since the sustainability of a business now depends so heavily on these roots. He also drew attention to the prediction by Commissioner Steven Wallman of the US Securities and Exchange Commission, that ten years' hence measures of intellectual capital will be the most watched numbers; financial accounts will take a back seat (on his approach to intellectual capital, see Wallman, 1996). The knowledge economy is upon us when Microsoft is worth more than General Motors. Future earnings potential comes to depend more and more on the quality as well as the scale of a firm's intellectual capital – the sum of its human and structural capital (Figure 1).

Figure 1. The new company balance sheet

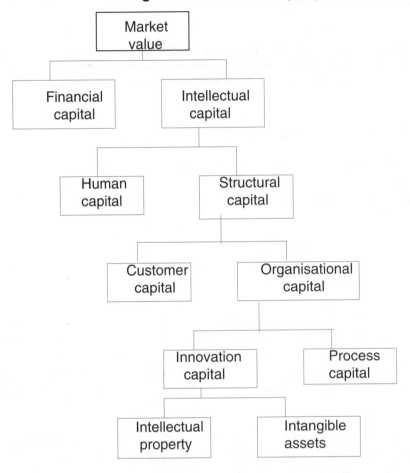

Source: Skandia, 1996, p. 4.

In some major respects the message from Skandia was remarkably similar, but in a different language, to that of subsequent presentations by SOL (a single-country rather than a multinational services company like Skandia) and by ABB (technically a manufacturing rather than a services multinational). Skandia's President and Chief Executive believes that the business revolution is "about daring to open the flow of ideas and propose that which has never been considered before; about tearing down walls between what were previously independent units; about fostering a climate of knowledge-sharing within the group that is conducive to creativity and value creation." (Skandia, 1996, p. 2).

However, for sustained competitiveness more is required than vision, more even than a good strategy. Percy Barnevik, Chairman of ABB and also of the Wallenberg holding company, Investor, is reported to have characterised business as 5 per cent strategy and 95 per cent implementation. The implementation priority identified by Skandia is innovation (Box 1).

> ### Box 1. Hardware, software and wetware
>
> "As the industrial age emerged, economists adopted a new economic metaphor based on the *factory*. Capital, labour, and now materials were the basic inputs. Manufactured goods replaced food as the typical form of output. For a person or a nation, investing in capital goods like machinery and plant became the new path to riches.
>
> Now, the *personal computer* is displacing the factory as the icon that stands for economic activity. People in the computer business now classify economic inputs into three new categories: hardware, software and wetware (or brainware, since the brain is a "wet" computer). Innovation is now understood as the driving force behind increases in wealth...
>
> Production makes hardware. Education makes wetware. ***Innovation makes software***. Innovation is a uniquely important kind of economic activity because software is something we can write down and communicate to others. Its value increases in proportion to the number of users. In a world with billions of people, this means that new software can create enormous value."
>
> *Source:* Professor Paul Romer, in Skandia, 1996, p. 3.

The goal is to achieve "a multiplicative effect in order to enhance rapid knowledge sharing and develop new business applications. The critical success factor is not only the nucleus of new ideas, but more so, their implementation. This can be facilitated by having the right company culture, leadership and infrastructure." (Skandia, 1996, p. 4).

In their different ways, all five companies which were the subject of presentations have been prepared to undergo radical change to achieve "the right company culture, leadership and infrastructure" to survive profitably with new technologies in an increasingly competitive market-place. The role of government in this process of self-transformation appears to be both direct, for example in educational provision, and indirect, for example its role in creating conditions which would foster rather than inhibit innovation. Innovation encompasses not only product and process innovation but organisational innovation. As Skandia itself demonstrates, that implies working collaboratively across generational, cultural and departmental borders within Skandia and across borders with external competence partners; and developing ways of measuring, appraising and rewarding innovative performance by teams and by individuals.

Dr Liisa Joronen, President and Chief Executive Officer of SOL Services, Finland, provided the seminar with a contrast which was also a complement to the Skandia story. SOL is a cleaning and waste-management company. It is a family company, operating very profitably all over but only in Finland, and with high levels of customer and employee satisfaction.

SOL's way of doing business is partly reflected in one of Dr. Joronen's axioms: "the more competitive work becomes the more it requires flexibility, trust, freedom and commitment. On the other hand, the more you free your people the more you need goals, measurements and rewarding". What she presented to the seminar was one of those paradoxical, loose/tight business structures.

In her own words, some of its characteristics are:

◊ "Freedom to work when, where and how an employee chooses, so long as self-set targets and customer needs are met...

◊ The absence of organisational charts, job titles and status symbols, including secretaries and company cars, own rooms and even own desks...

◊ An open-book policy on company performance...

◊ Employee involvement in the selection of name SOL, yellow colour and design of offices...

◊ The creation of individual work goals by employees. These goals are then agreed after individual target-result discussions.

◊ A compensation system with both fixed and variable salary. The variable salary which is linked to an employee's ability to reach the targets she or he has created, can be up to 30 per cent of the fixed salary.

◊ Voluntary participation in various training courses..."

The evolution of SOL was presented as a campaign against structures which prevent change and cause workers to shut off their brains when they come to work – therefore they do not use the knowledge and skills they have and measure time instead of results. As one independent source points out, such an organisation looked so "cooky" to one reporter that he asked: "Have you gone completely crazy, Mrs Joronen?" However, to use Skandia terminology, these "soft values" underpin "hard values". The same source (Tillier, 1996/97, pp. 70-75) reveals that:

◊ SOL's profits last year were US$5 million and they rise every year;

◊ annual growth is 22 per cent;

◊ big companies, such as Nokia and Telecom Finland, as well as hotels, hospitals and airports are among its customers;

◊ half the workers are part-timers, Joronen does not pay top wages, but a Cornell University study found 70 per cent of staff considered themselves "very happy" and strikes are unknown;

◊ the workforce has grown from 2 000, when Joronen took over her father's cleaning business and set up SOL, to 3 600 today; and she is still adding staff in a country with 17 per cent unemployment.

Like Skandia, SOL is goal-oriented, heavy on measurement if light on paperwork, and has geared its reward system to results. Operationally, it is obsessive about flexibility and customer orientation (Box 2).

Mr Anders Narvinger is President and Chief Executive of Asea Brown Boveri AB. By way of contrast with SOL, he drew from the experience of a truly global electrical engineering group with over 200 000 employees in 140 countries and annual revenues of US$34 billion. In ABB's pursuit of new markets and increased competitiveness, Narvinger identified a number of key developments which neatly illustrated three of the principal components of the changing structures of the firm:

Shifts in strategic objectives of the firm

In spite of its historic specialisation in products for the generation, transmission and use of electricity, ABB – like its competitors – is transforming itself into a more knowledge-based company, with growing emphasis on services, systems and plants (Figure 2). Narvinger pointed out that General Electric is generating 60 per cent of its profits, and rising, from the production of services. ABB already spends annually 8 per cent of its resources on R&D. But the significant change is the extent to which it is concentrating effort on building networks, integrating processes and developing knowledge. Instead of selling "bits and pieces", ABB is moving to providing complete life cycle maintenance for whole functions. To stay competitive ABB has to "find new niches with a greater emphasis on total undertakings and an increased content of knowledge rather than on low prices".

Figure 2. Market trends

From products to solutions

Integration

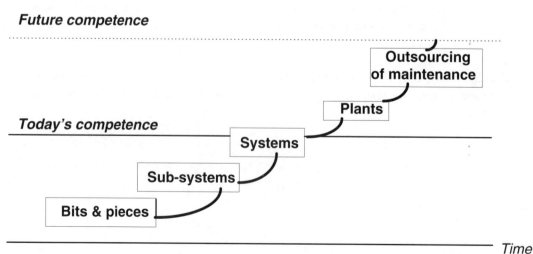

Source: ABB.

Changes in spatial strategies (globalisation and local adaptation)

Few multinationals better exemplify the importance of being both global and local. Narvinger reminded the seminar that only 35 per cent of world trade is inter-regional and that a large part of that inter-regional trade takes place internally within global organisations. These organisations account for no less than a half of current trade. It has a very high knowledge content.

In the most recent *World Economic Outlook,* the IMF described globalisation, in a way which perfectly fits ABB, as "the growing interdependence of countries worldwide through the increasing volume and variety of cross-border transactions in goods and services and of international capital flows, and also through the more rapid and widespread diffusion of technology." ABB is at the forefront of an unprecedented cross-border transfer of technology as it creates firms in new markets. Its 300 employees in Central and Eastern Europe in 1990 are 29 000 today, and its 15 000 Asian employees at the beginning of the 1990s are 30 000 today, and still growing. It is the changing product strategy and the accompanying transfer of know-how and technology which enables local companies to become more competitive in these fast-growing markets. In this way ABB is becoming a major exporter and importer of both services and goods in those countries in which it has companies.

Changes in the organisation and profile of the workforce

Competitiveness in these new markets has changed the prerequisites for nationally based organisations in the Western World, of which Swedish ABB is a fair example. In 1960 the Asea work force was 65 per cent blue-collar and 35 per cent salaried. Today there are more salaried than blue-collar employees, and the boundaries between the groups are being erased: "It is really outmoded to talk about two separate groups of employees." The objective now is a single agreement covering all employees in a flexible, knowledge-intensive organisation, where the demands for multi-skilling and continuous learning require much greater attention to "job enrichment, job rotation, the creation of internal and external networks and the finding of new career routes".

ABB's solution to its need to become more competitive is "a multi-domestic business strategy". It is to be "both global and local, both small and large, both centralised and decentralised". It is to become more and more a knowledge-based service company.

Peter Petersen, President of Swatch AG, described the phoenix-like company transformation which enabled a considerable part of the Swiss watch industry to come back (commercially) from the dead. This was a story of non-adaptation and then of adaptation. Technical innovation – quartz watch technology was a Swiss invention – was not matched by commercial innovation. By the 1970s Swiss watches had declined from a world market share of 50 per cent to about 12 per cent in the face of a competitive onslaught led by countries such as Japan and Hong Kong. In a few years the number of jobs in Swiss watchmaking shrank from over 90 000 to fewer than 40 000. Without a low-price, high-quality quartz watch the decline would continue. With traditional Swiss production methods there was no hope of producing this.

The solution was to "throw away the book". The main features of the transformation:

◊   Two of the industry's "big names" were merged into one company, Swatch.

◊ Design, as a marketing concept and instrument, and a fundamental part of branding, was advanced to a lead role.

◊ Production was revolutionised. Instead of an essentially hand-made product with over 100 parts, the specification was for a high-quality quartz watch with just 51 parts, manufactured by a fully-integrated, automated process.

◊ The production technology had to make possible low-cost, high-quality production in a high-cost country. Production in the 1970s was concentrated in the Canton Berne-Jura. Government (tax advantages) and banks (new capital) were prepared to be understanding and supportive to a firm which rebuilt employment and did not turn to outsourcing beyond the national borders, if at all. Swatch has 25 factories and produces almost 90 per cent of components for its own movement. This absorbs about 40 per cent of output, the other 60 per cent going to other Swiss watch makers.

Douglas Worth, former Vice President of IBM Corporation, struck some of the same notes as Petersen, but he also posed questions for governments about the public policy environment for business.

When the value of a blue chip multinational's shares drops to a quarter of its previously steady value this signals a failure to adapt to technological, organisational and commercial change. As was the case with Swatch, the eventual response was along now-familiar lines:

◊ R&D was safeguarded, not falling below US$5 billion a year (from US$8 billion a year) even in the darkest days, since knowledge creation had become more rather than less important to the long-term sustainability of earnings;

◊ an average eight-year product cycle had to be squeezed down to an average two years, and to three months in the PC and software side of the business.

◊ old production habits were abandoned: services business grew fast, components were built for competitors and research brought into the market-place far, far faster.

All multinationals remark on the continuing idiosyncrasies of doing business in different states, or as one person put it, "constrained enterprise in constrained markets". Government can kill enterprise with regulation. In one IBM plant in one state approximately 500 different permits were required. It took another multinational – not IBM – five years of knocking on doors to persuade the government to let it set up a local company. But in another state, far away from the United States, IBM was able to get a new plant into production in 75 days from an initial meeting, in one room, with all the regulators whose permissions were required.

Research perspectives

The business perspectives were in a sense anecdotal. But anecdotal, in effect case study, evidence can still be true. It offered powerful and concrete insights into a changing reality, from the perspective of the individual firm. The four keynote speakers from the research community were looking at the same changes from the outside; and from a vantage point which: *i)* enabled them to look easily across sectors and economies; and *ii)* facilitated the analysis of the implications which these changes have for public policy.

Gordon Betcherman, Executive Director, Human Resources Group, Ekos Research Associates Inc. Canada, warned against any search for a "quick fix on organisational innovation". Looking across countries, or just at the five business cases presented to the seminar, the heterogeneity of effective corporate responses to technological and market changes suggests a flexible country- or even region-specific approach to governmental support for change. But the imperative to provide a supportive infrastructure is strong in view of the constraints on macroeconomic policy and a "growing perception that macro goals regarding productivity, employment and income distribution (and, ultimately, social goods regarding integration and cohesion) may be served by micro policies that ultimately play out at the level of the enterprise."

Betcherman identified knowledge generation and innovation as the intervening link in this chain: "In one direction ... knowledge and innovation drive economic growth (and, thus, the possibilities for income and job creation) while, in the other direction, they themselves appear to be shaped to an important degree by organisational strategies, structures and practices." Non-anecdotal, system-wide empirical evidence and robust generalisations on strategies, structures and practices are proving difficult to assemble; and the task is complicated by the depth of cultural/institutional differences between, for instance, Anglo-Saxon countries, north European countries, Japan and the "catch-up" economies.

In spite of these problems, Betcherman summarised the preliminary research findings into three packs on:

1. *The relationship between "flexible" organisational innovations and productivity, employment and income distribution*

◊ So far, research shows a positive association between these flexible systems and enterprise performance measures such as productivity and sales.

◊ But there is little evidence to indicate that highly innovative enterprises who succeed in "doing more with less" lead to net employment creation.

◊ However, flexible organisational systems do alter the composition of labour demand in favour of more skilled workers.

◊ A culture of continuous learning accompanies organisational innovations, the value put upon human-capital investments by firms increases, but these investments are concentrated on the well-educated and skilled "core", not on the less skilled workers on the "periphery".

2. *The barriers to the diffusion of these innovations which are most relevant for policy makers*

◊ Financial markets, enterprise accounts and public accounts all operate with information which is seriously inadequate to assess the expected return on intangible investments. In addition to this information-based market failure, investment is constrained by the real danger of the investor being unable to capture the returns on the investment in some intangibles, such as training.

◊ Most recent organisational change has been a management-led initiative. The apparent short-term divergence of interest between employers and employees threatens the long-term co-operation which is essential to any durable workplace change which entails a fundamental redefinition of responsibilities, roles and relationships.

◊ There is a long list of institutions and built-in public policies which can impede organisational innovation which is built on intangible investment:

- "corporate governance and financial market institutions that emphasize shareholders' short-run interests;

- labour-market institutions that allow firms to "externalise" adjustment costs;

- industrial-relations institutions that discourage labour-management co-operation regarding workplace issues;

- employment standards and regulations that impose costs which have the effect of deterring hiring; and

- weak education and training institutions which do not generate the necessary supply of skilled workers."

3. The role of governments in supporting these forms of innovation

◊ In pursuit of "macro" policy goals relating to productivity growth, income growth and distribution, employment and social cohesion, governments can: *i)* facilitate the production of public goods which assist the diffusion of best-practice organisational innovation; and *ii)* help to redress market failures which lead to sub-optimal investment in intangibles.

◊ In pursuing these policy goals, governments are constrained by: *i)* fiscal pressures; *ii)* the necessity to operate in a non-traditional way across departments and even sovereign jurisdictions; and *iii)* must therefore take on new and difficult roles as brokers, catalysts and knowledge generators to provide "an enabling environment for organisational change".

◊ The specifics of the policy agenda include:

- basic skills education as the key to entry in the knowledge-based economy which is unlikely to be privately funded;

- support for the efficiency of human-capital markets through information, counselling and standard setting;

- promotion of education/labour market linkages; and

- guaranteeing effective counteraction to the access-narrowing, polarising effects of human-capital markets.

◊ Beyond education and training, the agenda includes:

- disseminating information on workplace innovation;

- providing SMEs with consulting support on organisational change and investing in intangibles; and

- brokering sectoral or national institutional partnerships.

◊ Last, but by no means least on the policy agenda, governments have to:

 – counter the economic insecurity created by typical characteristics of the flexible enterprise economy, *e.g.* downsizing, outsourcing and more contingent employment, with their knock-on effects on unemployment, inequality and poverty; and

 – find solutions for the weakening of traditional sources of security such as unions and the social safety net, and the growing risks placed upon individuals.

◊ Since greater economic insecurity seriously threatens social cohesion and popular support for a growth-oriented agenda, governments have to invent new "institutions and policies that offer security not as protection *from* change, but as the ability *to* change."

The British researcher from the University of Reading, **Professor John Dunning,** engaged in a most helpful mapping exercise. He provided the seminar with a schematisation of the current stage in the evolution of market-based capitalism (Box 3), contrasted the emerging paradigm of the firm with the old paradigm (Box 4), and delineated the emerging paradigm of national government and the old paradigm (Box 5).

Box 3. Features of three stages of market-based capitalism

	17th – early 19th century	19th century – later 20th century	Late 20th century onwards
1	Land-based (Agri-business)	Machine-/finance-based (Manufacturing)	Finance-/knowledge-based (Services)
2	Feudal/entrepreneurial	Managerial/hierarchical	Alliance/heterarchical
3	Local/regional	Regional/national	Global/local clusters

On the one hand, Dunning's work elsewhere (Dunning, 1997*a*) suggests that:

◊ the boundaries of market capitalism's main organisational forms – firms, markets and governments – are becoming more porous and more interdependent;

◊ globalisation requires a re-evaluation of the best way in which these forms should respond to the costs of organising resource allocation;

◊ globalisation increases the importance of the systemic role of national governments and requires them to pay more attention to the integration or harmonization of their policies with those of other governments; and

◊ it is necessary to alter our mental maps to accommodate the implications of alliance capitalism (Dunning, 1997*b*) for the boundaries of economic activity.

On the other hand, Dunning reminded participants that what there is on the ground to hinder or assist the competitiveness of a firm still matters: "While the intangible assets of firms have become increasingly mobile across national borders, the location of their creation and use has become increasingly influenced and determined by the presence of spatially immobile clusters of complementary value-added activities."

Box 4. Towards a new paradigm of the firm

	Old paradigm	New paradigm
* Functions of the firm	* (a) As an organiser of human and physical resources and of financial capital * (b) As a producer of goods and services at lowest possible price.	* (a) As a creator and organiser of knowledge-based assets. * (b) As an innovator, learner and continuous product improver.
* Competitive advantages	* Possession of, or access to, specific tangible and intangible assets, input sources and markets.	* Core competence (*e.g.* technological/ organisational), but also the ability to harness, learn from and initialise competences of other firms, including those in spatial clusters.
* Modality of organisation	* Hierarchical; with top management providing most of entrepreneurship, planning, division of tasks, and taking key decisions with respect to innovations and human resource development.	* Towards top management providing goals, visions and standards, but increasing decentralisation of entrepreneurial responsibility to line managers. More subsidiarity; more heterarchical intra-firm knowledge sharing and learning.
* Relational (External)	* Arm's length relationship with suppliers and customers. Governments and competitors generally regarded as adversaries.	* Closer on-going alliance and network relationships to achieve and sustain competitive advantages. Increased role of trust, forbearance and mutual commitment.
(Internal)	* Generally arm's length between different product divisions and/or functional areas, under general direction of top management.	* A more holistic and integrated approach to innovation and production. More co-operation between labour and management and different departments of firm. A "sink or swim" philosophy.
* Spatial dimension	* Mainly domestic, plus arm's length trade and "stand-alone" foreign investment.	* Increasingly to benefit from regional and global markets; and to engage in integrated cross-border production and trade.
* FDI	* Mainly to exploit existing competitive advantages and gain access to foreign markets.	* To both exploit and augment existing competitive advantages through, for example, strategic asset acquiring FDI and strategic alliance formation.

Dunning stressed certain features of contemporary capitalism, compared with those of previous stages (Box 3). In particular, he picked out two main features of alliance capitalism:

◊   the growth of inter- and intra-corporate co-operative ventures; and

◊   a recognition of the need for governments and firms to work together if the social goals of the former are to be significantly achieved.

He contrasted the neo-classical model of the firm as an organiser of human, physical and finance capital, all bought on the open market and assuming a given level of technology (or intangible assets), with the new model firm, a creator of assets rather than a utiliser of existing assets (Box 4).   The assumption of a given level of technology or set of intangibles is abandoned.   The firm is both *creator* and *organiser* of intangible and knowledge-based assets and an *exploiter* of networks with other clusters of knowledge assets belonging to supplying firms, to customers and to universities.

Box 5. Towards a new paradigm of the national government

	Old paradigm	New paradigm
* Functions of government	* As a direct participator in domestic asset creation and allocation wherever markets fail. * To intervene directly in economic affairs to promote social goals.	* As initiator and sustainer of a dynamic market-based economic system: to foster a variety of social, strategic *et al.* goals.
* Degree of autonomy in policy formation	* Considerable, while power of constituents to "move with their feet" limited. Most governments pursue macro-organisational policies independently of each other.	* Limited in a world of mobile created assets. Convergence of economic structures among many governments has led to increasing competition between governments for mobile assets.
* Relational (a) with firms	* Generally adversarial in sense that governments are likely to intervene to control anti-competitive or socially unacceptable behaviour of firms.	* Partly the old paradigm is still relevant, *e.g.* in respect of anti-monopoly legislation; but, increasingly, governments are seeking to work with firms to promote competitiveness of indigenous resources and capabilities and/or the access of firms to global markets.
(b) with other governments	* Only limited institutional competition or harmonization of policies, *e.g.* in respect of trade. * Few supra-national governance agencies. * Limited subsidiarity.	* As created assets become more mobile over space, there is both more competition and more co-operation between governments. Yet, as regional and supra-national governance plays an increasing role, so does subsidiarity and the functions of sub-national units.
* Organisation of government	* Mainly hierarchical * Little co-ordination between departments. * Involved in macro-organisational decision taking (*e.g.* with respect to technology, education, transport and communications, trade and the environment). * Tendency for wasteful duplication of tasks and inefficiency in the implementation.	* Lean, catalytic, competitive and mission driven governments; and a more holistic approach (involving heterarchical interactions among departments).
* Spatial dimension	* Trade, FDI, etc., judged mainly by effects of comparative advantage, employment and taxation.	* Recognition that being a player in a global economy via, *e.g.* FDI, brings benefits via tapping into foreign assets and learning experiences. Issues of trade and FDI looked at from viewpoint of enhancing competitiveness of indigenous resources and capabilities and/or promoting dynamic comparative advantage.

Dunning concluded by pointing to research findings that those countries who are most willing and able to adjust their micro-management programmes to support the competitiveness of the resources and capabilities within their borders are those which have so far been the most successful in the emerging global economy.

Caveats from earlier presentations were strongly reinforced by **Professor Lars Engwall** from the University of Uppsala in Sweden. In his view, the typical firm is a node in networks rather than an island in the ocean, plays follow-my-leader rather than acting independently, and struggles to make sense of the past rather than planning ahead. In such a firm, the manager is more a puppet on a string than a conductor of an orchestra, is not too well informed and satisfies instead of pursuing optimum solutions. There was support from the floor for his reservations about any clear causal explanations for the major changes which are under way in some firms in certain sectors. In the place of generalisable models of the relationship between a firm and its business environment, he emphasized the importance of context in choosing management solutions to problems of adaptation. Rather than problems leading to solutions by way of rational management, he observed managers with ready-made solutions looking for a problem which would fit. In keeping with this somewhat sceptical approach, he observed that most innovations occur when people in the sub-units of a firm do what they are not expected to do.

From all of this it followed unsurprisingly that the scope for white knights coming in to rescue and reorganise firms being outpaced by change seemed to be limited. Instead, Engwall favoured a less dramatic, patient exploitation of a firm's tacit knowledge, depending as this does on the industry- or even firm-specific competence of managers, *i.e.* of those who are thoroughly familiar with a firm's context, including the potential for exploiting interactions with other firms.

Swinging back once more from average behaviours to firms with exceptional capacities for coping with technological and market change, **Professor James Markusen** from the University of Colorado, United States, focused attention on that group of firms which drive foreign direct investment, on the characteristics of source and recipient countries, and on policy lessons from foreign direct investment.

Box 6. Firm and industry characteristics of multinationals

*   High ratios of R&D relative to sales.

*   A high value of knowledge-based, intangible assets such as blueprints, formulae, patents, organisational procedures, brand and reputational capital.

*   New and/or technically complex products.

*   Large numbers of scientific, technical and other white-collar workers.

*   Plant-level scale economies are not associated with multinationality.

*   Above a threshold size, firm size is of minimal importance.

Markusen's review of studies of foreign direct investment identified certain characteristics which are often, though not always, associated with multinationals breaking into or expanding in new (spatial) markets (Box 6). Above a certain threshold size of firm, neither firm size nor plant size seemed to be of any great importance. All the characteristics positively associated with multinational direct investment were features of knowledge-intensive production and products.

The foreign direct investment process is best understood in terms of country characteristics (Box 7) combined with firm characteristics.

Box 7. Foreign direct investment: source and recipient country characteristics

* High income countries are the major source and major recipients of foreign direct investment, which is "horizontal" or "market seeking". Direct investment is more concentrated among such countries than is GNP or trade.

* So high volumes of direct investment are associated with *similarities* among countries in relative factor endowments, not differences.

* Outward direct investment is positively related to a country's endowment of skilled labour and is significantly or negatively related to its physical capital endowment.

* The evidence is mixed on whether tax avoidance and/or risk diversification motivates direct investment, but political risk discourages it.

* A minimum threshold level of per capita income, strong infrastructure, high skill levels and intellectual property protection all have positive effects.

* Agglomeration effects are important in direct investment.

* Direct investment does not lead; it *follows* growth.

* Firms producing advanced products and services for high-income consumers constitute the bulk of multinational activity. Investments in developing countries are often "vertical" or "resource seeking", fragmenting the production process geographically into stages in order to exploit factor-price differentials between countries. Exceptions – market-seeking investments in developing countries – are to be found particularly in very large developing countries such as China and India, and in highly protected markets.

Over the last 25 years, FDI is primarily a developed-to-developed country phenomenon. Even the increase in FDI flows in the present decade is almost entirely due to liberalisation in China, *i.e.* China's introduction of more of the institutional characteristics of developed countries.

From his study of recent trends and of a wide range of analyses, Markusen distilled some conclusions about pro-investment policies for developing countries which are not irrelevant for many developed countries (Box 8). Markusen raised a range of key issues for policy, one of the most important being the need for a new international accountancy framework.

Box 8. Some policy implications

*   Strong infrastructure is more important than low taxes:

     – primary and secondary education
     – legal institutions, *e.g.* property rights and IPP, contracts, labour law
     – facilitating infrastructure, *e.g.* utilities, telecoms, transport.

*   Skilled labour is at least important as cheap unskilled labour:

     – FDI tends to be complementary to local skilled labour, not a substitute
     – FDI does not occur at the lowest level of the skills ladder
     – FDI may increase the gap between skilled and unskilled wages.

*   Credible commitments to liberalisation policy are crucial:

     – big countries: internal deregulation
     – small countries: commitment to openness
     – macro policies
     – treaties as commitment devices, *e.g.* Mexico
     – privatisation as a commitment device
     – tough international institutions may also be a commitment device.

*   Agglomeration, linkages can be crucial to success:

     – backward to infrastructure
     – deregulated trade in services, finance and insurance
     – liberal temporary residence
     – co-ordination among branches of government (trade, investment, regulation and immigration).

There is some evidence that FDI tends to increase competitiveness in the relevant sectors and to produce beneficial spillovers for recipient countries in terms of new technologies, improved market access and the flexibility of factor markets. But analysis of the impacts of FDI suffers from the obsolescence of company, public and balance of payments accounting systems. Knowledge capital of one or another kind is becoming more and more critical to competitive success in cross-border trading, but knowledge trading is nearly impossible to monitor because intangible assets and knowledge transfers are often so difficult to measure. What Dunning described as "non-equity alliance formation" exemplifies hidden knowledge transfers, which may be intra-national or international. Such transfers may be vital to the competitiveness of firms in specific markets, but they never appear in balance of payments or corporate accounts because they are one side of a barter arrangement in which the ally also receives some unacknowledged *quid pro quo*. Existing trade data, based on tangibles and openly traded services, give signals about increasing or failing competitiveness which are more and more misleading as the knowledge intensity of reported and unreported cross-border trading increases. It is more and more difficult to know for sure where value is being created.

A difficult agenda for governments

By the end of the seminar it was plain to see that there was widespread agreement that the paradigm of the firm is changing, and that the role of government in relation to business has to change – and is beginning to change – for this reason, if for no other. Given that the five companies which were used as case studies were very far from being a representative sample, there was also a clear preference for diffusion of good practice in building corporate capacity to change more quickly and radically rather than diffusion of any single model of "the new firm". No such model was identified and there was scepticism about its feasibility, given the continuing importance of context, *i.e.* of the sectors and markets in which firms operate, and the range of technologies and of inter-firm alliances which can contribute towards what is, for a given firm, a unique matrix of knowledge assets.

Product, process and organisational innovation were all exemplified in the five case-study firms. One of the respects in which these firms were unrepresentative is that they are all competitive success stories, albeit that at least two underwent radical re-orientation and restructuring in order to bring them back from the brink of competitive extinction. The key to these successes – business imagination and creativity – remained mostly implicit and unexamined throughout the seminar. Of course, these phantom drivers change shape over and over again if anyone attempts to grasp them. One of the outstanding problems for governments is that the structures of firms are now becoming almost as "slippery" as these drivers. Commissioner Wallman (1996, pp. 141-142) has underlined the difficulties of dealing with the emerging "virtual firms", *i.e.* linked clusters of legal entities which work together with suppliers, employers and customers in relationship-based transaction systems and which may well be much larger and operate across even more borders than the consolidated entities of today. The behaviour of firms like ABB and IBM supports Wallman's view that such networking and continuous adapting of the outer edges of the firm will apply as much to non-service firms as to service firms like Skandia and may gradually become the norm.

The researchers and their survey-based evidence complemented the compelling and idiosyncratic messages from the histories of individual businesses. Earlier reviews (OECD, 1996) have documented the way in which the new knowledge-based international economy of learning individuals, organisations and economies is emerging out of the machine-based economy which dominated the developed country world for much of the 20th century.

The seminar revealed a consensus that governments have to develop a new and very taxing role if countries are to benefit socially as well as economically from the inescapable development of the new international economy. The autonomy of national governments is limited by the intangibility as well as the mobility of so many of the critical assets of the most competitive firms. Co-operation between governments has to grow at the same time as competition between governments increases – a movement which parallels the simultaneous increases in co-operation and competition between firms. The management of the knowledge and regulatory infrastructure within which firms operate has to balance strategic objectives concerning employment and income distribution with objectives concerning competitiveness and growth. But the instruments with which governments can counter market failure or improve the efficiency of markets are more than ever limited in their effectiveness by the porousness of national markets to global market forces and by profound weaknesses in the measurement of the value of intangible assets and of knowledge transfers.

The new role of government

The concerns and hopes of the Swedish government, as outlined in his welcome address by **Anders Sundström,** the Minister of Industry, illustrated some of the typical issues for OECD governments. The top priority is curing unemployment when most new jobs have to be created in and by the private sector. The Minister saw only two strategic options for government:

◊ to improve competitiveness by cheapening labour in an economy based on low pay and a low-value currency; or

◊ to achieve the same objective by basing production on highly skilled and well-paid labour, constant development of new technology and constant renewal of high value-added products.

The government and country still depend heavily on Sweden's multinationals, which account for over 80 per cent of all exports and close to 100 per cent of all industrial R&D. A strategy which favours high skills and knowledge-intensive goods and services requires an appropriate competitiveness policy. The small firm and the local area have come increasingly into the policy focus. The Minister drew the conference's attention to three different kinds of measure which can be used to implement such a strategy:

◊ changing institutions, not just laws and regulations, but also those in which the social partners are the principal actors, such as the wage bargaining system;

◊ investing in physical infrastructure such as roads and railways, but also high-quality telecommunications;

◊ countering market failures by helping firms with subsidies or incentives, which only works well if a country has appropriate institutions.

For its part, the Swedish government is very actively deploying all three types of measure, making tax and social security systems more small-firm-friendly, deregulating telecommunications and linking knowledge providers together into a national network to improve access for small firms. The two areas in which the Minister was particularly hoping to learn from the experience of other countries were:

◊ how best to regulate the knowledge-based economy; and

◊ how to develop policies which will engage local and regional players more closely.

It was revealing that the Minister illustrated the first issue in terms of finding regulatory regimes which fitted both a large-firm, scale-intensive industry like paper and pulp but also a "new", small-firm industry like multimedia, whose cost-structure is totally different. In a country with a long history of centralised government, the government's growth policy now requires all counties to develop their own growth strategies, and central government took this position on analytical as well as democratic grounds.

Joanna Shelton, Deputy Secretary-General of the OECD, emphasized the extent to which the challenges for governments which are entailed by innovation and by organisational changes transcend borders between sectors, nations and cultures. In spite of this, governments are by no means powerless to help their firms and workers to adapt and profit from the changing business environment. Among the priority areas for government action which she identified were: *i)* facilitating the access of small and medium-sized firms to technology and to the managerial and organisational know-how for absorbing technology; and *ii)* adopting policies which would improve the access of such firms to venture capital.

The Deputy Secretary-General also stressed the need for greater consistency in public policy making in the face of globalisation and technological levelling. This means, horizontally, coherent inter-linkage across the wide range of relevant policy areas; and, vertically, giving sufficient stability to framework conditions to encourage investment with a long-term payoff.

The borderless economy?

Everett Ehrlich, Under-Secretary to the US Department of Commerce, argued that cheap, fast and accessible information processing was already dissolving the organisational structure of American transnational enterprises and would in due course do the same to multinationals in Europe and Asia, depending on the structural openness of constituent economies.

On this view, the transnational corporations which made everything everywhere and sold it to everyone were originally seen as the most effective organisations to manage business information across national borders – in effect the means of global integration. This pyramidal model of the firm was then undone by an information revolution which fragmented the largest companies along the lines of stages of production, product segments and regions. As a result, "the transnational enterprise has gone from its everything-everywhere-everybody model to one that focuses on sustainable, value-creating, differentiating skills and abilities and that then finds external partners that lever them."

The result, Ehrlich argued, "will be global integration, but not one under the command of the transnational enterprises. Instead it will occur through the network of partnerships, joint ventures, co-production and sourcing agreements, research collaborations, and other alliances and relationships formed under this new model." Relationship management becomes a key business challenge.

Ehrlich noted that currencies stubbornly refuse to converge to purchasing power parity values, and that investors worldwide do not appear to have the same attitudes to inflation or risk, just as Dunning had earlier remarked upon the continuing existence of risk-adjusted bond-rate differentials. In other words, the world's capital markets are slow to come together as one, even if capital is in principle the most fungible and potentially mobile commodity.

Governments who collaborate on joint stabilisation policies or the construction of common currencies are collaborating to increase borderlessness. In policy areas important for investment in intangibles in knowledge-based economies, such as competition and intellectual property policies, governments increasingly recognise the need to harmonize policy and practice in what used to be domestic policies. Borderlessness pervades government, the "creature of borders". Ehrlich even suggested that national policies or subsidies to innovation and diffusion, on regional development and on assistance to small and medium-sized enterprises could be regarded as vehicles for co-operation rather than pernicious competition between governments. But he admitted that "we are still far from that point".

In the European Union around 20 million, perhaps one-fifth to a quarter of the people who could be working, are sitting at home. Only a fraction are classified as unemployed. This is the European Social Model. The European Commission's Director-General for Industry, **Stefano Micossi,** pointed out that the minority of Europeans at work are finding it increasingly difficult to finance the non-working majority. He admitted that the policy debate in the European Union is not focused on the monstrosity of this Social Model, nor on the high labour costs which help to finance it, nor on the transport, energy and communications costs which are between 20 and 50 per cent higher than in the United States, nor on the widespread covert protectionism which continues to insulate so many firms from the market pressures which cause firms, institutions and governments to innovate.

This somewhat gloomy picture arises because the internal market, borderlessness within the European Union, has not been completed, notably in the highly protected services sector, and Member States are not really serious about enforcing internal market laws. European standards are set but mostly optional. Standards-setting bodies work slowly and tolerate much covert protectionism. Pervasive rigidities and distortions hamper the functioning of markets in goods and services and of factor markets and maintain high costs of production (capital and labour) and of other basic inputs such as energy, transport and communication services.

The role for the European Union and for Member States is to complete the European regulatory framework by deregulation, simplification and constructing new rules for the information society. At the same time, they have to extend international co-operation through bodies like the World Trade Organisation, for example by making more multinational agreements and fostering foreign direct investment and trade liberalisation, all to provide business with an environment which will both stimulate and enable firms to innovate technically, commercially and organisationally.

Professor Naohiro Yashiro from the Institute of International Relations at Sophia University, Japan, saw these same rigidities (non-tariff protectionism) in European markets as preventing European economies from benefiting fully from the growing division of labour which is both cause and effect of increased globalisation. He argued that the European, American and Japanese economies all faced severe structural problems and that low growth makes both macroeconomic reforms, *e.g.* Europe's single currency project, or microeconomic reforms more difficult and more necessary.

To escape into more competitive knowledge-based economies generating high growth is both technically and commercially feasible but requires attention to the social organisation of knowledge infrastructures and to public policy. Yashiro pointed out that most firms and markets still operate largely or entirely within national structures and cultures. It is the national economy, not a borderless economy, which is the fulcrum of change for governments, even though effective national reforms often cannot be implemented without a high degree of cross-national concertation.

Yashiro's focus was on human-capital formation and industrial competitiveness. Policies combating unemployment in Europe have failed. A large part of the solution to low growth everywhere and jobless growth in Europe lies in the potential of human capital to create high-quality employment. He recognised that the OECD countries have a comparative advantage in human-capital-intensive production over Newly Industrialising Economies, but exploitation of this advantage is critical to industrial competitiveness in a knowledge-based economy.

Yashiro's exposition of the basic economics of life-cycle continuous investment in firm-specific human capital in Japan perfectly illustrated the nexus which binds together human capital formation, employment practices and growth within one structure. The efficiency of this structure can be threatened. The Japanese model depends on firm-specific labour unions, employment security and seniority-based wages. Work-based learning is then a joint investment between workers (accepting early career wages below the value of their marginal productivity) and their firms. This worker investment encourages workers to stay with the joint investor in order to reap the rewards which are scheduled into the later years of working life. Not surprisingly, workers have a greater commitment to the profitability of their firm than many of the shareholders. There is little aggravation between "capital" and "labour" where the workers are capitalists who have invested in the firm by investing in themselves. Shareholders can sell, but workers are committed to their investment and its success. Firm-specific training is firm-specific investment by workers, and firm-specific unions represent the real stakeholders, long-term investors.

Long-term profit sharing between worker and firm, represented by seniority wages as well as annual bonuses, made this model work in Japan. The demand for training on these terms was induced by the benefits of a high growth rate. When real GDP growth fell to under 2 per cent in the first half of this decade it threatened the viability of the model at a critical moment in the evolution of the global market. "There is a vicious circle between the low economic growth and investment. Insufficient investment in physical and human capital is both cause and consequence of the low level of productivity increases and economic growth."

Yashiro's prescription for government included:

◊ Tax incentives and subsidies to stimulate human-capital formation.

◊ Policies to encourage more efficient use of human capital, *e.g.* reversing the trend to earlier retirement to improve output per person of working age, in order to reduce the cost of caring for the retired and assist inter-generational transmission of skills.

◊ Reduce minimum wages to encourage firms to hire young people and to invest in their human capital on-the-job. Also reduce over-generous unemployment benefit which inhibits the readiness of young people to accept low-wage jobs which involve self-investment in skills.

◊ By means of tax incentives, encourage introduction of profit-sharing wages, rather than fixed wages.

For all three speakers borderlessness was an incomplete agenda. The barriers to further globalisation, which also inhibit the development of the knowledge-intensive firm and the full exploitation of human capital, arise partly from the effects of low growth and semi-paralysed macroeconomic policy, partly from the difficulties which governments have in pressing through a wide range of structural reforms. Micossi reminded participants that monopoly (in Europe often in services) is one of the most pervasive and stubborn forms of market failure. It severely hinders innovation and the growth of competitive, knowledge-based firms. For him, effective competition policy was one of the most powerful levers available to governments who want to engineer a decisive shift towards a knowledge-based economy.

Throughout three days of excellent presentations and papers, many important insights came from or in response to interventions from the floor in plenary or workshop. The business perspectives of the seminar were characterised by one speaker as reports from ground level, as distinct from reports by academics and public policy makers circling at 30 000 feet. However, the perspective from 30 000 feet is not less useful for being so panoramic. Interventions mostly served to complement the more wide-ranging surveys from the researchers. For example, it was pointed out that:

◊ When governments react to events they are often reacting too late to symptoms, whereas the definition and implementation of infrastructure and appropriate policies for a knowledge-based economy requires that governments think and act long-term and act proactively.

◊ It is as necessary to reform information as it is to reform support infrastructures and public policies. Empirical data on investment in intangibles at a national level is often very inadequate (Hammerer, Herzog and Schwarz, 1997). We are used to producing statistics for macroeconomic analysis and policy making, but not for structural policies in a semi-borderless economy. Firms cannot be asked for data which they do not yet have. Measures of changing competitiveness and productivity and units of output from intangible assets are scandalously deficient. Where are the measures and policy instruments to leverage on the characteristic inputs, processes and outputs of knowledge-based economies?

Interaction between macroeconomic and structural policy

Ulf Jakobsson, Director of the Research Institute of Industrial Economics in Stockholm, offered a frank analysis of the macroeconomic problem of unemployment which faces Europe. Capital becomes more and more footloose and foreign direct investment becomes more and more important to the competitiveness of both the source and recipient economy. Whether this investment is contributing to long-term growth in investment or is a diversion of investment is a real question. Whichever it is, in a liberal world trade order with deregulated capital markets, the version of Keynesian macroeconomic policy practised by a country like Sweden up to the 1990s is no longer feasible and had to be abandoned.

Jakobsson was sure that growth policies cannot be an effective substitute for the labour market reforms which are a very high priority but which Sweden and most of the other EU Member States are doing their best to avoid. For Jakobsson, obsolete institutional structures and unreformed labour markets were the key to the high level of European unemployment, and organisational/commercial innovation of the kind illustrated by Swatch will be quite as important as the application of new technologies.

Everett Ehrlich, in his second presentation, commented upon the circumstances in which national monetary policy had ceased to be available to many countries as a countercyclical tool, *i.e.* the predominance of the Maastricht criteria in Europe and the consensus on eliminating the fiscal deficit in the United States. The new orthodoxy involves a shift in stabilisation policy from short to long term:

◊ "We are coming to see the most important aspect of our national budgets not as the stimulus they provide, but the kinds of spending they foster, their composition...

◊ The most important aspect of monetary policy is to stabilise the economy by preventing inflation and recession in the long run, not correcting for them in the short run. The more success we have at the former, the less we will need to pursue the latter."

In relation to Japan, Ehrlich argued that stabilisation policy cannot substitute for structural reform and that structural reform would make it easier to achieve stabilisation policy goals.

On this view, the goal of structural policy is to improve the "economic setting" which is created by the interaction of public sector policies and business decision making. Specific policy areas include regulatory initiatives, "the relative weight assigned to tomorrow's jobs compared to today's" in labour-market policy and the ways in which skill development is promoted in adults as well as children. But Ehrlich focused on three other areas:

◊ Well-designed innovation programmes are worthwhile but diffusion policies offer an even higher return. "Rather than think about how to create large numbers of new businesses we might think about how to make more of the existing ones successful. Diffusion policy goes directly to this objective."

◊ The quality of government decision making could bear improvement in areas like policy coherence across departments, *i.e.* from the standpoint of the firm, through appropriate outsourcing and hiring the right experience. The political will to tackle major structural economic problems – such as deregulation in Japan, entitlement expenditures and health care in the United States or the need for more entrepreneurship and labour market fluidity in Europe – might realise substantial gains to the economies concerned as well as to the governments.

◊ Globalisation undermines autarchy policies. Openness in trade, investment and corporate governance is a precondition to building an effective infrastructure for the greater competitiveness of a country's firms. Ehrlich returned to his earlier theme that the ability of the new information and communication technologies to "dis-integrate" firms means that the vertical value-creating chains which were formerly located and even hidden inside businesses are now being reassembled out in the open, as networks in which many (competitive) players can participate. Companies need to be free to find their places in such networks and need to be supported in this search.

Professor Luc Soete, Director of MERIT in the University of Maastricht in the Netherlands, accepted that the dominant macroeconomic policy criteria derived from the Maastricht treaty so much reduce the room for manoeuvre on macroeconomic policy that the effort to assist the emergence of the knowledge economy has to rely on structural policy. Macroeconomic policy is a blunt instrument at the best of times, but Soete pointed out that structural reform in Japan and in Europe would probably be less painful if their growth rates were better than those which they are currently experiencing. He reminded participants of earlier OECD work which had elaborated the relationship between the growing importance of knowledge – both the knowledge of individuals and the collectivised knowledge of firms and nations – and the astonishing reductions in the cost and increases in the range of knowledge acquisition, manipulation and diffusion as a result of the new information and communication technologies. He then identified five of the main structural policy challenges associated with this development, particularly as they have affected European economies.

1. Skills and knowledge as a complementary asset to the new information and communications technologies.

Physical capital formation was often the complement to earlier technological transformations such as the advent of the railroad or the motor car. Knowing how to use information typically depends on a person's skill level and tacit knowledge. The new asset complementary to the growth and use of information and communications technology is immaterial, human capital. Soete argued that the transformation of an emerging information society into a genuine knowledge society depends on a major development of the complementary asset, and that the European effort is seriously inhibited by the operation of four disincentives to traditional investment in education and training:

– The annual rate of knowledge acquisition in society at large is at least three times the rate at which the European working population is being rejuvenated. Without a spectacular effort to re-skill older workers, most knowledge acquisition will quickly become concentrated among about 20 per cent of the workforce.

– Knowledge obsolescence is increasing at much the same rate as knowledge acquisition.

– An increasing trend towards external labour-market flexibility has reduced the incentive to invest in general training where labour turnover is high.

– Fiscal consolidation in response to EMU convergence criteria has led to a matching tendency to reduce public spending on education just when the importance of education as a complementary asset for future competitiveness and growth has become critical.

2. Telecommunications, broadcasting and publishing: liberalisation and re-regulation

One of the most important jobs of government is to safeguard competitive forces so that new investment, markets and services flourish. In no field is there a greater regulatory challenge than in the creation, distribution and commercialisation of information. Soete identified dominance and abuse of market power, especially through vertical and horizontal integration across each major market segment: content creation (including publishing), service provision, distribution network and hardware equipment producers. He seriously doubted the capacity of the EU's current regulatory approach and available regulatory instruments to undertake a fundamental Europe-wide liberalisation and re-regulation involving both current and upcoming technological challenges to inter-network competition in the fields of telecommunications, broadcasting and publishing. At the very least, he argued for a transfer of regulatory power from national to Community level.

3. A role for public information services beyond enabling

Beyond economic enabling, Soete spelled out a proactive role for public-sector agencies as providers who can:

—   open up new market opportunities for private partnerships;

—   help to generate comprehensive and reliable information with a high level of accessibility, user friendliness and affordability for all people; and

—   undertake very risky pilot projects, without implying ongoing public sector provision of services.

4. Promotion of complementary organisational change in firms

Beyond the technology, the ability to innovate in information and communication technologies requires a coherent and complementary restructuring of the way in which work is organised – staff versatility, training, flexible hours, new pay systems, more team work, flatter hierarchies, review of company activities and outsourcing of some. If their organisational efficiency is to be raised sufficiently to exploit the new technologies, it will be essential that public policy focuses on helping SMEs in appropriate restructuring.

5. Uses of time

The rapidity, global range and potential interactivity of digital information transfer open up many opportunities both for more flexible production and for quicker responses to changes in demand. Service activities whose productivity used to be constrained by simultaneity of production and consumption have become far more tradeable because the time/storage dimension introduced by information technology makes possible a separation of production from consumption.

The nature of work, and conventions of place and time of work, are as vulnerable to radical transformation as the forms of production of goods and services. It was observed in one intervention that the latest household survey in the United States estimates the average working week at 41.8 hours. This results from compositional change. Where the working week tends to be reduced, in manufacturing, productivity is rising and employment is falling; whereas mind jobs are increasing as fast as muscle jobs are decreasing – and mind jobs can have really long hours. Increases in part-time and in casualised forms of work, and in the flexibility of work hours, after the fashion of SOL, are only the early signs of this transformation (see, for example, Boissonnat, 1995).

All these changes underline the vulnerability of (mostly) older workers to unemployment by reason of the increasingly rapid rate of obsolescence of existing skills, and the waste of human capital and threats to social cohesion which are inevitable if lifelong flexible working is not complemented by lifelong learning opportunities for all. Soete observed that qualifications ought to come with a maintenance contract, *i.e.* that competence updating should be compulsory instead of voluntary. EU economies can no longer afford uncontrolled obsolescence of people's competences. He agreed with one participant from Switzerland that on the whole incentives for human-capital formation are inadequate, and he argued for not closing off options too early in people's lives, for recurring investment, and, above all, for developing the capacity to learn as the critical competence for lifelong learning.

Best practice in shaping framework conditions which induce growth

In addition to thought-provoking interventions and discussions in plenary, the conference also broke into parallel workshops in order to facilitate the exchange of experience on key issues where government action is needed, and on best policy practice. The subjects of the workshops were quite distinct, but since they are also related to each other it was inevitable that there should be overlap in the content of the discussions. Arguments, points raised and conclusions are reported without attribution to participants because of the collective nature of the discussions and the synthesising of contributions in the course of reporting.

Intellectual property rights

The main focus for discussion on this issue was the adequacy of existing IPR instruments such as patents, copyrights and trade-marks to meet emerging needs. Treatment of specific instruments or needs revolved around two factors:

◊ how to strike the best balance between the two requirements which always have to be factored into any decision about IPRs, *i.e.* the need to reward innovation and so encourage risk taking by innovators and entrepreneurs and the need to maximise the social and economic benefits stemming from diffusion of innovation;

◊ the nature and extent of change which is required in the treatment of IPRs due to the arrival of new technologies and the increasing globalisation of business.

Three common features of current technological and economic change were seen to be particularly important when striking the balance between protection and diffusion:

◊ accelerating technological change is accompanied by an increasing need for rapid diffusion;

◊ the convergence of many new technologies – for example the current digital convergence between information and communication technologies highlighted by Soete – often extends

41

the scope of potential applications far beyond the capabilities of investors to exploit all the opportunities which have been created;

◊ the shorter life-expectancy of new applications may lead inventors to seek to harvest a maximum return as quickly as possible.

The use of IPR instruments to control the technologies they own has been complicated by changes in commercial practice as well as by the impact of new technologies. Examples reveal the wide variety of new pressures on firms and some of the reasons for thinking that cross-national responses, through the good offices of agencies like OECD, are as necessary as action by individual governments:

◊ Strategic research efforts launched by firms increasingly include efforts to develop standards agreed by partners at a pre-competitive stage. These private standards may provide earlier and more effective protection than IPRs, and they need to be taken into account in both policy and practice.

◊ Harmonization of national IPR systems has not kept pace with globalisation, in spite of some promising steps towards global harmonization like the recent agreement via the World Trade Organisation on Trade-Related Aspects of Intellectual Property. International R&D projects and even systems are becoming more common, both as transnational partnerships of firms and also with participation by academics and government scientists. The diversity of national practice on IPRs entails diverse effects on willingness to participate and on innovation in different firms and industry sectors. SMEs are in the front line of innovation in several key technologies, but the creation of such firms and their willingness to innovate can be inhibited by national IPR regimes which make it too costly and too risky to rely on IPRs to protect their innovations. In addition, there are real and hidden dangers in cross-national research collaboration, as in cross-national private-sector standard setting. These dangers arise because national authorities are not party to the content of these accords, which may be anti-competitive in their effects. This is even a danger within big public programmes of cross-national technological development, such as the EU's SPRITE, RACE and BRITE programmes (Canibano, Sanchez and Paloma, 1992, p. 9).

◊ For some firms and countries counterfeiting has become a major commercial issue because of inherent IPR enforcement difficulties and the non-comprehensive nature of international agreements. Moreover, the new digital technologies themselves pose a host of unprecedented challenges to copyright protection, including the problem of defining "disclosure" in an electronic environment. Specifics do need attention by all governments, for example the adaptability of IPR instruments to new fields such as biotechnology or greater recognition of innovation in services. But the evident mismatch between available IPR instruments and the current technological and economic environment caused members of one workshop to consider the need to reassess quite fundamentally the scope for appropriability as well as finding ways to improve the cross-national implementation of IPRs, possibly through a joint evaluation by Member countries and the OECD.

The social responsibility of enterprises

Goods and services whose benefits spill over to all sorts of people and organisations, and which cannot be assigned and charged to an individual consumer, are sometimes called public goods. This title can be misleading, since many goods and services which have this characteristic in part – quasi-public goods – do not have to be produced using publicly owned assets and public finance. Indeed, many enterprises generate highly valued spillover benefits for the community as a by-product of their private for-profit business. Only pure public goods, where it is impossible to charge individuals for exclusive enjoyment of the service or good, depend necessarily on tax-financed production.

One of the matters discussed in workshop mode was whether the balance of responsibility for producing quasi-public goods, especially services often tax-financed by governments such as education, basic research and general business infrastructure, has been shifting from the public to the private sector as governments seek reductions in public budgets. The second and related question was whether enterprises should assume responsibility for producing any of these services, and, if so, which ones. The conclusions which were reached reflected a strong consensus that the issue calls for a partnership between governments and firms from which both parties can benefit:

◊ The market system itself is a paradigm public good. One of the chief functions of government is to provide an institutional framework which is conducive to economic growth, innovation and structural change. This may involve initiatives such as re-regulation and privatisation as well as legal framing for transactions. To support the efficient working of a particular market such as the human capital market, information and counselling services need to be provided where the market will not supply, and standard-setting is an unavoidable government function.

◊ Increasing globalisation compels national governments to pay more attention to how their policies might be integrated and harmonized with those of other governments.

◊ Enhancement of human assets is strategically very important for competitiveness in the knowledge-based economy. Government has a clear role in providing basic education and training as a platform upon which firms and individuals can build. It has a clear role in financing basic research, which is unlikely to be funded from private sources. However, the border between basic skills and firm- or industry-specific skills may be blurred, so there is room for co-operation between tax-financed education and price-financed human resource development in industry – co-operation which may be informal or formal.

◊ Given the structure of technological and economic change, governments will have to take on new roles as brokers, catalysts, net-workers and partnership-builders. Governments can provide linkages, for example between education providers, industry and the labour market.

◊ Rapid structural adjustment can increase insecurity and erode popular support for growth policies based on innovation, flexibility and the efficiency of markets. A high priority for governments is to devise new ways to generate a reasonable level of personal security without diminishing the flexibility of the economy, and of labour markets in particular.

Knowledge infrastructures and flows

In many countries special attention is paid to technology diffusion, although this attention is often focused on very direct forms of knowledge transfer. The need for such attention is rooted in the difficulty which knowledge producers may experience in understanding user needs. The pattern in which knowledge is created is not necessarily the pattern in which it is usable. The market cannot always cope with the knowledge re-integration which may be required to link creation to use. To compensate for such market failure, government-provided intermediary services are critical. The effectiveness of intermediary institutions and services is in doubt in a number of countries. It may be necessary to undertake comprehensive and critical re-assessment, not least to ensure that publicly provided services do not undermine the supply of those services which the market can provide.

Such reassessment would focus not only on the architecture of the knowledge infrastructure and on knowledge flows, but also on specific issues which have already been identified, amongst which are:

◊ *Mobility within the service and technology community.* In some countries there is little such mobility between public and private sectors, which have completely different cultures. Yet indirect knowledge flows are of the greatest importance. Equipment-embodied knowledge transfer is complemented by embodied diffusion through occupational mobility and learning by interaction, and it is these last two routes which cannot be expected to work optimally without some attention.

◊ *It is necessary to balance mobility of persons with stability.* Otherwise there is a danger that the incentive for firms to invest in creating new knowledge, acquiring knowledge and embodying it, may be greatly reduced.

◊ *The root of the financing problem for firms is an inhibition which arises when the cost of knowledge creation or acquisition cannot be related to future earnings streams.* The investment rationale is not visible and intelligible. The link to the broader issue of intangible assets is clear: under-investment is a risk whenever the pay-off from innovation is obscure.

Intangible assets

Two main threads emerged from wide-ranging presentations and debate:

◊ In general, governments and academics tend to be somewhat "behind the game". This is the game played by some firms, a fast-increasing number, and by accountants and management consultants whose clients they are. These firms are very busy investing in intangibles, trying to measure the performance of the assets and to manage them.

◊ The action is going on in the private life of firms, with only occasional and extremely partial glimpses available to the public in general but in particular to regulators, competition authorities and the investing community. If public policy is to become more informed, coherent and well-designed, it has to address the "invisible reality" of firms which have become primarily organisers of knowledge and not rely on the "visible illusion" of company accounts. In doing this, the first steps are to develop an internationally understood language for intangibles and to measure what can be measured with the collaboration of firms. Only with a language and measures which are technically feasible and commercially acceptable to firms is it possible to address seriously the difficult policy agenda in areas such as competition, regulation, the efficiency of financial markets, innovation and R&D policies, and the reform of the business support infrastructure into one which is effective for knowledge-intensive businesses.

There is an agenda for firms and an agenda for governments. They are bound to interact; and it is upon that interaction that policy has to bear. There was explicit support for Baruch Lev's (1996) contention that, although the valuation of intangibles is not different in principle from the valuation of tangibles, reporting of intangibles should be prospective – focused on the sustainability of the earnings of the firm, as for instance, Skandia, believes – rather than being retrospective like conventional company accounts. This orientation seems to be critical. It was pointed out that it is what people believe about the future – perceptions – which drives investment in intangibles.

Those who have a stake in the efficient use, development, measurement and regulation of intangibles come to them from rather different angles. They include investors, industrial competitiveness policy makers, regulators, human capital accountants, financial analysts and national income accountants. The ratio of market to book value on Dutch, Swedish and US stock markets is around 2; and in extreme cases, often service firms with a very strong brand, it may be in the 10 to 20 range. On one estimate at least two-thirds of investment by the ten largest Swedish firms since 1990 has been in intangible assets, and it is this kind of investment which has become the chief suspect in explaining the value gap between book and market values. Recent investigations include a range of suggestive findings, for example that:

◊ on the Stockholm exchange the higher the knowledge-intensity of firms, the higher the rate of return on a stock portfolio; and that

◊ in the United States, the book-to-market-value gap of knowledge-based firms is increasing, that analysts use a wide range of non-financial data, that there is strong variation in its focus by sector and growth group, that the more analysts use such data the more accurate their forecasts become, that approximately one-third of investment decisions are based on non-financial data, that the most used non-financial information relates to strategy, management capability, innovativeness, and the ability of companies to attract and to keep talented people; and that

◊ detailed investigations of very considerable potential returns available from reorganising working conditions in Finland have been complemented by the findings of a study of the profitability of changes in work organisation, competence development and rehabilitation which arose from a major programme of the 1990s – the Swedish worklife experiment. Resultant reductions in sick leave and increases in productivity in 108 randomly selected participating Swedish organisations produced a median value of pay-back of 3.0 years.

The limitations of the balance sheet for reporting intangible assets were explored mostly in terms of technological development or human resources, where training investments at least are manageable using standard accounting practice. The mooted alternatives for human resource accounting – standardized human resource management, effect studies on training expenditures and satellite balance sheets – would assist several different stakeholders, and their development could be accelerated through a collaborative cross-national project in which firms, national governments and international institutions combined forces. There was further consideration of a proposed broadening of this same approach to cover all intangible assets and include critical issues such as capacity to generate future earnings, measurability and ownership. A project on investing in invisibles might be based on three main types of study, *i.e.* capital markets, management control and growth and employment.

The role of government in the knowledge economy

Professor Peter Sheehan of the Centre for Strategic Economic Studies in Victoria University, Australia, reminded the conference that governments, like firms and individuals, face a difficult learning process as they work out how to pursue the public interest efficiently and effectively in an increasingly global and increasingly knowledge-based economy. He listed certain features of the emerging knowledge economy which have direct implications for the nature of policy:

◊ The competitiveness of firms, industries, nations and regions can change more rapidly than ever before – witness the sudden shift in only the last five years when Japan's superiority in technology-based manufacturing processes gave way to the clear dominance of the United States in knowledge-based services.

◊ Systematic distortions of the incentives facing those with the ability to produce and apply knowledge for social benefit, for example those in SMEs or in universities, have been the subject of government attention for years, but successfully tackling such distortions has become much more urgent given their position at the core of a knowledge economy.

◊ For a similar reason, it has become increasingly urgent to address the imbalance between investment in services which generate social welfare, *e.g.* global fibre networks, and in those which will generate good returns in the market-place, *e.g.* pay TV. The imbalance arises either because producers have great difficulty capturing the benefits or because consumers are unable to pay.

◊ Employment policy cannot accommodate fast enough to the speed at which economies are becoming service activity economies. Sheehan emphasized that, although purchasing power and employment are shifting to the services sector, value added is not and the knowledge-intensity of employment in the emerging economy can be exaggerated. Inter-personal skills rather that muscles are at a premium.

◊ The wage or skill profile of an occupation is not a good guide to employment prospects. Education and skill requirements are changing rapidly, in different ways, in different industries, in ways that are difficult to foresee. This argues for strong generic education and training mechanisms very sensitively linked to the process of change in firms and industries.

◊ The net effect of many of these changes is to increase inequality of opportunity and of incomes. It will require strong and continuous countervailing action to reverse this trend.

◊ Governments cannot leave entirely to the discretion of firms and other agencies the choice of organisational adjustment process in the face of globalisation and rapid technological change. The choice is between very flexible factor use – downsizing, restructuring, contracting out, casualisation of labour – and internal adjustment methods such as retraining and job reassignment, which may not be rapid enough to use as the sole means of adjustment.

◊ The United States apart, structural reform to ease the birth pains of the knowledge economy is no substitute for macroeconomic policies which permit economic growth rates consistent with reduced levels of unemployment.

◊ The structural changes implied by the emergence of the knowledge economy affect both revenue flows to governments and expenditure demands upon them – many of these effects can be influenced by policy.

Sheehan raised doubts about the viability of the traditional model of government in which the Treasury/Finance departments have the prime responsibility for maintaining the efficient operation of the economy. In this model the other functional groups of departments, *i.e.* Industry/Science and Technology,

Labour/Employment, Education and Training, in isolation from, or even in competition with, each other, are required "to assist in improving the efficiency of firms and markets, to influence the exogenous development of technology and skill, to contribute to the take-up of best practice inputs by firms and to help to manage the adjustment process forced on individuals and firms by market processes". He went on to note that "the exogeneity of production inputs and the automaticity of market processes provides a rationale for discrete government functions, independently administered and co-ordinated only at the level of Cabinet decision making".

Sheehan argued that the principal assumptions of this familiar model are now unsafe; the processes of technology and skill formation are inherently indigenous, competitive strength depends on continuous recreation, full information is persistently lacking and there are strong and irresistible feedback mechanisms linked to the global economy. Successful operation of any of the major government functions requires "substantial and systematic input from the other areas if its objectives are to be achieved". New forms and mechanisms of policy co-ordination are therefore essential, and Sheehan detailed some of the Australian, and particularly Victorian, experience with large-scale institutional and policy experimentation. Two of the key lessons which he drew from that experience were that:

◊ long-term success in achieving a new level of policy co-ordination requires a broad consensus in support of bold institutional re-engineering; and

◊ systematic co-operation with the private sector helps to change the behaviour of the public sector and to create a more competitive private sector.

He emphasized the length and difficulty of the learning process for government in trying to find a new model appropriate to a knowledge economy, and one which works well in a particular country.

Some conclusions

It is an inconvenient irony that knowledge about the creation, distribution and management of knowledge is remarkably fragmented. A succession of OECD conferences has documented this fragmentation and demonstrated the huge areas of ignorance about the creation, use and competitiveness-value of knowledge assets. More strikingly than ever, this conference showed that there is a valuable and urgent role for the OECD, which is to help Member governments and other stakeholders, especially firms, to reduce their information costs and exploit potential synergies within an international knowledge base – knowledge about the knowledge economy – which is so unnecessarily and so uneconomically compartmentalised.

Out of the many insights provided by participants, three might be highlighted in conclusion:

◊ The agenda for governments who wish to promote industrial competitiveness is peculiarly difficult because it requires a willingness to adopt new roles and ensure a degree of policy co-ordination which is still rare. Severe constraints on public finances have robbed governments of the means, even if they have the will, to engage in large-scale and widespread interventionism. Piecemeal, low-cost interventionism may be common but attracted few supporters. The consensus favoured a far more profound degree of co-ordination across policy areas than heretofore. This had to be combined with a sustained and patient search for ways:

–   to measure the characteristic activities of the knowledge economy, *i.e.* flows of knowledge-intensive goods and services where the location of value creation is obscure, knowledge transfers in a greater and greater variety of forms, and a continuing evolution in the ways in which knowledge assets are formed; and

–   to articulate an almost-new partnership style of government, where policy making and implementation becomes a process open to knowledge creators and users, and government adopts the role of provider less often and the role of promoter, regulator, catalyst or broker more often.

Government cannot do this refocusing alone. In addition to private-sector and knowledge-network partners, participants emphasized that firms need transparency and consistency of policy across national borders, requiring heightened levels of inter-governmental collaboration.

Nor was the conference a simple exercise in constructing wish lists. The difficulties of achieving this kind of agenda were fully appreciated, especially in view of: *i)* the perpetual corruption of government by vested interests; and *ii)* the habitual reluctance of governments to surrender sovereignty through regional or world-wide agreements. The well-known macroeconomic targets in the European Union were contrasted with the absence of EU targets for structural reform. The reluctance of many governments to go beyond reactive and piecemeal microeconomic interventions was set against a rationale for non-marginal structural reform in areas like labour market or competition policy.

◊   Governments will and must remain powerful framers of the business environment even in a more global, knowledge economy. They will still have to make choices between market-reliant, market-regulating, market-supplementing and market-displacing strategies. A reconstruction of the environment for business is necessary as foreign direct investment and information services become more and more important features of the global economy, and as the knowledge intensity of internationally traded goods and services increases. If massive government failure is to be avoided, governments have to find ways of engaging effectively with increasingly protean entities – knowledge-based, increasingly virtual firms – in a process which amounts to recurrent learning for governments.

◊   It was a common view that it would be premature on the international level for bodies like the OECD to try to jump towards recommendation of international standards on matters such as accounting, information technology, Stock Exchange regulation or competition policy. The practice of the most forward-looking firms, and the state of data on intangibles at national level, suggest that the appropriate collective action cross-nationally, apart from existing initiatives, is to pool and share experience. In particular, the identification of feasible options and good practice in measuring knowledge flows and stocks, and in reporting and managing intangibles, was strongly supported. A partnership project between firms and governments would be essential for any collective learning in which knowledge about the measurement and management of knowledge was collated, exchanged and analysed. The purpose would be to improve understanding among governments and firms of the feasibility and likely gains and losses of various policy options for governments wishing to promote industrial competitiveness in the knowledge economy.

REFERENCES

ANDREASEN, L.E., B. CORIAT, F. DEN HERTOG, R. KAPLINSKY (eds.) (1995), *Europe's Next Step: Organisational Innovation, Competition And Employment,* Frank Cass, London.

BOISSONAT, J. *et al.* (1995), *Le travail dans vingt ans,* Rapport de la Commission Présidée par Jean Boissonat, Editions Odile Jacob, Paris, October.

CANIBANO, L., M. SANCHEZ and M. PALOMA (1992), "Technological Development: An Accounting Challenge", paper presented at the Fifteenth Annual Congress of the European Accounting Association, Madrid, 22-24 April.

CAPELLI, P. *et al.* (1997), *Change at Work*, Oxford University Press, Oxford.

DUNNING, John H. (1997*a*), "Reconfiguring the Boundaries of International Business Activity", in G. Boyd and A.M. Rugman (eds.), *Euro-Pacific Investment and Trade*, Edward Elgar, Aldershot, pp. 1-18.

DUNNING, John H. (1997*b*), *Alliance Capitalism and Global Business*, Routledge, London and New York.

HAMMERER, G., A. HERZOG and K. SCHWARTZ (1997), *Immaterielle Investitionen*, Peter Lang, Frankfurt am Main.

LEV, Baruch (1996), "The Boundaries of Finincial Reporting and How to Extend Them", paper presented at the Conference on Changing Workplace Strategies, Human Resources Development Canada/OECD, Ottawa, 2-3 December.

NONAKA, I. and H. TAKEUCHI (1995), *The Knowledge Creating Company: How Japanese Companies Create the Dynamics of Innovation,* Oxford University Press, Oxford.

OECD (1996), *Employment and Growth in the Knowledge-based Economy*, Paris.

SKANDIA (1996), *Power of Innovation*, Intellectual Capital Supplement to Skandia's 1996 Interim Report.

SKANDIA/MARKET ACADEMY OF STOCKHOLM UNIVERSITY (no date), *Welfare and Security*.

TILLIER, Alan (1996/7), "Liisa Cleans Up", in *Scanorama*, December 1996/January 1997, pp. 70-75.

WALLMAN, Steven M.H. (1996), "The Future of Accounting and Financial Reporting. Part II: The Colorized Approach", in *Accounting Horizons*, Vol. 10, No. 2, June, pp. 138-148.

Part I

The Changing Nature of the Firm

Chapter 4

TECHNOLOGY AND THE CHANGING BOUNDARIES OF FIRMS AND GOVERNMENTS

by

John H. Dunning
Emiritus Professor of International Business, Rutgers University, United States

Introduction

There are signs that the world is entering into a new stage of market-based capitalism which may be distinguished from those which preceded it in three main ways. First, in contrast to the *land-based* capitalism of the pre-industrial era and *machine- and finance-based* capitalism of the 19th and much of the 20th century, the capitalism of the 1990s is becoming increasingly *knowledge-based.*[1] At the same time, created intangible assets have replaced natural tangible assets as the main source of wealth creation in industrial societies; this is demonstrated, *inter alia*, by the rising importance of services, relative to that of goods, in the gross national output of most countries.[2]

Secondly, the territorial horizons of capitalism – as proxied by the spatial sourcing of inputs and the location of production and the markets served by firms – have continuously widened from the sub-national to the national and macro-regional and now, increasingly, to the global. Over the last two decades, for example, the growth of world trade has consistently outpaced that of world output, while in the mid-1990s the sales of the foreign affiliates of multinational enterprises (MNEs) exceeded that of world trade by 10-15 per cent (UNCTAD, 1996). However, while the intangible assets of firms have become increasingly mobile across national borders, the location of their creation and use has become increasingly influenced and determined by the presence of spatially immobile clusters of complementary value-added activities. Thus, in the words of Ann Markusen (1994), globalisation presents us with a paradox of "sticky places within slippery space" (Markusen, 1994).

Thirdly, the dominant organisational modality of market-based activity is evolving from that of *hierarchical* capitalism to that best described as *alliance capitalism.*[3] While retaining many of the characteristics of hierarchical capitalism, the distinctive feature of its 21st century successor is the growing extent to which, in order to achieve their respective economic and social objectives, and to meet the dictates of the international market-place, the main stakeholders in the wealth-creating process need to co-operate more actively and purposefully with each other. The critical features of alliance capitalism are, first, the growth of ongoing inter-firm co-operative ventures; second, the emergence of closer and more clearly delineated intra-firm relationships; and third, the recognition by governments and firms alike of the need to work together if the societal economic goals, for which the former is ultimately responsible, are to be achieved.

These features of contemporary Western-based capitalism, which are compared with those of previous stages in Table 1, are having a profound effect on our understanding of the role of firms, markets and non-market institutions – including governments, at all levels; and on the extent and form of the interaction between them. Each, of course, reflects a series of dramatic and far-reaching world economic and political events which have occurred over the past 20-30 years. In this chapter, we will concentrate on one such event, *viz.* the impact of recent technological advances, which, we believe, alongside the renaissance of market-based economic systems, and the emergence of several new players in the world economy, have been the critical factor affecting the nature and functions of the leading actors on the global economic stage, and the attitudes and actions of policy makers. Let us briefly deal with each of these aspects of technological change in turn.

Table 1. Features of three stages of market-based capitalism

A Western model

	17th century – early 19th century	19th century – later 20th century	Late 20th century onwards
Primary source of wealth and form of activity	Land-based: Agriculture and forestry	Machine-/finance-based: Manufacturing	Finance-/knowledge-based: Producer and consumer services
Spatial dimension	Local/regional	Regional/national	Regional/global: but with some national or sub-national clusters
Principal organisational form	Feudal/entrepreneurial: Major decentralisation of economic authority	Managerial/hierarchical: Generally adversarial economic relationships	Alliance/heterarchical: More co-operative economic relationships

Towards a new paradigm of the firm

The firm has long been the main unit of production in a market-based economy. But, it is only comparatively recently that economists have considered the firm as a *creator* of assets, as well as a *utiliser* of assets. Most of the neo-classical theory of the firm, for example, was concerned with how given a certain level of technology – the human, physical and financial resources which a firm might acquire in the open market, might best be used to produce the output of a particular good or service at the lowest possible cost.

Today, not least as a result of a series of watershed advances in technology, but also of changing consumer preferences, a firm's commercial success or competitiveness is more likely to be judged by its ability to innovate new products and to upgrade the quality of its existing products. In turn, this ability will be affected by the correctness (or otherwise) of a whole set of strategic decisions, such as those to do with choosing the right location in the world both to produce or acquire, and to exploit wealth-creating assets; and how best to co-ordinate the search for, and deployment of, those assets. For example, in the international arena, should it be via foreign direct investment (FDI), co-operative ventures or arm's length trade?

It is the combination of technological change and the opening up of regional and global markets which has been the primary cause of the reconfiguration of the kind and range of value-added activities undertaken by firms, their spatial dimensions and their organisational forms. Thus, for example, MNEs are increasingly seeking to both exploit and augment their home-based technological assets from foreign locations[4] and are doing so both by deepening their value-added activities in these locations and by engaging in synergistic alliances with foreign firms. It is the growth of these alliances that is extending the "soft" boundaries of firms and fostering alliance capitalism. At the same time, many MNEs and other large firms are downsizing the range of their value-added activities[5]; however they are not replacing these by arm's length transactions, but by a series of ongoing and "hands-on" technological and marketing relationships with their new suppliers, customers and competitors.

In Table 2 we set out some of the main components of the emerging paradigm of the firm in a knowledge-based economy, and compare and contrast these with the more traditional paradigm contained in most textbooks on microeconomics. Clearly, not all firms fit into the new paradigm, but most do in one way or another.

The facts and ideas set out in Table 2 are largely self-explanatory. We would, however, make three comments which encapsulate both the main thrust of actual events and the development of scholarly thinking:

◊ Since an integral feature of a knowledge-based economy is that of change and uncertainty, and the continual upgrading of intellectual capital, it is imperative that any new paradigm of the firm should pay particular attention to these elements. This is now being increasingly accepted by economists and business strategists, and particularly by those who view the firm as a dynamic institution which is continually reconfiguring its resources and capabilities by innovation and learning experiences.[6]

◊ Second, since the competitive advantages of firms relate as much to their ability to identify, access and harness assets which are complementary to their core competencies, as to these competencies themselves, any new paradigm of the firm must encompass extra-firm value-added activities within its purview. As articulated by Professor Engwall in Chapter 5 of this volume, the idea of the firm as an "island of conscious power" is giving way to the firm as "a node in a network of intra- and inter-firm relations". The conceptual framework for this reconfiguration has been set out in another paper by the author (Dunning, 1995 – reprinted in Dunning, 1997a), but, essentially, this gives more attention to the net benefits of alternative organisational options open to firms as they seek to forge productive intra- and inter-firm collaborations. The question here is: What are the optimum combinations of these alternative forms, and how far are these combinations dependent on the value of contextual variables (such as industry-, country- and firm-strategic specific circumstances)?

Table 2. Towards a new paradigm of the firm

	Old paradigm	New paradigm
Functions of the firm	(a) As an organiser of human and physical resources and of financial capital. (b) As a producer and marketer of goods and services at lowest possible price.	(a) As a creator and organiser of knowledge-based assets; and as a co-ordinator of these and other assets. (b) As an innovator, learner and continuous product improver; and searcher of new markets. (c) As a nexus of transactions.
Competitive advantages	Possession of, or access to, specific tangible and intangible assets, input sources and markets.	Possession of core competences (*e.g.* technological, managerial, organisational, etc.), but also the ability to harness, learn from and internalise competences of other firms, including those in spatial clusters.
Organisational structure	Mainly hierarchical, with top management providing most of the entrepreneurship, planning and strategic initiatives; and taking key decisions with respect to innovations, division of tasks and human resource development.	Towards top management providing goals, visions and standards, but increasing decentralisation of entrepreneurial responsibility to line managers. More subsidiary; more hierarchical intra-firm knowledge sharing and learning.
Relational (External)	. The firm as an "island of conscious power". . Arm's length relationship with suppliers and customers. . The firm as a node in a network of relationships. Governments and competitors generally regarded as adversaries.	Closer "hands-on" alliance and network relationships to achieve and sustain competitive advantages. Increased role of trust, forbearance and mutual commitment as relationship building factors.
(Internal)	Generally arm's length between different product divisions and/or functional areas, under the general direction of top management.	A more holistic and integrated approach to innovation, production and marketing. More co-operation between labour and management and between different functional areas of firm. A "sink or swim" philosophy.
Spatial dimension	Mainly domestic, plus arm's length trade and "stand-alone" foreign direct investment.	Increasingly geared towards regional and global markets; and engaging in integrated cross-border production, trade and inter-firm alliances.
FDI	Mainly to exploit home-based competitive advantages, and to secure access to foreign input or output markets.	To exploit, leverage and augment existing competitive advantages, through, for example, strategic asset acquiring FDI and strategic alliance formation.

◊ Thirdly, any new paradigm of the firm must pay particular heed to the spatial configuration of economic activity (and, in particular, to that forged by foreign direct investment and cross-border alliances) as a means of exploiting and enhancing its core competencies. Because of the growing importance of macro (supra-national) and micro (sub-national) regions as economic units, issues such as the economies of regional integration and those of the spatial agglomeration of related activities are now gaining increasing attention. Here, some interesting work is being done both by economists and industrial geographers as they seek to identify both optimum spatial areas for particular kinds of economic activity, and the ingredients of industrial clusters which best promote the interests of members of the cluster. From the firm's perspective, the main question of interest revolves around how best to organise its portfolio of unanchored assets across geographical space; and how, in turn, this balance is affected by industry- and firm-specific contextual variables.

The ability of most firms[7] – both large and small – to cope with the demands of the knowledge-based globalising economy essentially rests on the extent to which they can summon the necessary organisational capacity to respond to the challenges posed by these three features.

Towards a new paradigm of national government

We have suggested that alliance capitalism is currently being fashioned by technological change, as is the spatial dimension of business activity. But, it has been the renaissance of the market system and the liberalisation of individual markets, together with the acceptance by governments of the benefits of regional economic integration, and the need for a more systemic harmonization of investment and trading regimes, that has set a new macroeconomic and organisational environment that has conditioned the reactions of businesses to technological change.

Thus, in recent years, most national governments – of both developed and developing countries – have substantially reduced barriers to trade and FDI; and (for good or bad) have permitted, and even encouraged, more cross-border mergers and acquisitions. In many instances, governments (including sub-national authorities), in the belief that they compete with each other to acquire scarce created mobile assets, have stepped up their incentives to foreign investors.[8] Others have recognised the need to improve the supportive (domestic) services for such investment over which they have some control or influence, e.g. human and physical infrastructure; and, where it is desirable to do so, to foster the spatial agglomeration of related activities.

In seeking to respond to, and indeed influence, the events of the last two decades, and those likely to occur in the next two decades, governments – and particularly Western governments – need to draw upon a new paradigm of governance. Paradigms which have stood the test for most of the present century are no longer appropriate for the knowledge-based and globalising economy of the later 1990s. Table 3 summarises some of the ways in which the characteristics and scope of governments in the economic realm have changed, and are continuing to change. Again, these are reasonably self-explanatory, but we would highlight four distinctive and inter-related features of the new paradigm:

◊ In a global economy, in which knowledge-related assets can flow easily across national borders, national governments have only a limited autonomy in their economic strategies and policies.[9] In effect, many governments do compete with each other for such assets, even though trade in these, or their rights, is rarely a zero sum game.

◊ In spite of the deregulation and liberalisation of many markets, the role of governments in affecting the creation and utilisation of immobile assets, critical to the economic prosperity of the constituents under their jurisdiction, is increasing. This is because market failure is generally more pronounced in the provision of these assets – and especially those complementary to the core competencies of firms – than in the provision of natural assets.

This market failure – in its various guises[10] – is especially noticeable in the less specialised areas of human-resource development, in innovatory activities, and in the provision of capital-intensive public goods, which have a long pay-back period.

◊ We earlier suggested that the more successful firms in the contemporary world economy are restructuring the scope and depth of their value added (by externalising their non-core activities); and revamping their organisational structures (*e.g.* by flattening their hierarchical pyramids). Likewise, we believe, if they are to be successful in the pursuance of their economic and social strategies, governments need to reconsider the content of their tasks and the way in which they co-ordinate these, both internally and with other economic institutions. Elsewhere (Dunning, 1994) we have argued that while globalisation may require national governments to surrender some of their traditional tasks to the market-place, those which remain are no less vital to the economic welfare of their constituents. Therefore, we would assert that, even allowing for the reformulation of the role of government suggested by such scholars as David Osborne and Ted Graebler (1992), the need for strong, efficient and entrepreneurial government is as great as it has ever been.

◊ One consequence of the above three features is that the optimum locus or *level* of governance is requiring re-examination. On the one hand, one is seeing an increasing role for sub-national areas of governance as, in their location strategies, firms are the spatially "sticky" resources provided. On the other, new or strengthened supranational governance institutions may be necessary in order to minimise market-distorting policies by national governments to attract inbound FDI or foster domestic production.

Although some East Asian governments are well on the way to accepting the new paradigm of government, their Western counterparts are, for the most part, reluctant to embrace many of its facets. This is partly because old attitudes, opinions and habits – not to mention institutional rigidities – die hard; governments usually take a short-term perspective on the likely consequences of their actions.

Table 3. Towards a new paradigm of national government

	Old paradigm	New paradigm
Economic functions of government	. As a direct participator in domestic asset creation and allocation wherever markets fail. . To intervene directly in economic affairs to promote social and strategic goals.	As initiator and sustainer of a dynamic and knowledge-based market economy: to foster a variety of social, strategic *et al.* goals.
Degree of autonomy in policy formation	Considerable, while power of constituents to "move with their feet" limited. Most national governments pursue macro-organisational (*i.e.* management) policies independently of each other.	Limited in a world of mobile created assets. Convergence of economic structures among industrial countries has led to increasing competition between governments for unanchored assets and markets.
Relational **(a) with firms**	Generally adversarial in the sense that governments are likely to intervene to minimise anti-competitive or socially unacceptable behaviour by firms.	Partly the old paradigm is still relevant, *e.g.* in respect of anti-monopoly legislation; but, increasingly, governments are seeking to work with firms to promote competitiveness of indigenous resources and capabilities, and/or their access to foreign inputs and markets.
(b) with other governments	. Only limited institutional competition and/or harmonization of policies, *e.g.* in respect of trade. . Few supra-national governance agencies. . Limited delegation of economic responsibility to sub-national authorities.	As created assets become more mobile over space, there is both more competition and more co-operation between governments. Yet, as regional and supra-national governance plays an increasing role, so does subsidiarity and the functions of sub-national units.
Organisation of government	. Mainly hierarchical. . Little co-ordination between departments or agencies. . Involved in macro-organisational decision taking (*e.g.* with respect to technology, education, transport and communications, trade and the environment). . Tendency for wasteful duplication of tasks and inefficiency in their implementation.	Lean, catalytic, competitive and mission-driven governments; and a more holistic approach towards the functions and actions of departments within governments.
Spatial dimension	Trade, FDI, etc., judged mainly by effects on the domestic economy's comparative advantage of resource usage, employment and taxation.	A recognition that being a player in a global economy via, *e.g.* FDI, brings benefits via tapping into foreign assets and learning experiences. Issues of trade and FDI looked at from viewpoint of enhancing competitiveness of indigenous resources and capabilities and/or promoting dynamic comparative advantage.

To some extent, the problem is educating the decision takers in government. Here, the fault lies partly with the academic community. We have just not got over the message that there is a fundamental difference between the kind of government action necessary to help overcome endemic market failure and to facilitate the upgrading of the resources within their jurisdiction, and that which seeks to replace or modify the behaviour of firms in the belief that central planning and regulatory mechanisms can do a better job in advancing economic and social welfare than can markets. We have not got over the message that, to optimise their efficiency and response to market signals, firms require the availability of created assets and a wealth-creating ethos which, frequently, only governments can provide. We have not got over the message that increasingly *what* governments do and *how* they do it, is much more important than *how much* government involvement should there be.

To some extent, too, the problem is one of re-forming opinions and attitudes towards the role of governments. There is need for a new vocabulary to promote the image of government as a public good rather than as a necessary evil. We need a *perestroika* of government. We need to recognise that, just as "Fordism" is an outdated method of organising work, so the kind of government interventionism appropriate to "Fordism" is outdated. And, just like the emerging managerial structure of 21st century firms, we need governments to be lean, flexible and anticipatory of change. The new paradigm of government should eschew such negative or emotive sounding words such as "command", "intervention", "regulation", and replace them by words such as "empower", "steer", "co-operative", "co-ordination" and "systemic". Moreover, not only must governments recognise the need for a far more integrated and holistic system of organising their responsibilities (which demands a "spider's web" rather than a "hub and spoke" relationship between the various decision-taking initiatives and the core of government); but, all those affected by governments, and particularly ordinary tax payers, must learn to take a more positive view of the benefits which only the former can produce.

The changing role of firms and governments

Finally, what are the respective tasks of firms and governments in a knowledge-based economy and in an age of alliance capitalism as compared with those exercised in earlier eras? Here it might be useful to refer to Figure 1, which illustrates the three main organisational mechanisms for resource creation and allocation in a market-based economy, and depicts four situations in which each of these mechanisms plays a rather different role.

In Situation 1, as, for example, is the case of a purely communist society, neither private hierarchies nor markets play any part in the creation and allocation of resources: each is assumed to incur unacceptably high transaction costs and/or to promote unacceptable social goals. By contrast, in a purely market economy, private buyers and sellers are the sole determinants of the level and composition of goods and services produced and traded. Governments play a minimal role, while firms engage in a single value-added activity, the inputs for, and outputs of, which are bought and sold in the open market. In this scenario, the transaction costs of the market are assumed to be negligible, while those of hierarchies and governments are both assumed to be positive (see Situation 2).

Figure 1. The triad of organisational mechanisms

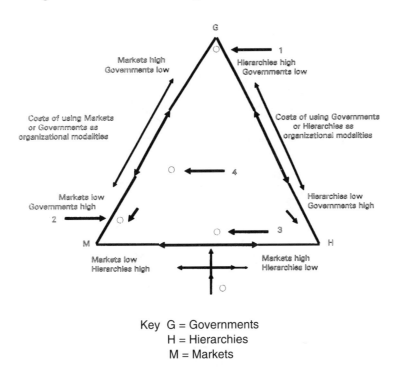

Key   G = Governments
      H = Hierarchies
      M = Markets

In a hierarchical-market-managed economy, economic activity is organised partly by markets, and partly by multi-product firms which govern the deployment of resources and capabilities which might otherwise have been co-ordinated through the market (see Situation 3). [11] This situation suggests that different kinds of economic activity require different modes of governance, and that the greater the market failure, the more likely its functions will be performed by, and within, hierarchies.

In a mixed economy (see Situation 4), governments, along with markets and hierarchies, may either directly engage in production and transactions or they may indirectly influence the structure of resource creation and allocation, which, otherwise, would be decided by the other two members of the triad. Such a tripartite arrangement presupposes that governments perceive that, in the case of some activities at least, neither markets nor hierarchies, by themselves, can achieve socially optimum results, and hence that some additional organisational modality is required.

It is, I think, generally acknowledged that changing economic, political and technological forces over the last one-and-a-half centuries have resulted in a substantial realignment of the costs and benefits of the three main modes in organisation of cross-border economic activity. Figure 2 illustrates the direction of these shifts. For example, in the mid-19th century, international transactions were mainly organised by arm's length markets. There was some government intervention, but large managerial hierarchies were in their infancy. Over the following century, while the relative significance of governments and markets in determining the level and terms of international transactions fluctuated, that of hierarchies continued to increase. However, no less noteworthy was the changing extent and character of the interaction between the triad of organisational entities, which, in the main, took on an adversarial form.

Figure 2. Changes in the configuration of the triad of organisational mechanisms

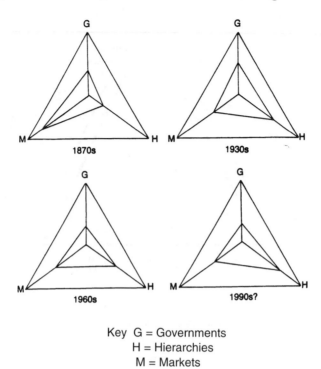

Key G = Governments
H = Hierarchies
M = Markets

What then of the situation of the knowledge economy in the late 1990s, and the prospects for the next decade or so? Consider, first, business corporations. As we have seen, all the evidence points to the further pushing back of their territorial boundaries, and to a larger number of them initiating regional or global production and marketing strategies, particularly within the OECD countries. In addition, the organisational forms of these strategies are likely to become more pluralistic as firms pursue a more holistic approach to their transborder operations. The boundaries of firms are becoming increasingly blurred as they forge new allegiances and as their networking with other firms becomes multi-focused. While it is probable that internalised cross-border bonding will increase, other less formal exchange relationships are likely to proliferate as firms interpenetrate each other's territories. More and more, the large international firm is becoming an orchestrator of a set of geographically dispersed, but interdependent, knowledge-based assets. Some of these, which represent its core competencies, it will wish to own; others (which may be no less important to its commercial success), it will either jointly supply with other firms or purchase from its global network of suppliers.

Next, consider the role of governments. We are currently in the midst of a wind of change towards the liberalisation of markets, and a reduction of government interventionism in the production process. However, while accepting the dramatic changes now occurring in the economic management of the erstwhile communist countries, the role of government in affecting the organisation and competitiveness of economic activity in knowledge-based economies has in no way diminished. Several of the most market-oriented national administrations have consistently pursued strategies and policies which have had a very fundamental impact upon the manner in which intellectual capital is created and used. In a variety of ways, and to achieve many diverse objectives, governments are increasingly taking actions which, taken as a whole, have repercussions on the nature and behaviour of firms far in excess of anything that the kind of industrial policies practised by Western nations in the 1970s ever achieved.

The fact is that governments do themselves a disservice by belittling their role as a promoter and sustainer of the efficient organisation of knowledge-based resources. It is the consensus of many studies that national governments have played a critical role in influencing the success or failure of post-war industrial economies; and that it is not the countries with the least government involvement which have performed the best, but those which have worked most closely and efficiently with hierarchies and markets to promote the most efficient and cost-efficient allocation and upgrading of resources under their jurisdiction. These are also the same governments which acknowledge that, while they, as resource managers, must lessen their intervention and reduce their own costs of governance, markets and hierarchies do sometimes fail, and that a systemic and integrated approach is needed if economic activity is to be optimally organised.

Finally, what of the characteristics of markets? Despite the current fashion towards the deregulation and liberalisation of markets, we suspect that the unaided efficiency of that particular exchange mechanism for many goods and services in the knowledge-based economy of the later 1990s is likely to fall in the 1990s. This is partly because we foresee a greater supra-market control over the conditions of supply of a whole range of products, *e.g.* to reduce information asymmetries, harmonize technical and safety standards and advance environmental goals, and partly because the interdependence between, and the risks associated with, the markets for intermediate products seem likely to increase. We also think it probable that there will be a recasting of international supervisory or control mechanisms to take account of the specific attributes of global production, and also to minimise the adverse effects of "beggar-thy-neighbour" strategic behaviour, *e.g.* with respect to investment incentives, on the part of national governments. At the same time, future developments in information and communications technologies may well reduce the costs of organising corporate networks; while a combination of the opportunities afforded by regional integration and the fear of regional protectionism is prompting firms to become insiders in both Western Europe and the United States.

Conclusions

The age of alliance capitalism and the maturation of the knowledge economy is, then, demanding a reconfiguration of the role of each of the three main organising mechanisms in a market-oriented economy; and, indeed, of the very structure of capitalism itself. Such a reconfiguration is primarily the result, on the one hand, of a shift in the origins of wealth in most industrial societies from natural resources to created assets and especially all forms of knowledge – and, on the other, of the widening geographical spread of all kinds of value-adding activity.

In the late-20th century market-based economies, as in earlier phases of capitalism, the privately owned and managed firm remains the critical wealth-creating agent. But, over the years, and particularly in the last two decades, the criteria for its success, the ingredients of its core competencies and its territorial boundaries have all changed; as, indeed, have its relationships with other firms.

Similarly, the emergence of an innovation-led global economy, with all its uncertainties and the difficulties of national macroeconomic management, has demanded that national governments reconsider their role, and how, in particular, their actions, for good or bad, may affect the dynamic comparative advantage of resources and the competitive advantages of firms in world markets. Also, because firm-specific created assets are increasingly mobile across national boundaries, national governments need to recognise and take account of each other's macro-organisational policies if they are to attract and retain mobile investments; and also to reappraise the instruments and policies which may best achieve that objective. In so doing, they may, and do, affect the functions and boundaries of firms; and this means that any discussion of the changing nature of the firm which does not consider the changing role of government, will be inadequate.

Indeed, it is the interaction between the new paradigm of the firm and that of government which, at the end of the day, will determine the nature and scope of the firm in late-20th century alliance capitalism. Here we see a movement towards a more co-operative and synergistic relationship between governments and firms, in which each is acknowledged to have a unique, but complementary role in a knowledge-based economy and in advancing the economic welfare of its constituents. While, to a certain extent, the respective roles of the state, firms and markets have always been recognised, it is only as we approach the 21st century that a holistic and integrative approach to the organisation of wealth-creating activities is being seriously considered. Even so, in most OECD countries, such an approach is still very much at an early stage and, this being so, the current changes in the nature of firms are simply a foretaste of those yet to be experienced.

NOTES

1. Or what some commentators (*e.g.* Edvinson, 1997) have referred to as intellectual capital.

2. For further details see, for example, *World Development Report* (World Bank, 1996), Tables 11 and 12.

3. The implications of alliance capitalism, a term originally coined by Michael Gerlach (1992), and also called "relational'", "collective", and "stakeholder" capitalism, are explored in a new book by the current author, *viz.* Dunning (1997*a*). In that book, we accept that the current wave of strategic *et al.* alliances could lead to a reconfiguration, rather than a replacement, of hierarchical capitalism. Here the eventual impact of the rash of mergers and acquisitions on the organisational structure of US industry towards the end of the last century should not be ignored (Chandler, 1990).

4. One estimate (Dunning, 1996) suggests that between 20 and 25 per cent of R&D undertaken by the world's largest industrial corporations is located outside their home countries, while patent statistics confirm that an increasing proportion of patents registered by firms in the United States are in respect of innovations arising from their foreign subsidiaries.

5. *i.e.* disinternalising activities both along a value chain (*e.g.* horizontal disintegration).

6. See, for example, various articles in a special issue of the *Strategic Management Review*, Vol. 17, Winter 1996, edited by J.C. Spender and R.M. Grant.

7. We say most because there still remain some firms which engage in more traditional sectors, but even here communication and related technologies are requiring considerable restructuring of their activities.

8. According to UNCTAD (1995), between 1991 and 1994, of 373 changes in the foreign investment regimes made by over 50 countries, 368 were in the direction of liberalisation or more aggressive promotional procedures.

9. Clearly, the extent of such autonomy depends upon the economic and other characteristics of the country in question, not only its size and resource structure; compare, for example, that of the United States with that of Singapore.

10. As set out at length in the literature, *e.g.* in Chang and Rowthorn (1995), by Dunning (1994) and by several contributions in Dunning (1997*b*).

11. Relative to the number of goods and services produced in the world economy, the number of separate and discrete economic activities required to produce and market these goods and services has increased. In other words, the transactional intensity of economic activity has risen.

REFERENCES

CHANG, H.-J. and R. ROWTHOLM (eds.) (1995), *The Role of the State in Economic Change*, , The Clarendon Press, Oxford.

CANTWELL, J. (1991), "The Theory of Technological Competence and its Application to International Production," in D.G. McFetridge (ed.), *Foreign Investment, Technology and Economic Growth*, University of Calgary Press, Calgary.

CHANDLER, A.D., Jr. (1990), *Scale and Scope: The Dynamics of Industrial Capitalism*, Harvard University, Cambridge, MA.

DUNNING, J.H. (1994), *Globalization: The Challenge for National Economic Regimes*, The Economic and Social Research Council, Dublin.

DUNNING, J.H. (1995) (reprinted in Dunning 1997*a*), "Reappraising the Eclectic Paradigm in the Age of Alliance Capitalism", *Journal of International Business Studies 26* (3), pp; 461-493.

DUNNING, J.H. (1996), "The Geographical Sources of Competitiveness of Firms: The Results of a New Survey", *Transnational Corporations 5* (3), December.

DUNNING, J.H. (1997*a*), *Alliance Capitalism and Global Business,* Routledge, London and New York.

DUNNING, J.H. (1997*b*) (ed.), *Governments, Globalization and International Business*, Oxford University Press.

EDVINSON, L. (1997), *Intellectual Capital Development*, Skandia, Stockholm.

GERLACH, M.L. (1992), *Alliance Capitalism: The Social Organization of Japanese Business*, Oxford Press, Oxford.

GRABHER, G. (1993) (ed.), *The Embedded Firm*, Routledge, London and Boston:, pp. 116-137.

GRANT, R.M. and C. BADEN-FULLER (1995), "A Knowledge-based Theory of Inter-firm Collaboration", *Academy of Management Best Paper Proceedings*, pp. 17-21.

MARKUSEN, A. (1994), *Sticky Places in Slippery Spaces: The Political Economy of Post-War Fast Growth Regions*, Rutgers University Working Paper No. 79, New Brunswick Center for Urban Policy Research.

OSBORNE, D. and T. GAEBLER (1992), *Reinventing Government: How the Entrepreneurial Spirit is Transforming the Public Sector*, Addison Wesley, Reading, MA.

SPENDER, J.C. and R.M. GRANT (1996) (eds.), "Knowledge of the Firm", *Strategic Management Review*, Vol. 17, Winter, Special Issue.

UNCTAD (DTCI) (1995), *World Investment Report 1995: Transnational Corporations and Competitiveness,* UN, Geneva and New York.

UNCTAD (DTCI) (1996), *World Investment Report 1996: Transnational Corporations, Investment, Trade and International Policy Arrangements,* UN, New York and Geneva.

WORLD BANK (1996), *World Development Report*, Oxford University Press, Oxford.

Chapter 5

HUMAN-RESOURCE ASPECTS OF THE CHANGING NATURE OF THE FIRM: ISSUES, EVIDENCE AND PUBLIC POLICY IMPLICATIONS[1]

by

Gordon Betcherman
Canadian Policy Research Networks and Ekos Research Associates
Ottawa, Canada

Concerns about productivity, employment and income distribution rank high on the agenda of individual governments. As national (and sub-national) governments and the OECD have grappled with these issues through the 1990s, there seems to have been a shift in emphasis away from traditional macroeconomic policies to a more micro focus. This is not to say, of course, that macroeconomic policy and the environment it creates are no longer important. But the growing interest in the micro side across much of the OECD region reflects two developments. The first is the fiscal and political constraints that most governments have been experiencing on the macro front during the 1990s. The second is the widening perception that, for various reasons, the changing nature of economic activity is heightening the importance of production inputs that are only indirectly related to the macro environment and that ultimately play out at the level of the enterprise.

The driving force behind this changing nature of economic activity has been a radical shift in what economists have variously called "enabling" or "general purpose" technologies (Lipsey, 1996). The key development here, of course, has been the revolution in information and communication technologies which has led to a reconceptualisation of production. As Freeman and Perez (1988) have argued, however, this reconceptualisation involves much more than a simple recalibration of the neo-classical production function; it also involves a new "technoeconomic paradigm" – *i.e.* the web of institutions, policies and practices by which economic activity is organised. This web has many strands, operating at a number of levels including society-wide, in particular markets and within individual firms.

By now, we have learned from the "new" economic growth theorists that the critical factors underlying growth are "intangible" assets that create knowledge and generate innovation. The optimal technoeconomic paradigm for this economy, then, is one that supports efficient investment in these assets. At the same time that these factors drive economic growth (and, thus, the possibilities for income and job creation), the capacity for knowledge creation and innovation, themselves, appears to be shaped to an important degree by organisational strategies, structures and practices. It is through this set of links that the nature of the firm becomes so central to macroeconomic objectives.

This shift in the technoeconomic paradigm calls for changes in the strategies, practices and behaviours of all of the economic stakeholders. Lipsey (1996) disaggregates the responses into two components: the "policy structure" and the "facilitating structure". The latter includes the physical capital embodying the specific technologies, human capital, organisation of production facilities, the financial and managerial organisation of firms, the organisation of industries, infrastructure and financial institutions. Among the various areas where changes in the facilitating structure are occurring, this chapter is concerned with innovation in the workplace including the reorganisation of work and human resource management practices including training. The underlying motivation of these changes has been to improve enterprise flexibility and increase investments in intangible assets.

As we will see below, these workplace changes do appear to contribute to organisational performance and, by extension, to the overall economy. However, the transition to new workplace systems is not unfolding in seamless fashion. The diffusion of practices that effectively enhance flexibility and support intangible investment has been fairly narrow. And the workplace change that has occurred seems to have contributed in some instances to economic insecurity and polarisation. Thus, while governments do not have any overriding interest in what happens within individual firms, for both efficiency- and equity-related reasons they must be concerned with the nature of the changing organisation.

The challenge for policy makers is how to stimulate the adoption of organisational strategies and practices that foster the knowledge generation and innovation which underlie productivity and employment growth, on the one hand, and lead to acceptable income distributions and high rates of economic participation, on the other. This challenge is heightened by the fact that governments cannot achieve these objectives with traditional policies but will require new knowledge and approaches, themselves, if they are going to contribute to supporting desirable workplace change. It is also important to keep in mind that the particular policy interventions and strategies will differ country by country, reflecting different contexts across the OECD area.

This paper covers these issues by addressing four questions:[2]

◊   What changes are occurring in the workplace and how widely are they being diffused?

◊   What is the evidence on the impacts of workplace change?

◊   What are the barriers to diffusion?

◊   What is the role of governments in supporting workplace innovation?

The diffusion of workplace change

"Workplace change" is a broad concept that encompasses strategic, structural and behavioural dimensions.[3] At least in recent times, it has been largely employer-initiated and typically in response to intensified competition and new technological opportunities. The fundamental thrust of much of the organisational change that has occurred throughout the OECD area has been to enhance organisational flexibility. Following the characterisation adopted by the OECD (1986) a number of years ago, there are two broad types of flexibility strategy. *Numerical* flexibility relates to the establishment's ability to vary its workforce by hiring and firing, by altering hours of work, by using non-standard employees or by subcontracting or outsourcing. *Functional* flexibility relates to the establishment's capacity to reorganise how work itself is carried out within the firm. Flexibility strategies can be oriented towards either the internal operations of the firm or on the relationships between the firm and external markets and agents, or both.

A key thing to emphasize is that workplace change designed to enhance flexibility can take many forms depending on a host of national and even industry- and firm-level characteristics. Certainly at a national level, there are differences in terms of how enterprises are pursuing flexibility strategies. The OECD (1997, forthcoming) has identified four dominant "regional" approaches to organisational change representing countries with Anglo-Saxon traditions, the Northern European countries, Japan and the "intermediate" or "catch-up" countries. These differences largely reflect differences in the traditional organisational paradigms and their attendant strengths and weaknesses.[4]

Workplace change typically entails complementary bundles of practices in one or more of the following three overlapping areas:

◊ *work organisation*, which involves changes in the production process, how work is organised, job responsibilities, work allocation and organisational structure;

◊ *human resource management practices*, which can cover a range of personnel management areas including hiring and firing, compensation, information sharing and decision making, training and scheduling;

◊ *industrial relations practices*, where in unionised environments, new strategies or institutional structures alter processes between labour and management.

We have already emphasized that the precise form of workplace change will differ across firms. In a sense, then, there is no single "best practice", all the more so when the frame of reference is international. However, the OECD (1997, forthcoming) does identify a "loosely defined 'model'" of an emerging organisational system which incorporates some of the following: more complex jobs, more multi-skilling and overall upskilling; ongoing training; reduced hierarchy; greater communication and distribution of responsibility; compensation incentives; increased focus on "core" activities; and more inter-firm links.

At the core of the emerging systems, then, are two connected features. We have already discussed the first – the goal of enhanced flexibility which, as we have seen, can take a variety of forms. The second (related) key element of organisational change involves investments in "intangible" assets which are central to the innovation and knowledge creation that drive growth under the new technoeconomic paradigm. These intangibles include investments in human and organisational capital (through training and work organisation, for example), management structures, technology, software, links with other organisations and market development. Of these, it is human and organisational capital investments that are at the heart of the workplace changes which provide the focus for this chapter.

Patterns of diffusion

How widely have these organisational changes diffused? Before turning to this question, a couple of points of caution should be made. First, there are significant gaps in our knowledge which reflect the intrinsic difficulties involved in assembling system-wide empirical evidence on the organisational variables of interest (*e.g.* strategy, structure, practices). These variables, for the most part, are intangible and thus not easily captured in a quantifiable sense. Moreover, the nature of the evidence that is available is complicated by the fact that different researchers have used various definitions and methodologies. And finally, as we have seen, the international context raises additional complexities because of significant variations across countries due to cultural, historical and institutional factors.

These qualifications notwithstanding, there has been progress recently in terms of estimating the diffusion of organisational change (and its impacts which will be summarised in the next section). On the basis of analysis in a number of Member countries, the OECD (1997, forthcoming) estimates that about one-quarter of all enterprises have adopted flexible organisational or workplace systems of one form or another. The patterns, if not the forms, do appear to be similar across countries. Incidence is highest among larger firms than among small and medium-sized ones.[5] It also tends to be highest in industries exposed to international competition and where competitiveness is determined primarily by quality and product/service innovation.[6] Finally, close links between organisational and technological change have been consistently observed. Organisational changes, both in terms of internal processes and relations with external markets, often have been initiated as new technology has been introduced and has penetrated deeply within enterprises.

Impacts of organisational change

Workplace innovation potentially has a wide range of impacts. It can affect various aspects of enterprise performance and different sorts of outcomes for employees. At a macro level, the cumulative effect of these changes can have both social and economic consequences for the labour market and society.

For a number of reasons, it is difficult to empirically identify these outcomes. There are various issues that come into play in attempting to measure the impacts of organisational change on firms and on workers.[7] It is far from straightforward to establish appropriate workplace measures and then to clearly establish linkages between these and outcomes. Identification of causality can be especially problematic. To offer one illustration, enterprises that invest in intangible assets through training, for example, may also report positive performance trends in terms of, say, revenues. Is training leading to performance improvements or do successful companies simply have more resources to make investments, intangible or otherwise? Or, is there a virtuous circle of investment and performance gains and further investment? Furthermore, since organisational innovation is often part of broader enterprise changes (*e.g.* as part of a process of technological change), it is often problematic to isolate its effects. None of these relationships can be unambiguously identified using available data sets.[8]

Keeping in mind the data and methodological limitations, outcomes research has been accumulating, especially on the enterprise side. This body of analysis generally shows a positive association between organisational systems built on flexibility and intangible asset investments and enterprise performance measures such as productivity and sales. There are two lines of evidence supporting this conclusion. One comes from case studies of firms that have introduced these types of organisational innovations.[9] The other comes from quantitative surveys that demonstrate statistically significant links (if not causality) between flexible organisational practices and enterprise performance measures.

The precise mechanisms underlying these links, however, are only imperfectly understood. Research does indicate that organisational innovation is most effective when it includes complementary "bundles" of practices. It also seems to require support from all of the key stakeholders, from senior management through the supervisory level and from labour. Decision makers must also recognise that organisational investments tend to have long time horizon strategies and, thus, they must be prepared to wait for the benefits. Failure can occur for a number of reasons then and, indeed, the payoff from organisational change is not guaranteed.[10]

While it is the evidence associating flexible organisational systems with improved firm performance that can be expected to drive their further diffusion within industry, public policy makers are concerned most about macro impacts. In this regard, to the extent that organisational innovation does improve enterprise performance, it can be assumed to contribute to aggregate economic performance as well.

What about impacts related to labour-market variables and income distribution? Unfortunately, there is little evidence to indicate whether the boost to productivity and growth spills over into net employment creation.[11] On the one hand, conventional economic theory would unambiguously say that it would; however, on the other hand, rationalisation is a clear objective of many flexible organisational strategies and casual observation reveals that highly innovative enterprises are "doing more with less". A priority for future research is to clarify the transmission mechanisms between production and employment under the new organisational models. The suspicion now exists that these may be different than was previously the case.

While the impacts of flexible organisational systems on the overall level of labour demand may be uncertain, it is clear that they change the composition of that demand in favour of more skilled workers. The advanced technology that generally accompanies (or drives) flexible systems, plus the precision, flexibility and dependability required in these organisations, call for a workforce with firm-specific and, in particular, very strong general employability skills. Thus the diffusion of flexible systems increases the importance of human-capital investment. And, indeed, surveys indicate that training and a culture of continuous learning tend to accompany organisational innovation. However, they also suggest that human capital investments are concentrated on the well-educated and skilled employees in the "core" and not on those less-skilled workers in the "periphery".[12] In this way, then, workplace innovation may be contributing to the wage polarisation evident in some OECD countries.

"Best practice" organisational change

So, are there "best practices" whose wide diffusion is in the public interest in the sense of contributing to aggregate economic, employment and social goals? As our brief review of the impacts of organisational change suggests, there are no magic answers. Flexible systems can lead to positive performance outcomes for firms and, presumably, to economic efficiency gains, at least in the short run. The benefits for workers, again at least in the short run, are not as clear. New organisational systems, as they have typically been introduced, seem to provide opportunities for challenging work, material benefits and human capital investment for some segments of the population (especially high-skilled workers), but not necessarily for the full spectrum of the labour force.

In the final analysis, much more thinking needs to go into defining "best practice" organisational innovation. However, the way forward would seem to involve the recognition that sustainable innovation must incorporate a long-run view of efficiency. Key questions for policy makers, then, should include the following: is it based on investments in "intangibles," including human and organisational capital? Does it provide workers with opportunities to enhance their employability and, thus, longer-run economic security? Are there productivity gains and mechanisms for sharing those gains? Thus, a complete assessment requires that various perspectives be incorporated and that the long-run effects be considered.

Barriers to diffusion

There are a variety of reasons why "best practice" organisational innovations may not diffuse to an optimal extent on their own.[13] Many of these relate to problems associated with investing in intangibles. In this section, we will briefly discuss three barriers to diffusion that are especially relevant for policy makers: market failures, divergent interests of the stakeholders and unsupportive institutional environments.

Market failures

Market failures stem from both information barriers and externality issues. Information barriers occur at a number of levels. One that is attracting increasing attention concerns the functioning of financial markets and their limitations in terms of gaining access to and interpreting information relevant for evaluating the expected returns from investments in intangible assets. It is clear that these markets do take into account these assets – management quality is an obvious example. However, most experts believe that this accounting is partial and unsystematic.[14] As a consequence, intangible investments are probably undervalued.

One source of this problem is the limitations of enterprise accounting frameworks which tend to measure intangible assets incompletely.[15] These frameworks at best measure the costs but rarely the returns associated with these investments. Reviews of accounting practices in the area of training, for example, reveal this. Surveys show that a substantial proportion of firms do not regularly track training expenditures and only a minority attempt to formally measure impacts.[16] In other human resource areas the situation is almost certainly even worse. A related information barrier for firms pertains to the difficulties many experience in accumulating information about intangible investments and in managing relevant knowledge within the firm.

The externality problem relates to the risks associated with intangible investments, whereby enterprises have no guarantee that they will capture the returns to investments that are not firm-specific.[17] Thus, the aggregate level of investment will be sub-optimal. This problem has been most frequently considered within the area of training where firms, having invested in the training of an employee (with at least some general skills component), may lose that worker to another company before they have fully benefited from the performance gains that result from the training.[18] Less attention has been paid to the externalities that may be associated with other types of human and organisational investments. At any rate, it seems likely that this is becoming an increasingly important issue for firms implementing various flexible employment systems, such as using temporary and other non-standard workers. In these arrangements, investments in training and other human resource development strategies will be made less frequently.

Divergent interests

A second barrier relates to divergent interests of employers and employees. Employers typically evaluate change in terms of its effect on performance and competitiveness; employees judge change more often in terms of its impact on job security, on job quality including health and safety and access to learning opportunities and on earnings. Over the long run, these interests do converge; however, in the short run, they can be opposing interests. This issue of divergent interests manifests itself in different ways in different countries because of cultural and institutional variations.

This divergence heightens a natural unwillingness to take the risks inherent in redefining roles, responsibilities and relationships, which is necessary in changing workplace systems. To complicate the situation further, much of the recent organisational change has been dominated by management-led initiatives in response to crisis situations. This is a difficult setting in which to generate the co-operation and long-range planning that research has shown is important in achieving effective, durable workplace change.

Unsupportive institutional environments

Institutional frameworks and public policies also act as impediments to the introduction, diffusion and sustainability of organisational innovation built on intangible investment. These can involve a wide range of institutions. Naturally, these barriers and their effects differ across countries because of major institutional differences.

One institutional barrier is corporate governance and financial market institutions that emphasize shareholders' short-run interests. This can have the effect of directing management priorities away from the long time horizon necessary for investing in many intangibles. This "capital impatience" has received particular attention as a problem in the North American context (Kochan and Osterman, 1995). Various labour-market institutions may also come into play. For example, the design of unemployment insurance systems in some countries allows firms to "externalise" adjustment costs which can act as a disincentive to human-resource investment. Collective bargaining laws can have the effect of discouraging labour relations innovations that support labour-management co-operation regarding workplace issues. Employment standards and regulations can impose costs which have the effect of deterring hiring. Weak education and training institutions can limit the supply of workers with the general employability and more specific occupational skills that seem to be prerequisites for effective flexible organisational systems.

The role of government

Government interest in organisational change cannot stem from any particular concern about what happens in individual workplaces *per se* but rather how "best practice" at the micro level can serve traditional macro policy objectives relating to productivity growth, income growth and distribution, employment and social cohesion. Thus governments have an incentive to produce, or facilitate the production of, public goods that support the diffusion of best practice organisational innovation. They also have a role in considering how to redress market failures that lead to a sub-optimal level of innovation and investment in intangibles.[19]

At a general level, then, governments must assess how they can contribute to a framework that is supportive of "best practice" organisations. It is very important to emphasize, however, that the appropriate strategies will differ from country to country because of differences across the OECD area in terms of what "best practice" is, what the major barriers are, as well as differences in terms of political philosophy.

In thinking about a more specific policy agenda, governments face real constraints. In a sense the most straightforward one is the fiscal pressures that now restrict the sorts of solutions most public administrations can pursue. A second constraint stems from the intangible aspects of the "new economy" – and, by extension, the sorts of organisations that are suited to it and thus should be fostered. Value is increasingly created by fluid enterprises that are constantly revising their own internal operations as well as changing the nature and content of their interactions with external actors and markets. This creates unprecedented challenges for governments in observing what is happening and in identifying where and how they can usefully get involved.[20]

Even where a clear policy rationale exists, governments are increasingly uncertain about how to proceed. This uncertainty is heightened by two other developments. First, conventional policy "silos" (*e.g.* human resources, industry, treasury, etc.) are often no longer appropriate since many of the issues need to be dealt with horizontally. Second, global integration is increasingly raising the prospect of competitive policy regimes and the need to consider the attractiveness of national and sub-national policies for mobile factors of production such as capital and highly skilled labour.

To return to the notion of the new "technoeconomic paradigm" discussed in the introduction, it seems clear that, at the cutting edge at least, there is substantial change now in what Lipsey (1996) calls the "facilitating structure", which includes the organisational issues considered in this chapter.[21] For this organisational change to be more diffused and effective in its implementation, Lipsey's (1996) "policy structure"- the political and economic institutions that provide the context for economic activity – must also respond. This will require new roles and new skills on the part of governments. Control and direct provision of services will be less central functions, while information and knowledge generation, offering technical resources and support, and brokering alliances between different interests will become more important.

In substantive terms, what can governments do to support organisational change that will contribute to important macroeconomic and social goals? Since human capital investment is at the core of the knowledge generation and innovation that underlie such change, the clearest priority is education and training. As a starting point, human-resource development policy must provide basic-skills education which is a key to entry in the knowledge-based economy and is unlikely to be funded from non-public sources. Governments can also support efficient human-capital markets through information, counselling and standard-setting; indeed, a number of trends are heightening the information challenge in these markets. They must also promote linkages within the education sector and between that sector and the labour market. Finally, human capital markets appear to generate outcomes that have a polarising effect and a priority for public policy is to guarantee that selective access problems are confronted.

However, governments must go beyond education and training, and address a range of other concerns in support of organisational innovation. One is to foster the diffusion of best practices through gathering and disseminating information on workplace innovation; providing consulting support on organisational change and investing in intangibles (especially for small enterprises); and brokering sectoral or national institutional partnerships.

And, ultimately, governments must be concerned with how economic security can be provided in a flexible-enterprise economy. Workers everywhere are concerned about downsizing, outsourcing and the growth of contingent employment and the implications of these trends for unemployment, inequality and poverty. These concerns are heightened by the fact that, as the current of economic life seems to have become more turbulent, traditional sources of security (*e.g.* unions and the social safety net) have weakened with the result that the associated risks have increasingly shifted onto the shoulders of individuals and away from the collectivity.

Ultimately, high levels of economic insecurity have the potential to erode popular support for growth-oriented economic agendas founded on innovation, flexibility and the efficiency of markets. At the same time, a failure to confront the security issue could potentially threaten social cohesion. For these reasons, governments must place a high priority on how to provide security in the new environment. How this is achieved is another question, whether it is through a re-invented safety net or (more likely) through very different institutions and policies that offer security not as protection *from* change, but as the ability *to* change.

NOTES

1. This is a revised and extended version of a paper presented at the International Seminar on "The Changing Nature of the Firm" held in Stockholm in February 1997 and sponsored by the Swedish Ministry of Industry and the OECD. The revisions have benefited from the discussion at the seminar and the ensuing conference, "Industrial Competitiveness in the Knowledge-based Economy: The New Role of Government".

2. I have considered these questions in more extended fashion and in a somewhat different context in a report on the conference, "Changing Workplace Strategies: Achieving Better Outcomes for Enterprises, Workers and Society," sponsored by Human Resources Development Canada and the OECD in December 1996. See Betcherman (1997).

3. The term itself is widely used, but at times its meaning is not precise. To complicate things further, other labels – "organisational innovation", "flexible organisations", "high-performance workplaces", to offer just a few examples – are often used interchangeably with workplace change.

4. To illustrate, firms in the Anglo-Saxon countries traditionally have adopted organisational strategies that have emphasized numerical flexibility, relying on labour markets that have been relatively unregulated. In Northern Europe, where markets have been more regulated but where consensual labour relations systems have accommodated more bipartite negotiation and agreement, organisational systems traditionally have been based much more on well-developed internal employment systems that provided considerable functional flexibility. The differences in the current direction of innovation reflect this history. Many firms in the former group are now trying to become more functionally flexible while much of the innovation in Europe depicts a drive to establish more external flexibility, especially in the numerical sense.

5. It should be recognised that most data instruments are better suited to capturing organisational changes in larger firms where the process is more likely to be formalised and codified than in small firms.

6. Relatively high incidence rates have been found in certain manufacturing industries. Less is known about organisational innovation in services but it is now becoming apparent that many firms in some service industries such as financial services, communications and a range of business services are undergoing workplace changes analogous to those occurring in manufacturing.

7. There is a well-developed literature concerned with the methodological issues associated with measuring outcomes on firms (*e.g.* OECD, 1996; Ichniowski *et al.*, 1996; and Huselid, 1995). Less attention has been paid to issues around measuring outcomes for employees.

8. One promising data development is the Workplace and Employee Survey being undertaken by Statistics Canada, with support from Human Resources Development Canada. This is not only a linked employer-employee survey, but plans are to make a longitudinal panel with both firms and workers followed over time. This panel dimension may allow for improved identification of causal relationships.

9. The case study literature from the United States is reviewed in Ichniowski *et al.* (1996). Four examples of European companies (Asea Brown Boveri AB, Skandia Insurance, SOL-palvelut, and Swatch AG) with innovative organisational systems were described at the Stockholm seminar. In each case, successful enterprise outcomes were attributed to the flexible organisational strategies and to the investment in intangibles.

10. One common pitfall is "fad-based" innovation where firms introduce popular change strategies that may be inappropriate for their situation. Some of the literature documenting this syndrome is reviewed in *The Economist* (1997).

11. Qualitative evidence gathered through public opinion surveys indicates that a number of labour market developments, including flexible workplace models, may be reducing job security. Certainly, they reduce *perceptions* of security. However, job-tenure data (at least from North America) does not support this perception since it shows that tenure has remained relatively unchanged through the 1980s and 1990s (*e.g.* Farber, 1995; Green and Riddell, 1997).

12. Evidence from training surveys shows the unequal distribution of workplace training with workers who already have high stocks of human capital receiving a disproportionate share (*e.g.* de Broucker, 1997).

13. Or, alternatively, these may be obstacles to firms in terms of maximising the effectiveness of organisational change initiatives.

14. For a review of the issues, see the summary document (OECD, 1997) of the "Accounting for Intangibles: The Case of Human Resources" seminar organised by the OECD and Human Resources Development Canada in Ottawa, December 1996.

15. Practices and developments in human resource accounting are reviewed in Drake (1997), which reports on the OECD Helsinki seminar.

16. For example, in a recent Canadian survey, Betcherman, Leckie and McMullen (1997) found that 43 per cent of establishments with training programmes did not regularly track these expenditures and only 36 per cent reported they undertook formal impacts analysis. Follow-up case studies revealed that these figures probably overstate the accounting endeavour in that there is little uniformity in terms of how these firms measure the costs and benefits; their interpretation of formal impacts analysis can include methods that lack rigour; and there is virtually no consideration of more informal modes of training investment.

17. For a recent treatment of these issues, see Booth and Snower (1996).

18. According to human capital theory, employees should fund general skills training, usually through lower wages. However, it is not always straightforward to apportion costs where training, as is so often the case, has both general and firm-specific elements. Even where it is clearly of a general nature and thus appropriately employee funded, various behavioural and institutional factors can make it difficult for this to occur.

19. In these cases, there is increasing onus on governments to show how any possible interventions improve on the imperfect market outcome.

20. An interesting list of challenges posed by "new economy" organisations for policy makers was presented by Leif Edvinson of Skandia Insurance Co. at the Stockholm seminar. This list focused on the "imaginary" nature of value-creating firms, the importance of investments in intangibles and the balance between global and local activity.

21. This new organisational paradigm was summarised by John Dunning in his presentation to the Stockholm seminar.

REFERENCES

BETCHERMAN, Gordon (1997), *Changing Workplace Strategies: Achieving Better Outcomes for Enterprises, Workers and Society,* Summary Report of a Conference sponsored by Human Resources Development Canada and the OECD, Ottawa, December 1996.

BETCHERMAN, Gordon, Norm LECKIE and Kathryn McMULLEN (1997), *Developing Skills for the Canadian Workplace: The Results of the Ekos Workplace Training Survey,* Canadian Policy Research Networks, Ottawa.

BOOTH, Alison L. and Dennis J. SNOWER (1996), *Acquiring Skills: Market Failures, Their Symptoms and Policy Responses,* Cambridge University Press, New York.

de BROUCKER, Patrice (1997), "Job-related Education and Training: Who Has Access?" *Education Quarterly Review,* Vol. 4, No. 1, Statistics Canada Catalogue No. 81-003-XPB.

DRAKE, Keith (1997), "Human Resource Accountancy in Enterprises: Recent Practices and New Developments", in OECD/Ernst & Young Center for Business Innovation, *Enterprise Value in the Knowledge Economy: Measuring Performance in the Age of Intangibles* (forthcoming).

FARBER, Hank S. (1995), *Are Lifetime Jobs Disappearing? Job Duration in the United States, 1973-1993,* Working Paper No. 5014, National Bureau of Economic Research, Washington, DC.

FREEMAN, Chris and Carlota PEREZ (1998), "Structural Crisis of Adjustment" in Giovanni Dosi *et al.* (eds.). *Technological Change and Economic Theory,* Pinter, London.

GREEN, David A. and W. Craig RIDDELL (1997), "Job Durations in Canada: Is Long-term Employment Declining?", in M.G. Abbott, C.M. Beach and R.P. Chaykowski (eds.), *Transition and Structural Change in the North American Labour Market,* IRC Press, Kingston, ON.

HUSELID, Mark A. (1995), "The Impact of Human Resource Management Practices on Turnover, Productivity and Corporate Financial Performance", *Academy of Management Journal,* Vol. 38, No. 3.

ICHNIOWSKI, Casey *et al.* (1996), "What Works at Work? Overview and Assessment", *Industrial Relations,* Vol. 35, No. 3, July.

KOCHAN, Thomas A. and Paul OSTERMAN (1995), *The Mutual Gains Enterprise,* Harvard University Press, Boston.

LIPSEY, Richard G. (1996), *Economic Growth, Technological Change, and Canadian Economic Policy,* C.D. Howe Institute Benefactors Lecture, Vancouver.

OECD (1986), *Labour Market Flexibility: The Current Debate,* Paris.

OECD (1996), *Technology, Productivity, and Job Creation*, Paris.

OECD (1997), "Accounting for Intangibles: The Case of Human Resources", unpublished report of a technical meeting jointly sponsored by the OECD and Human Resources Development Canada, Hull, Quebec, December 1996.

OECD (1997), *Flexible Enterprises*, Paris (forthcoming).

THE ECONOMIST (1997), "Instant Coffee as Management Theory", 25 January.

Chapter 6

FOREIGN DIRECT INVESTMENT, COUNTRY CHARACTERISTICS AND LESSONS FOR POLICY

by

James R. Markusen
University of Colorado, Boulder
Universitat Pompeu Fabra, Barcelona

I have been asked to explore the interplay between changing firm and country characteristics over time, and what role national policies can play in determining the outcome. Since several speakers will focus more closely on the nature of firms engaged in direct investment and in other forms of international business, I will concentrate more on the country characteristics and what lessons recent history suggests for public policy.

First, I will quickly review evidence on the characteristics of firms that engage in direct investment. It is important to establish that foreign direct investment (FDI) is associated with firms and industries that are relatively intensive in the use of skilled labour and that these firms are closely associated with knowledge-intensive production. Much of the value of the multinational firm lies in various forms of knowledge-based assets rather than in physical capital. These assets range from blueprints, formulae, patents, to organisation procedures, to brand and reputation capital. Some of the specific characteristics of multinationals (relative to all firms) identified in studies are as follows:

Firm and industry characteristics of multinationals

◊ multinationals are associated with high ratios of R&D relative to sales;

◊ multinationals employ large numbers of scientific, technical and other "white-collar" workers;

◊ multinationals tend to have a high value of "intangible assets" (roughly, the market value of the firm minus its book value of capital);

◊ multinationals are associated with new and/or technically complex products;

◊ plant-level scale economies are not associated with multinationality;

◊ multinationals are associated with product-differentiation variables, such as advertising, trade-marks, and brand identification;

◊ a "threshold" level of firm size seems to be important for a firm to be a multinational, but above that level firm size is of minimal importance;

◊ multinationals tend to be older, more established firms.

FDI not only varies significantly across industries, but also varies considerably with respect to source and host countries. Characteristics of source and host countries combine with firm characteristics to forge an understanding of the investment process. Existing evidence indicates that FDI is overwhelmingly a developed-to-developed-country phenomenon. Direct investment is much more concentrated among high-income countries than is GNP or trade. This is partly explained by the knowledge-intensity and high-tech nature of the goods and services produced, and by the fact that the market for the same goods and services lies in relatively high-income consumers. The sales of European affiliates in the United States, for example, have grown from about 88 per cent of the value of European exports to the United States in the early 1980s to about 122 per cent in 1993.

Evidence suggests that the overwhelming part of direct investment remains "horizontal" or "market-seeking". Firms producing advanced products and services for high-income consumers constitute the bulk of multinational activity. The theory of the multinationals explains the association of horizontal multinationals with knowledge capital, by noting that this capital often has a public-goods or joint-input characteristic within the firm. Blueprints, for example, can be supplied to additional production facilities without lowering the value of these assets in existing plants. Physical capital usually does not have this property. In this theory, multinationals are thus exports of the services of knowledge-based assets to foreign subsidiaries.

A second type of direct investment is termed "vertical" or "resource-seeking". It occurs when firms geographically fragment the production process by stages, with the stages generally located where the factors they use intensively are relatively cheap. US firms, for example, often ship components to Mexico for assembly, with the output shipped back to the United States. US and Japanese firms do the same types of assembly work in South-East Asia. Despite the well-known examples of this type of activity, vertical direct investment has been quantitatively much less important than horizontal investment, although they are difficult to distinguish in the data. Specific country characteristics of direct investment include:

Country characteristics

◊ High-income countries are both the major source and recipient countries. Most direct investment seems to be *horizontal*.

◊ High volumes of direct investment are associated with *similarities* among countries in relative factor endowments and per capita incomes, not differences.

◊ Vertical direct investments, when they can be identified, often go to middle-income countries with inexpensive skilled labour.

◊ Outward direct investment is positively related to a country's endowment of skilled labour and insignificantly or negatively related to its physical capital endowment.

◊ Direct investment is not primarily motivated by tariff avoidance or measurable transport costs.

◊ There is mixed evidence that tax avoidance and/or risk diversification motivates direct investment. Political risk discourages inward investment.

◊ Infrastructure, skill levels and a minimum threshold level of per capita income are important determinants of inward direct investment. Intellectual property protection has a positive effect.

◊ There is evidence that agglomeration effects are important in direct investment.

◊ Evidence suggests that direct investment *follows* growth; it does not lead it.

The overall picture is that direct investment is primarily from high-income, developed countries to other high-income, developed countries. That portion of direct investment that does go to developing countries seems to be either motivated by market-seeking motives in large markets such as China, or by resource-seeking motives, particularly low-wage assembly labour. Still, it is important to note that in the latter case, direct investment does not go to the poorest countries, but is concentrated among middle-income countries with good infrastructure and good supplies of skilled labour. Multinationals do not enter at the bottom of the development ladder (with a few possible exceptions such as mining or petroleum extraction).

I have looked hard to find trends in the 1990s that depart significantly from those of the previous two decades. But much of what I see is a matter of degree, not of qualitative change. Investment to developing countries did rise significantly in the 1990s. But much, if not all, of this is explained simply by liberalisation in the developing countries; there is no apparent role for more exotic explanations. A further look at this increase of FDI flows to developing countries reveals that it almost entirely due to liberalisation in China. The poorest countries have not received a larger share of flows.

Several specific items have received attention in the business press. First, there has been a strong increase in international mergers and acquisitions (M&A) in the mid-1990s. Yet a careful look at the data reveals two things: *i)* there was a strong renewal of FDI of all types in this period, so that M&A did not actually increase as a percentage of all FDI; *ii)* the early 1990s was something of a relative low point so, in a sense, M&A activity has just returned to its level of the late 1980s. Second, privatisations and liberalisation of rules regarding investments in infrastructure in developing countries and in Central and Eastern Europe (CEE) have received considerable attention. The importance of both may have been somewhat exaggerated, but clearly infrastructure investments will remain important to firms in telecommunications, construction and utilities from Western Europe, North America and Japan.

Trends (or lack thereof)

◊ FDI slowed down in the early 1990s, but still outpaced growth in GNP and world exports. FDI into *both* developing and developed countries has now recovered.

◊ Much has been written about a surge in mergers and acquisitions. But M&A have not increased as a share of all FDI (running between 40 and 60 per cent) except viewed from the perspective of the early 1990s, when they were very low.

◊ FDI to developing countries surged in the 1990s, but viewed as a share of all inward investment, the increase was more modest. As a share of the stock of inward investment, it remains small.

◊ A major reason for the surge in investment into the developing countries was liberalisation in China, which was receiving close to 40 per cent of all flows to developing countries in the mid-1990s. A very small, but rapidly increasing, share goes to Central and Eastern Europe.

◊ Privatisations have been an important source of FDI, but they are not a large proportion of FDI inflows into developing and CEE countries (about 5.6 per cent).

◊ Rules and restrictions applying to infrastructure investments have been significantly liberalised in many developing countries but, again, this is rarely a large portion of a country's inward investment (about 5-13 per cent of developing countries' FDI inflows).

I see no great shift from the general pattern of the last two decades: FDI inflows as well as outflows are concentrated among the high-income, skilled-labour abundant countries. More inflows will occur to the middle-income countries and very large LDCs.

The following tables give some brief statistics that lend support to some of the assertions made above. The first documents the continued high growth of direct investment in the world economy relative to both trade and world GDP. The second notes the increase in direct investment to developing countries in the 1990s, but then goes on to note that this increase is concentrated in China, with the poorest countries in the world receiving a slightly lower share; a share that is much smaller than their share of world income. This helps establish that FDI remains a high- and middle-income country phenomenon, and that poor countries cannot count much on FDI as an initial stimulus to growth.

Table 1. Annual growth rate, all countries

Percentages

	1986-90	1991-94
FDI inflows	24.7	12.7
FDI stocks	19.8	8.8
Sales of foreign affiliates	17.4	5.4
GDP at factor cost	10.8	4.3
Exports of goods and non-factor services	14.3	3.8

Table 2. FDI inflows and outflow, share in total

Year	Developed		Developing		CEE	
	In	Out	In	Out	In	Out
1983-1987	76	95	24	5	0	0
1988-1992	78	93	21	7	1	0
1993	62	85	35	15	3	0
1994	59	83	39	17	3	0
1995	65	85	32	15	4	0
Share of inward FDI to developing countries going to:						
	China		Least developed (48 countries)		LDC share of world GDP	
1984-89	10		2		4	
1990-92	15		2		5	
1993	38		2		4	
1994	39		1		4	
1995	38		1		4	

Source: UNCTAD *World Investment Report*, 1996.

Let me mention a few policy implications, focusing on those that are most relevant to developing countries. These are conclusions that I draw from a wide range of studies which attempt to assess the successes and failures of countries in attracting foreign investment. I list them first and then provide a brief discussion.

Policy implications (developing countries)

◊ Strong infrastructure is more important than low taxes:

  – Primary and secondary education;

  – Legal institutions – property rights and IPP, contracts, labour law, etc;

  – Facilitating infrastructure – utilities, telecoms, transport, etc.

◊ Skilled labour is at least as important as cheap unskilled labour:

  – FDI tends to be complementary to local skilled labour, not a substitute;

  – FDI does not occur at the lowest level of the skills ladder;

  – FDI may raise the gap between skilled and unskilled wages.

◊ Credible commitments to liberalisation policies are crucial:

  – Big countries – internal deregulation;

  – Small countries – commitment to openness;

  – Macro policies;

  – Treaties as commitment devices (for example, Mexico);

- Privatisation as a commitment device;

- Tough international institutions can be a commitment device.

◊ Agglomeration, linkages can be crucial to success:

- Backward to infrastructure;

- Deregulated trade in services, finance, insurance;

- Liberal temporary residence;

- Co-ordination among branches of government (trade, investment, regulation, immigration).

◊ Evidence weakly in favour of inward FDI:

- Pro-competitive effects;

- Spillovers – technology, labour skills, market access.

It is beyond the scope of this brief paper to present detailed references and a literature review. Most of these results and the references which support them can be found in my review articles (Markusen, 1995, 1997). The first set, involving infrastructure, reflects the finding that infrastructure, broadly defined to include education and legal systems, is important for attracting direct investment, whereas there is no strong case to suggest that taxes are a big disincentive. This suggests that moderate taxes are acceptable, provided that they are spent on providing intermediate public goods. Evidence suggests that, as discussed above, skilled labour is very important. Multinationals do not enter countries just because there is an abundance of cheap unskilled labour.

It is even further beyond the scope of this presentation to go into macroeconomic management, but the paper would probably be incomplete without one sentence (this one) emphasizing that multinationals seek stability and a business environment which they know and have confidence in. The fourth point notes some results from survey evidence, which emphasizes that firms need a variety of support services. These include good infrastructure as noted above, but also inputs from the business service sector including finance, banking, insurance and telecommunications. There have been many disaster stories about developing countries in which one branch of government is trying hard to attract investment while other branches are, directly or indirectly, putting immense obstacles in front of the same firms.

The points noted above hardly do justice to the huge literature on the effects of direct investment on host economies. This is a terribly complex topic to address empirically, and limited progress has been made. At this point just about all that we can say is that there is weak evidence to the effect that inward direct investment seems to have more beneficial effects than costs. Often there are a variety of favourable impacts on local firms: pro-competitive effects on firms in the same line of business; and forward-backward linkage effects on firms in related businesses. There seem to be a variety of favourable labour-market effects, especially the transmission of new skills to local workers and managers. Multinationals seem to have an external effect on local firms' exports, perhaps by helping to develop better international channels and contacts.

I will conclude by noting that a study of multinational firms and direct investment is needed in order to help appreciate the changing nature of world economic activity. We are currently stuck with an outdated international economic accounting framework in which trade in goods is heavily emphasized. While there are service accounts as well, they often do not pick up the huge volume of "trade" in services that goes on within multinational firms. These firms are supplying subsidiaries with services of a wide variety of forms of knowledge capital, intangibles that are not identified very well in our statistics. A new approach that more accurately reflects the transition to the knowledge-based economy would be welcome.

REFERENCES

MARKUSEN, James R. (1995), "The Boundaries of Multinational Firms and the Theory of International Trade", *Journal of Economic Perspectives* 9, pp. 169-189.

MARKUSEN, James R. (1997), "Integrating the Multinational Enterprise into the Theories of Trade and Location", in P. Braunerhjelm and K. Ekholm (eds.), *The Geography of Multinationals*, forthcoming.

UNCTAD (1997), *World Investment Report 1996*, United Nations, Geneva.

Chapter 7

FIRMS, EXECUTIVES AND MODELS OF ACTION: DOMINANT VIEWS *VS.* EMPIRICAL BUSINESS RESEARCH

by

Lars Engwall
Department of Business Studies, Uppsala University, Sweden

Introduction

Neo-classical economic theory has had a considerable influence on the general perception of how economic systems work. Especially in recent years, which have been characterised by deregulation, appeals to the market have been commonplace. Even though economic research since the 1930s (Chamberlin, 1933; Robinson, 1933) has pointed out that competition is frequently limited and that the perfect market model can be questioned also on other grounds, it nevertheless appears to be used as the basis for important considerations concerning the operating conditions of firms. However, it is not just our view of firms that might be discussed, but also the prevailing concepts of management's activities and models of action. The reason for an examination of this kind is found in empirical research on firms and their activities. These studies point out that the commonly held ideas on firms, executives, and models of action are not in complete agreement with reality. It is therefore the object of this paper to present an account of these differences between the prevailing concepts and the empirical scientific studies.

Firms

The predominant view of firms seems to encompass three important components, namely that they: *i)* lack permanent relations with buyers and sellers; *ii)* act independently of their competitors; and *iii)* make long-range strategic decisions. The empirical studies support alternative perspectives.

Firms that lack relations with buyers and sellers

In the classical model, firms are seen as a number of small islands in a great ocean (Håkansson and Snehota, 1989). The market determines a price and the firm must accept production for subsequent sale at this price. The market is anonymous. The firm is a relatively closed system and has no contacts with its counterparts. Research in the area of industrial marketing has shown, however, that in practice most firms have numerous and long-lasting relations with various counterparts. Just as links between various production stages can be observed within a firm, it has been found that production processes in one firm are linked to production processes in a number of other firms. Consequently, modern economies come to form large networks whose nodes are various firms (Hägg and Johanson, 1982; Forsgren *et al.*, 1995). If we focus in on a firm, we see that its suppliers, in turn, have suppliers that, in turn, ... etc. Likewise, it is common for a firm's customers, in turn, to have customers, etc. This trend has even been reinforced in recent years, since the larger firms, in particular, have tried to concentrate on their primary activity and let others take responsibility for subcontracts. Links and dependencies among firms have also been strengthened by so-called capital rationalisation, meaning that firms have reduced their inventories to a minimum. In the extreme case, input goods for one day's production arrive at the firm in the morning and the firm's own products leave before evening. Research also shows that the various firms interact to a great extent in the area of technical development. Thus, it has been maintained on empirical grounds that successful development work is based on continuous contacts with demanding customers, since they specify what will be needed in future products (*e.g.* Håkansson, 1989).

Thus, marketing research gives us a picture of firms that have been able to identify customers and suppliers. In this way, they have succeeded in developing long-term relationships. This mode of operation goes against traditional economic rationality, in that the firm does not constantly change partners due to changes in pricing. Instead, it is characterised by another more long-term economic rationality. Long-term relationships reduce the risk of problems with quality and delivery times. In this way, the technical nucleus is protected against disturbances that can have devastating economic repercussions in both the short and long term. In the short term, production disruptions cause a direct loss of income due to shutdowns and in the long term they can scare off customers due to a loss of confidence.

Firms that act independently of one another

However, it is not just firms' relationships with their suppliers and customers that differ from the perfect competition model. Conditions are different when it comes to competitors, as well. After all, most "markets" are dominated by a small number of firms. This means that executives, boards, stockholders, analysts, financial journalists, etc., can observe what actions the actors in a certain arena take. Since the relationships between cause and effect in the business world are far from clear, there is a tendency for executives to be pressured into following the behaviour demonstrated by other actors on the scene. This is also in agreement with the theories promulgated by the above-mentioned economists Neil Chamberlin and Joan Robinson during the 1930s. They limited their arguments to pricing, however, and pointed out that on limited markets it is not possible to deviate from the dominant firm's pricing. The same mechanism is also relevant, however, to other actions. The content and marketing of tabloids provide one example we see every day. They are reminiscent of both the children's game "follow my leader" and the principle of "tit for tat".

In principle, the case of the tabloids is a relatively innocent one. Of course, we may have our views of how journalism is progressing, but the economic consequences for the nation are limited. The situation was worse when financial markets were deregulated in the 1980s. The idea at that time was that deregulation would create better working markets for the benefit of citizens and society alike. Instead, in many countries the result was financial crises that, to a considerable extent, were intensified by the "follow the leader" behaviour of the banks. As a result of the new conditions, those few actors who were involved egged one another on to take actions that were hardly well thought out (*e.g.* Engwall, 1994, 1995). Banks established themselves abroad and attracted borrowers who had been turned down by others. They vied to purchase insurance firms and provide credit for risky investments. Those who endeavoured to keep a cool head were criticised for their passivity. Studies on the Swedish business press (Hadenius and Söderhjelm, 1994) show that even financial journalists were a driving force. Instead of critically analysing the heated atmosphere, they helped drive up the temperature even more.

Firms' tendency to follow one another is also the predominant component of the theories developed by the so-called neo-institutionalists (DiMaggio and Powell, 1983; Meyer and Rowan, 1977; Powell and DiMaggio, 1991; Scott, 1995). In certain cases, this occurs because the state or industry organisations establish various rules of accepted behaviour. In many cases, however, it is simply the tendency of firms to adapt to one another that leads to homogeneity within a certain line of business.

Long-term strategic decisions

The traditional view of economic rationality has led to the concept that a firm operates with long-term strategies. This concept developed after World War II because military thinking spread throughout the business world. Igor Ansoff's book *Corporate Strategy* (1965) is an important exponent of this view. He has had numerous successors, of whom Harvard professor Michael Porter was the most successful, with his *Competitive Strategy* (1980) and subsequent books. However, these concepts are normative, indicating what firms should do. Studies on what they actually do reveal quite different patterns. They point out, instead, that strategic decisions are extremely complex and that in firms, too, they are characterised by political processes (Mintzberg, Raisinghani and Théorêt, 1976; Pettigrew, 1973). Strategic decisions are also highly dependent on a firm's past history (Kimberly *et al.*, 1980). It is even common for a firm's strategies to result, to a high degree, from a desire to create meaning for the future from a firm's past history (Kinch, 1987; Mintzberg and McHugh, 1985; Pascale, 1984). Thus, corporate culture and profile have become important elements in modern management literature and among firms (Alvesson and Berg, 1992; Smircich, 1983; Smircich and Morgan, 1982; Trice and Beyer, 1984).

In summary

The upshot of the arguments presented above is that firms, as social phenomena, are much more complex than indicated in the traditional perfect competition model. Firms have extensive contacts with their suppliers and customers. Long-term relationships are common and important for the industrial system to work. Firms can also observe the behaviour of their competitors and they tend to mimic what others do. They, themselves, are complex structures in which decisions are made, to a great extent, by political processes rather than by long-term strategic decisions.

Executives

With regard to executives, too, there are certain prevailing views that are belied by empirical studies. According to these notions, the executive is in control of his firm's activities, he is fully informed, and he is able to find optimal solutions.

The executive is in control of his firm's activities

In 1951 Sune Carlson published a book entitled *Executive Behaviour* which has long been considered a classic. It presented an empirical study in which Carlson had studied the work of ten chief executives, using the diary technique, among other tools. The book pointed out that executives live highly fragmented lives. The most frequently quoted passage is the following (Carlson, 1951, p. 52):

> "Before we made the study, I always thought of a chief executive as the conductor of an orchestra, standing aloof on his platform. Now I am in some respects inclined to see him as the puppet in a puppet-show with hundreds of people pulling the strings and forcing him to act in one way or another."

Since then, it has been shown that Carlson's results with his ten chief executives were not unique. Similar studies by Henry Mintzberg (1973) of Canada and Rosemary Stewart (1967) of England found the same conditions (see also Carlson, Mintzberg and Stewart, 1991).

What is more, studies on large firms have shown that executives have a difficult time monitoring the behaviour of their subordinates. Through specific skills, customer relations, or other power bases, subordinate units are able to make executives dependent on them (Pfeffer and Salancik, 1978; Andersson, 1997).

The executive as fully informed

Traditional economic theory and classical management literature assume that those making decisions are well informed. They have access to all the information they need and, based on this information, they are able to make the correct decisions. Once again, empirical studies have shown that this is seldom the case. The key figure who pointed to this lack of access to information and the inability of human beings to process this information is the American Herbert Simon, who received the prize in economic sciences in memory of Alfred Nobel. Alone and with his co-workers, he has stressed the cognitive limitations of human beings (March and Simon, 1958; Cyert and March, 1963). Thus, limited rationality has become an important concept for those who study firms.

It is easy for a more and more complex world with an increasing amount of information to understand what Simon and his colleagues have pointed out. After all, it is a common conception that change has never been as rapid as it is now. But the limited availability of information does not apply to the outside world alone. It also applies within the firm. Once again, it may be stated that subordinate units lead a life of their own and that executives are unable to stay informed of what occurs within these units. Thus, it often happens that subordinate bosses act contrary to the intentions of their superiors. Purely from a control standpoint, this must be seen as reprehensible. History has shown, however, that in a number of cases this has been advantageous to the firm. After all, many new products have seen the light of day as a result of fiery spirits who pursued their ideas against the wishes of their superior executives. One example of how such disobedience can save a company is American Express. By directly disobeying his boss in the United States, the company's Paris representative was able to develop the traveller's check, thereby creating a base for the development of what was then a stage-coach company into a financial firm (Grossman, 1987).

Executives who make optimal decisions

Another premise behind the dominant picture of the executive is that he is able to make optimal decisions. He selects the solution that is best for the firm among various available alternatives. Here, too, studies on decision-making point to deviations from optimal behaviour. Instead, in their book *A Behavioral Theory of the* Firm (1963), Richard Cyert and James March present the view that executives are forced to choose satisfactory rather than optimal solutions. Part of the reason for this is the above-mentioned limited availability of information. But this is not the only explanation. One additional complication is that the firm's goals are not always clear and unambiguous. Profitability can be measured over different periods of time. Various interests within the firm make a number of different simultaneous and contradictory demands on its actions. In this way, different interests must be weighed in a decision-making process that is political in nature. This, in turn, means that the results of an executive's work are judged to a great extent by social processes (Berger and Luckmann, 1966). What is good management at a given time depends on the prevailing values in society at the time.

In summary

The prevalent picture of the executive is that he is in full control of his firm. He holds the highest position and decides what his subordinates will do. Reality tends to look a bit different. The executive lives an extremely fragmented life and, to a great extent, is controlled by external events. He also has the same human cognitive limitations as everyone else and, consequently, he is unable to assimilate all the available information. Moreover, he is forced to choose satisfactory rather than optimal solutions. Not all this is bad, however. There are many examples of how the executive's lack of control has been for the good of the firm. If this is the case, then the obvious question is what role does the executive play. His most important functions are probably working as a uniting force internally and helping deal with various external relations within the industrial network discussed above.

Models of action

The previous discussion has dealt in various ways with the actions of the firm and of the executive. If we take a closer look at the various models of action that are recommended, then we see that the prevailing view has three conceptions: *i)* the relationship between cause and effect is clear; *ii)* models of action are general; and *iii)* solutions are selected as a result of problems that have arisen. Alternatives may be suggested to these conceptions, as well.

Clear relationship between cause and effect

The classical model on decision making is based on the idea that there is a clear link between the measures that are accepted and their effects. Thus, it is common to interpret certain results as the effect of a previous measure. But social systems are far too complex for this to be a correct interpretation in all cases. For a firm, there are so many interacting factors that we cannot be sure of cause and effect. Like the man who ate his first banana as his train entered a tunnel, causing him to think the fruit led to blindness, firms are in danger of drawing false conclusions concerning cause and effect. Positive effects are interpreted as the result of steps that have been taken when, in reality, they are dependent on outside changes. Thus, it appears that certain measures lead to effects that do not really exist. This, in turn, can cause certain models of action to spread and be used more extensively even though in the best case they have no effect and in the worst case they may be downright harmful.

The generality of models of action

Ever since Frederick Taylor's *Scientific Management* (1911), management models have been presented to a great extent as general, *i.e.* applicable to all types of firms under all conditions. Since the greater part of management literature comes from the United States, we may slightly twist the well-known General Motors saying and say the message has been that "what is good for General Motors is not just good for the United States – it is good for every company in the entire world." This trend has been reinforced during the post-war period by a growing management literature and the desire of large American consulting firms to achieve the advantages of large-scale production (see the discussion of neo-institutionalists above).

This trend toward standardization is countered by research results dating back to the 1960s, which point out the need to consider a firm's tasks and context when choosing organisational solutions (Lawrence and Lorsch, 1967; Pugh and Hickson, 1976). In other words, it is important not to organise and run all firms like automobile plants. Internally, it is important to observe how various activities are linked together and how worker incentives are set up. With respect to the outside world, it is particularly important to observe the nature of interaction with customers. The bank crises in various countries provide yet another example. They show that banks would have done well to realise that borrowers at a bank differ radically from appliance purchasers since the former, unlike people who buy dishwashers, are expected to return the goods after a stipulated period of time. This circumstance places special demands on the choice of customers.

Several researchers have also pointed out the significance of cultural differences in business (Hofstede, 1980, 1992). In addition, we must consider how national systems regulating enterprise are set up (Roe, 1994). This means that a knowledge of business conditions in various contexts is extremely important. Thus, studies on international business stress that lack of knowledge is the greatest obstacle to a firm's internationalisation (Johanson and Vahlne, 1977).

Actions as solutions to arising problems

The traditional view of the sequence between problems and solutions is that problems come first and their solutions follow. Once again, however, there is evidence that this relationship is not so clear. Because of the cognitive limitations of individuals, they tend to use the solutions they have learned in the past. Thus, there is a risk that the order between problems and solutions will be reversed. Individuals or groups of individuals who have learned certain solutions want to utilise these solutions in as many contexts as possible. This behaviour, which is perfectly rational to those involved, is the main characteristic of the so-called Garbage Can Model, put forward by James March in conjunction with Johan Olsen of Norway (March and Olsen, 1976). Its implication is that in large organisations we may expect the use of standardized models for solving problems. This tendency also explains many of the fads that may be observed in management circles that have been criticised in some recent management books (Hilmer and Donaldson, 1996; Huczynski, 1993; Micklethwait and Woolridge, 1996).

In summary

The arguments presented above show that the relatively clear relationships offered by natural science are not available within firms. Actions are carried out in an extremely complex context, which means it is quite difficult to determine their effects. To reduce this uncertainty, we must consider the various special conditions of a firm. Thus, general solutions can be questioned at a time when there are strong forces moving toward standardization. Moreover, we must remember that solutions that are implemented are not always a result of problems that have arisen, but are often more a consequence of previous experience by the individual actors.

Conclusions

The consequences of the research results presented above are that the prevailing view of firms, executives, and models of action should be revised. With regard to *firms*, it is important to remember that they are linked to one another to a great extent by long-term relationships in large industrial networks. Firms also tend to copy one another's behaviour and to be highly dependent on their past history. These observations mean that measures based on the prevalent market model may be expected to have effects other than those anticipated.

With regard to *executives*, the studies stress the difficulty of their work. Combined with the results on firms, this means that executives' specific knowledge of their firm and their line of business is of extreme importance. This, in turn, means that the "white knight", who comes from the outside and saves the firm, is probably overrated. At the same time, competence in the form of quiet knowledge and personal networks seems to be underrated.

Finally, regarding *models of action*, the empirical research stresses the importance of subjecting them to critical evaluation. This is particularly true of standard solutions that spread rapidly from company to company and from one line of business to another. After all, the success of a model in one context is no guarantee of success under different conditions. However, a critical attitude toward new models of action requires considerable courage, since social processes can readily convert these models into established truths.

There are two possible reactions to the discrepancy between the results presented in this paper and the predominant notions of firms, executives and models of action. The first is that the established models are correct, nonetheless, and that the observations that have been made are only coincidental deviations from these models. According to this view, we may expect that, in time, reality will come to imitate the models. The other reaction is that it is time to revise our thinking and that new models must be developed. The latter alternative is the one many business researchers have chosen. The studies they have conducted and are conducting hardly indicate that reality is adapting itself to the established picture. Their impression is, rather, that new models and modes of thinking must be created. Decision makers of various kinds would probably do well to adopt this view.

REFERENCES

ANSOFF, Igor (1965), *Corporate Strategy*, McGraw-Hill, New York.

ALVESSON, Mats and Per-Olof BERG (1992), *Corporate Culture and Organizational Symbolism*, de Gruyter, Berlin.

ANDERSSON, Ulf (1997), *Subsidiary Network Embeddedness. Integration, Control and Influence in the Multinational Corporation*, Doctoral Thesis No. 66, Department of Business Studies, Uppsala University.

BERGER, Peter L. and Thomas LUCKMANN (1966), *The Social Construction of Reality: A Treatise in the Sociology of Knowledge*, Doubleday, Garden City, NY.

CARLSON, Sune (1951), *Executive Behaviour*, Strömbergs, Stockholm.

CARLSON, Sune, Henry MINTZBERG and Rosemary STEWART (1991), *Executive Behaviour, Reprinted with Contributions by Henry Mintzberg and Rosemary Stewart*, Acta Universitatis Upsaliensis, Studia Oeconomiae Negotiorum 32, Almqvist & Wiksell International, Uppsala.

CHAMBERLIN, Edwin H. (1933), *The Theory of Monopolistic Competition*, Harvard Economic Studies, Cambridge, MA.

CYERT, Richard M. and James G. MARCH (1963), *A Behavioral Theory of the Firm*, Prentice-Hall, Englewood Cliffs, NJ.

DiMAGGIO, Paul J. and William W. POWELL (1983), "The Iron Cage Revisited: Institutional Isomorphism and Collective Rationality in Organizational Fields", *American Sociology Review*, Vol. 48, No. 2, pp. 147-160.

ENGWALL, Lars (1994), "Bridge, Poker and Banking", in D.E. Fair and R.J. Raymond (eds.), *The Competitiveness of Financial Institutions and Centres in Europe*, Kluwer, Amsterdam, pp. 227-239.

ENGWALL, Lars (1995), "Bankkris och bankorganisation", in *Bankerna under krisen. Fyra rapporter till Bankkriskommittén* ["Banking Crisis and Bank Organization", in *Banks in the Crisis. Four Reports to the Banking Crisis Committee*], Fritzes, Stockholm, pp. 131-206.

FORSGREN, Mats *et al.* (1995), *Firms in Networks. A New Perspective on Competitive Power*, Acta Universitatis Upsaliensis, Studia Oeconomiae Negotiorum 38, Almqvist & Wiksell International, Uppsala.

GROSSMAN, Peter Z. (1987), *American Express. The Unofficial Story of the People who Built the Great Financial Empire*, Crown Publishers, New York.

HADENIUS, Stig and Theresa SÖDERHJELM (1994), *Bankerna i pressen* [*Banks in the Press*], Report to the Banking Crisis Committee, Fritzes, Stockholm.

HÄGG, Ingemund and Jan JOHANSON (eds.) (1982), *Företag i nätverk* [*Firms in Networks*], SNS, Stockholm.

HÅKANSSON, Håkan (1989), *Corporate Technological Behaviour, Cooperation and Networks*, Routledge, London.

HÅKANSSON, Håkan and Ivan SNEHOTA (1989), "No Business is an Island: The Network Concept of Business Strategy", *Scandinavian Journal of Management*, Vol. 5, No. 3, pp. 187-200.

HILMER, Fred G. and Lex DONALDSON (1996), *Management Redeemed. Debunking the Fads that Undermine Corporate Performance*, Free Press Australia, East Rosewill NSW.

HOFSTEDE, Geert (1980), *Culture's Consequences: International Differences in Work-Related Values*, Sage, London.

HOFSTEDE, Geert (1992), *Cultures and Organizations: Software of the Mind; Intercultural Cooperation and its Importance for Survival*, McGraw-Hill, London.

HUCZYNSKI, Andrzej A. (1993), *Management Gurus, What Makes Them and How to Become One*, Routledge, London.

JOHANSON, Jan and Jan-Erik VAHLNE (1977), "The Internationalization Process of the Firm – A Model of Knowledge Development and Increasing Foreign Market Commitments", *Journal of International Business Studies*, Vol. 8, Spring/Summer, pp. 23-32.

KIMBERLY, John R. *et al.* (1980), *The Organizational Life Cycle*, Jossey-Bass, San Francisco, CA.

KINCH, Nils (1987), "Emerging Strategies in a Network Context: The Volvo Case", *Scandinavian Journal of Management*, Vol. 3, No. 3-4, pp. 167-184.

LAWRENCE, Paul R. and Jay W. LORSCH (1967), *Organization and Environment*, Graduate School of Business Administration, Harvard University, Boston, MA.

MARCH, James G. and Johan P. OLSEN (1976), *Ambiguity and Choice in Organizations*, Universitetsforlaget, Bergen.

MARCH, James G. and Herbert A. SIMON (1958), *Organizations*, Wiley, New York.

MEYER, John and Bryan ROWAN (1977), "Institutionalized Organizations: Formal Structure as Myth and Ceremony", *American Journal of Sociology*, Vol. 12, No. 2, pp. 340-363.

MICKLETHWAIT, John and Adrian WOOLRIDGE (1996), *The Witch Doctors*, Heinemann, London.

MINTZBERG, Henry (1973), *The Nature of Managerial Work*, Harper & Row, New York.

MINTZBERG, Henry and Alexandra McHUGH (1985), "Strategy Formation in an Adhocracy", *Administrative Science Quarterly*, Vol. 30, June, pp. 160-197.

MINTZBERG, H., Duru RAISINGHANI and André THÉORÊT (1976), "The Structure of 'Unstructured' Decision Processes", *Administrative Science Quarterly*, Vol. 21, June, pp. 246-275.

PASCALE, Richard T. (1984), "Perspectives on Strategy: The Real Story Behind Honda's Success", *California Management Review*, Vol. 26, No. 3, pp. 47-72.

PETTIGREW, Andrew (1973), *The Politics of Organizational Decision-making*, Tavistock, London.

PFEFFER, Jeffrey and Gerald R. SALANCIK (1978), *The External Control of Organizations. A Resource Dependence Perspective*, Harper & Row, New York.

PORTER, Michael E. (1980), *Competitive Strategy*, Free Press, New York.

POWELL, William W. and Paul J. DiMAGGIO (eds.) (1991), *The New Institutionalism in Organizational Analysis*, Chicago University Press, Chicago, IL.

PUGH, Derek S. and David J. HICKSON (1976), *Organizational Structure in its Context: The Aston Programme I*, Saxon House, Farnborough.

ROBINSON, Joan (1933), *The Economics of Imperfect Competition*, Macmillan, London.

ROE, Mark J. (1994), *Strong Managers. Weak Owners*, Princeton University Press, Princeton, NJ.

SCOTT, W. Richard (1995), *Institutions and Organizations*, Sage, Thousand Oaks, CA.

SMIRCICH, Linda (1983), "Concepts of Culture and Organizational Analysis", *Administrative Science Quarterly*, Vol. 28, No 3, pp. 339-358.

SMIRCICH, Linda and Gareth MORGAN (1982), "Leadership: The Management of Meaning", *Journal of Applied Behavioral Science*, Vol. 18, No. 3, pp. 257-273.

STEWART, Rosemary (1967), *Managers and their Jobs*, Macmillan, London.

TAYLOR, Frederick W. (1911), *The Principles of Scientific Management*, Harper, New York.

TRICE, Harrisson M. and Janice BEYER (1984), "Studying Organizational Cultures Through Rites and Cermonials", *Academy of Management Review*, Vol. 9, No. 4, pp. 653-669.

Chapter 8

THE CHANGING NATURE OF THE FIRM

WHAT'S NEW? VELOCITY

by

Douglas C. Worth
Former Vice President, IBM Corporation, Washington

Several decades ago, Thomas J. Watson, Sr. said that IBM is not just a company but a movement forward. Indeed, it has been just that. For my 36 years with the company, the pace has always seemed fast.   My first days were spent plugging wires in control panels to create circuit paths for electro-mechanical collators, calculators and accounting machines. Now, if you wanted to actually see a circuit path with your naked eye, you'd have to enlarge a chip to the size of several football fields. An IBM mainframe that once filled a room is now five inches' square and a quarter of an inch thick. And while the capacity of IBM to invent and market its way along that increasingly fast-paced race has been formidable, it has also been fallible.

For nearly a decade, in the 1980s and early 1990s, we were spinning off market share to our competitors and stubbornly maintaining levels of employment that didn't fit our performance.   The concept of institutional re-invention has been popular; simply said, that means change that is total, not incremental or on the margin. Clearly, the 1993 vintage leadership at IBM had set its sights on aggressive change and it has been remarkably successful. I note this point to this audience, largely academics and governmental officials, because I would also assert that all large institutions that want to maintain their relevance to the microeconomy need change. An especially prescient management instructor once told my class, "no matter how brilliant you may be today, it will never be good enough for tomorrow."

Key to IBM's resurgence has been a focus on time to market. One plus of our oft- praised *and* maligned culture has been our faith in invention and a significant, continuing commitment to R&D. During even our darkest days, we maintained a vigorous multi-billion dollar research and development effort. At the same time, we reduced our product cycle from eight years - rather like a GATT Round - to less than two years. Indeed, nearly 80 per cent of our product line was not on the market 18 months ago. Technology is like strawberries. If you do not bring it to market very quickly, it may simply not be useable; other competitors may have invented their way past you. For instance, if you were to buy a stock of leading-edge parts for a PC and leave them unassembled for 90 days, you could not sell the resulting product for a profit.

Among the thousands of other changes absorbed by IBM in the last three years, a few are especially important:

◊ The shift in business volumes from hardware towards a heavier weighting for software and services, leveraging the intellectual assets of the company's talent pool.

◊ A move into technology and component sales to other companies, yielding a more efficient use of manufacturing investment and more competitive components – IBM's microelectronics unit went from a billion dollar loss to a billion dollar profit in one year.

◊ A winnowing of resource replication around the Corporation, a replication that was based more on organisational hubris and mirror-imaging than a real need. Every country aspired to the strength of IBM Germany (more than 30 000 employees) and every division had a considerable number of people dedicated to interfacing with other divisions.

◊ Leadership with a simple message: win in the market-place, be willing to change anything and trust each other. It's worked.

For business people as well as governmental policy makers, "economics is expectations expressed in money". At the same time, we both crave stability. We like to be able to predict and plan. The focus of the OECD, and of this conference in particular, is not just timely: I believe that there is an opportunity to put into play the elements of an expanded understanding between government and business enterprise. What is new in that enterprise is the velocity with which investment moves through the business cycle.

I would ascribe the source of this exponential change to invention enabled by technology, feeding on itself, permitting the management of the private enterprise model to alter its composition with stunning speed. At the same time, that invention is opening new possibilities for the customers for those goods and services, sometimes shifting demand so quickly that even the most sophisticated modelers cannot predict tomorrow. In the technology business, we have taken to thinking in "web years", that is, periods of three months. Recently, the model structure for a certain type of disk drive had shifted considerably. We were losing market share rapidly – "getting hammered", as we say. In order to reinvent, a new manufacturing facility was needed, tuning the old just wouldn't be adequate. Time was of the essence. We decided to put the new plant in Singapore, where the government is organised in such a fashion that an investor is met by a team of bureaucrats representing each relevant departmental interest and missioned to work at the investors' pace and not their own. Seventy-five days elapsed from handshake to production. In most places, we would not have received our first "permit" in that time. While the companies that produce these technological advances may be more vivid examples, one should not dismiss this phenomenon as irrelevant to the broader economy. Technology is pervasive in its application, enabling the same "modelling" and new market possibilities throughout industry. The demands for the health of the enterprise imply growth and that implies both product/service model shifts and market risks such as expansion into emerging markets, frequently with less favourable environments for business and capital.

Equally pervasive is the influence of government on the private enterprise model. To appreciate the macro and micro economic influence of public policy, one need only scan how public policy impacts business from the point where capital is sought through equity or debt to that where the financial flows from affiliates return the fruits of foreign direct investment or trade (Figure 1). For a multinational enterprise, that pervasiveness is exponential. In the days of punched-card technology, the cards were printed with the warning not to fold, bend, spindle or mutilate. At times, I have wished that we could have printed that warning on our business model. I need not speak at length about 12 US federal antitrust cases and an EC inquiry, need I? Seldom is there any long-term advantage for government to force an enterprise into a model that defies microeconomic gravity. Unfortunately, that is what frequently happens.

Figure 1. Public policy
Impacts on the business cycle

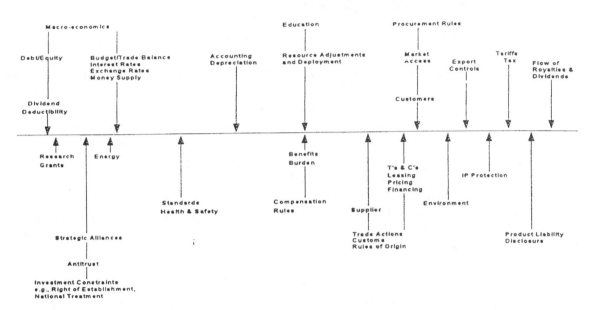

For example:

◊ The cost of debt is tax deductible, equity dividends are not. Is it any wonder that junk bonds spin out of control or that companies deploy assets to buy back their stock or that dividends are reduced in tough times?

◊ Policy makers' sentiment regarding government funding of research and development is on a scale somewhere between imperative and "corporate welfare" around the globe. I would suggest that there has been, and remains, a role for government: less development and more research, a mingling of government funding with academic and industry talent that can advance enabling infrastructure without constraining the market-place – open, not closed, standards – *e.g.* the Global Information Infrastructure (GII).

◊ The mere establishment of an enterprise may be precluded in some national market sectors. Try to get into the insurance business in Japan or look at the destructive results of market reserve on the Brazilian IT industry.

◊ Regulatory costs are imposed. For example, there are environmental regulations that dictate expensive processes rather than results, and local content requirements that raise the cost of key components.

◊ The quality of human resources is enabled. In one US city near an IBM manufacturing facility, the achievement level of the school graduates was so low and the direct cost of in-company remedial education so high, that we had to stop hiring out of that school system. In addition, we have put considerable resources into that and ten other large school systems [Chicago, Austin (TX) and Charlotte (NC), among others] where there is a demonstrated commitment to systemic change, standards and accountability. The consequences of failure in basic education are severe. If education is inadequate, scholastic re-tooling slow, then the firm must "rehire" to capture a shift in skill requirements. School systems must be responsive to evolving skill needs, producing analytical capability and an anticipation of the constant change that will be a part of life.

◊ Business terms and conditions are dictated. Often, elaborate contract terms are imposed, lease provisions inserted, artificial residual values required. In some countries, the use of local agents is mandated, increasing costs and, of necessity, prices. So much for efficiency.

◊ Import and export constraints are imposed. Disparate and often conflicting export control regimes can impede normal trade. During the Yamal pipeline crisis in 1982, four of the "denied" companies (one each from Germany, Italy, the United Kingdom and France) were IBM customers, and we faced severe penalties for delivery of any IT equipment to any of them. In France, the government set out to "requisition" delivery to our customer, placing our general manager in the unenviable position of choosing between a French or a US prison sentence. Some years later, I recall a well-meaning US Secretary of Defense insisting that he could not decontrol the 286 microprocessor because it was too powerful to be allowed to fall into Soviet hands.

◊ Not so long ago, the US government responded to the pleadings of a group of "flat panel" manufacturers for protection from Japanese "dumping". In fact, all of these companies had made technological misjudgements and either wanted time to catch up or a distortion of the pricing model. After a long drawn-out legal battle, the US government put itself in the position of imposing a 63 per cent duty on a product that was not manufactured *at all* in the United States and drove laptop manufacture off-shore for several years, until the case was overturned in the Court of International Trade.

◊ Intellectual property rights are left exposed. IBM has been inventing steadily and massively since the first part of the 20th century. In the past several years, the company has been number one in the world in the filing of patents. So it is no surprise that IBM owns a rather large mountain of intellectual property or that it is often a target for those who would rather steal than spend. We once estimated our losses in excess of US$1 billion per year due to inadequate or purposefully lax enforcement. While the TRIPS Code negotiated in the Uruguay Round is most helpful, we have at least one competitor that is treading systematically around the globe attempting to undo that achievement by persuading governments to make legal the reverse engineering of software (decompilation). In some countries, there simply is no rule of law.

◊ Tariffs and taxes siphon off earnings and capital. In many countries, there is a penchant for double, even triple, taxation of the same income, largely through taxes on foreign-source income. Withholding taxes on remittances can be ridiculously high: 10, 25, even 35 – in the face of OECD norms of zero – per cent on royalties and interest and 5 per cent on dividends. Many countries have been bringing these and other self- defeating statutory tax rates down; I can only cheer them on. With regard to tariffs, the latest GATT Round, NAFTA and other regional trade liberalising efforts have made much progress, topped off last year by the precedent-setting Information Technology Agreement at the WTO which will yield zero tariffs globally on the productivity tools of the information technology industry and the users in the Global Information Society. It was especially noteworthy that Chinese Taipei cogently signed on before even becoming a member!

For the multinational enterprise, the algorithm by which its model is shaped through public policy is far from linear. A difference in the way a lease is characterised for tax purposes can result in double taxation of the same revenue stream, labour rigidities can inhibit a vital change in production volumes to address a market shift. Our experience is that it is 3.5 times more expensive to right-size a European workforce than one in the United States. This has important implications for the current model, as well as for future market share, of the enterprise that is slow to make the shifts demanded by their new market model. Often those who are "protecting jobs" are attempting to retain jobs that have been dead for several years.

In effect, there is a "demand bid", in contract bridge terms, to which an enterprise that wishes to remain competitive, relevant and healthy must respond. Part of that response is a fluidity that must be balanced with our old friend stability. You say, well, that's nothing new. We've always noted that the nimble succeed. But, I would argue that the new paradigm is one where *every* element of the model is subject to dramatic change, in *every* "product" cycle. This places high value on the enterprise that has fewer "parts" that engender inertia. As a metaphorical example, think of the small-scale printer business where devices were once built with hundreds of discrete parts, say 387 parts, each with its own product engineer, and even someone in development conceiving of the next generation of that part. The business took an enormous leap forward when a comprehensive redesign reduced the number of parts to 62 (now, even fewer). Costs dropped and the small printer business accelerated into a shortened cycle of change that has brought remarkable improvements to the market-place, in turn expanding the array of uses and the number of users.

The implications for government are, at one and the same time, simple and complex. Government must do its best to create a policy environment that permits that fluidity. To the extent that enterprises within your polity are constrained in ways that their competitors are not, they will quickly become uncompetitive, irrelevant and sick. Such firms cannot be fixed with infusions of private or public funds. They need fewer parts and a faster pace. The requirement is for fewer and less intricate regulations, fewer mandated long time lines, shorter regulatory review cycles, ease of relief from changed circumstances, an open and candid relationship between policy makers, regulators and private enterprise and, quite frankly, a mutual effort to educate the public with the facts as well as a rejection of rhetoric and political hyberbole. Governments should take the lead in encouraging the public to embrace technology and turn it to their individual advantage – to make technology their instrument of labour mobility.

If I may be so bold, I would suggest that government must view itself in a similar fashion. Substitute democracy (or the opportunity for self-realisation) for invention and think of citizens as "customers" for the goods and services of government. A responsive government, one that will "satisfy" its "customers" and bring them back for more, must be one with a faster-paced, more *fluid*, policy-making cycle. That would demand, I believe, a government with *fewer parts* (less entrenched bureaucracy and perhaps fewer arrows on the chart in Figure 1) and points to a structure that better enables the integration of ministerial action into a single logic stream of policy. That would include an element of accessibility and transparency that recognises the shared responsibility for the most important mission of government - to sustain and improve the standard of living of the people. During the seminar, one of my academic colleagues noted the classic view of the role of government in the economy, that is, to determine the public good and redress market failure. I replied that there were many governments that wouldn't know a public good or a market failure if one came up and bit them in the leg. Provocative, perhaps, but not off the mark. Too much of the bureaucracy is looking through a rear-view mirror and considers attention to a dialogue with the private sector to be inappropriate. Try antitrust and flat panels for size.

Indeed, most governments are either obtuse to changes in those public "goods" that might most appropriately or effectively be delivered by government or politically unwilling to say enough is enough. Public "goods" and *services* are not "free", microeconomically. Every employee carries a public burden, that is, the cost of providing those goods and services. The firm absorbs that burden in the form of taxes, pay rates and remedial training. Am I implying that there is no role for government, no public good? Of course not. What I would assert is that the efficient provision of public goods and services is essential to enable a "competitive" public burden.

The key is productivity. With few exceptions – education being the most important – productivity gains are induced by the private sector. Only a co-operative effort can yield governmental success in improving the standard of living. In pursuit of that success we will face uncertainty and confusion; the private sector calls those elements "risk". Risk is not to be feared but faced, with no embarrassment for the confusion. Indeed, it is a sense of certainty that leads to failure. The notion of dominance is ephemeral and backward looking. We need to be looking ahead, together. As government makes a determination of market constestibility and chooses carefully those instances where it believes that it must fulfill its mission to temper the market-place, there must be a successful search for an acceptable definition of what is indeed predatory. The interaction and interdependencies of government and the private enterprise have been expanded by invention and international intercourse that is relatively unfettered by war. In a peaceful world, attention to economics rises to a new priority. Nearly a truism, but the terms on which both government and the business enterprise must address this priority are coming upon us at breakneck speed.

The velocity of investment ... and change ... is "real time".

Part II

Are We Moving Towards a Borderless Economy?

Chapter 9

NOTES ON A BORDERLESS WORLD

by

Everett M. Ehrlich
Former Under Secretary for Economic Affairs, US Department of Commerce

Are we moving towards a borderless economy?

The answer depends on who is "we"?

The pressures for ongoing global economic integration are undeniable. They concern the rapidly declining cost of data processing, more effective transportation and communications and greater structural openness in individual economies. But the extent to which these pressures have produced integration depends on the aspect of the economy or class of actors we consider. We must consider separately businesses, capital markets and governments.

At the cutting edge of business in the advanced nations, integration is a fact of life. The interesting thing about that integration is not that it has come to pass but rather the manner in which it has occurred.

For most of the post-war period, analysts of the transnational enterprise (both critics and defenders) have seen it as the vehicle for bringing together the world's economies: the ascendance of the transnational enterprise would lead to an elite of global corporations that made everything, everywhere and sold it to everybody.

But that is not what has happened. Instead, this model of the firm proved to be an act of overextension and its own undoing. In part, it simply taxed the capabilities of any organisation, in terms of managerial attention, investment funds and R&D capabilities. Yet the prevailing view of managers was that the very scale of their enterprises lifted them above competition save with each other, and that any inefficiency associated with their size and sprawl (as measured by markets, product segments, regions or stages of value creation) was the price paid for the benefits of achieving global scale.

In retrospect, the everything-everywhere-everybody view of the transnational corporation and the integration that it would bring to the world economy was based on the premise that these organisations would ultimately prove to be the most effective form to organise and manage information and decision making. But this premise was undone by the burgeoning capabilities of information technology. The ongoing improvement in the price performance of computing and communications challenged this integrated, vertical model of the firm.

In an environment in which information processing is cheap, fast and accessible the organisational structure of the transnational enterprise was transformed from a compelling strategic advantage to an outmoded nuisance. Co-ordinating the various activities of the firm was no longer best accomplished by pyramidal structures that sent information up and down the chain of command for verification, distribution and action. Instead, information could be shared across the boundaries of the firm as easily as within it, if not more so.

The result has been the dis-integration of our largest companies along the lines of stages of production, product segments and regions. The ability to share production information – schedules, lay-outs, specifications, designs, and the like – has allowed companies to distinguish those stages of the production process in which their value-creating skills excel and those in which they do not, and to find the skills that complement their own. The most successful US automobile producers, for example, are those that have targeted product design and engineering and marketing, leaving the development and manufacture of components to networked "co-producers". The leading figures in the US computer industry are no longer the integrated producers – those who produced everything from the hardware platform to the operating system and application – but rather those who have specialised in one stage of the process or one component – Intel, Microsoft, Oracle, Novell, Hewlett-Packard. The same strategy of cross-company partnership is being used to fill out product lines or to market to geographic regions.

Simply put, the transnational enterprise has gone from its everything-everywhere-everybody model to one that focuses on sustainable, value-creating, differentiating skills and abilities and that then finds external partners that lever them. Rather than search for new activities to bring *into* the firm, modern companies now demand competitiveness in every activity, while looking for new activities to array *around* the firm.

This transformation is underway in the United States. Signs of it are also visible in Europe and Japan, but the less open markets for corporate control found in those areas have placed less pressure on their firms to adjust. As a result, they lag behind. But, in my view, these pressures for transformation are unrelenting and inevitable, and will play themselves out outside the United States just as they are now doing inside the United States.

The result will be global integration, but not global integration under the command of the transnational enterprises. Instead, it will occur through the network of partnerships, joint ventures, co-production and sourcing agreements, research collaborations and other alliances and relationships formed under this new model.

This is a desirable outcome: this new and different form of integration suggests more rapid diffusion of new technology, more specialisation and, therefore, better economic performance and a more open world economy.

Somewhere behind our corporations are our capital markets. Economists have long heralded the coming integration of the world's capital markets. The technology that links them already exists – the global computing and telecommunication network. A body of theory exists to describe capital market integration, complete with theorems that guide us to understand the results it will produce.

The only problem with all of this preparation is that it hasn't happened yet. Capital markets persist in showing a frustratingly national character. Interest rates have not yet obviously overpowered trade flows as the dominant determinant of exchange rates. "Covered parity" explanations of these phenomena are still more theoretical than actual. Currencies stubbornly refuse to converge to purchasing power parity values. At the same time, the isolation displayed by the Japanese stock market during its recent rundown shows that the global linking of equities is not yet at hand.

All of these results are surprising. Capital is the world's most fungible and potentially mobile commodity. Still, it has yet to become truly world-wide in its outlook, although there is no reason to believe that the process of integration in global capital markets has run its course. But while capital's horizons are ever expanding, it still demonstrates some old-fashioned charm, preferring to stay at home when possible.

To some extent this reflects the fact that global information networks have yet to eliminate all information gaps in those markets, or overcome the suspicions that impede capital's cross-border flow, be they about accounting, language or culture. If this is the case, then the prospects for further and rapid integration are clearly strong.

But there also may be weaknesses in the underlying theory. In essence, the idea that the world's capital markets will come together as one requires us to believe that all investors have the same reaction to inflation everywhere. If they do not, then why should inflation differentials narrow? But an investor in the United States is exposed to a far higher-level of US-based price risks than to price risks in other nations, if only because that investor consumes untraded US goods and services. And producers may view inflation risks in proportion to the nature of their markets or the structure of their costs. Investors in each nation, therefore, may not care equally about inflation in every locale, and may not, therefore, drive capital markets to produce the inflation-equilibrating result that real integration produces.

All told, our theories regarding "open economy macroeconomics", however elegant, need to wait for underlying reality to catch up with them. Sooner or later, it will.

The last group to consider is government. It is not surprising that a creature of borders be the least susceptible to borderlessness.

And yet we are seeing borderlessness pervade this last bastion. The international linkages inherent in stabilisation policy are now institutionalised. Nations have learned to act in concert to perform such once-national tasks as promoting capital standards or preserving the environment. Can such functions as promoting accounting standards, chartering and perhaps governing corporations or protecting intellectual property be far behind?

The growing borderlessness found in the first two spheres I've discussed – business and capital – is increasingly forcing itself on this third one. There are fewer and fewer domestic policies in our world. Technological subsidies, export promotion and regional development all now spill over in ways we have come to understand.

This linkage is not a secret: on the contrary, it is now the motivation for much of what we do. The problem is that we lack the institutions to allow us to step back from this competition of policies. There is no framework that allows us – economically – to disarm.

Policies such as subsidies to innovation and diffusion, regional development and assistance to small and medium-sized enterprises need not have a pernicious effect on other nations. In fact, many policies might be enhanced if they were viewed as vehicles for co-operation rather than competition. We are still far from that point. But unless we strategise as to how to get there, that point will never be reached.

Chapter 10

EUROPE'S INDUSTRIAL POLICY: PROMOTING OPENNESS, FLEXIBILITY AND INNOVATION

by

Stefano Micossi
Director General for Industry, European Commission, Brussels

The European economy in a changing environment

The world economy is changing rapidly under the twin impulses of globalisation and technological progress. Information and Communication Technologies (ICT) are driving both processes, leading to a revolution comparable in scope to the industrial revolution which took place two centuries ago.

These forces are radically changing the ways in which companies compete. Entry barriers are falling rapidly and protectionism is being reduced. All companies are becoming exposed to fierce international competition. The ability to manage knowledge and information and to incorporate them in core business strategy are becoming key elements of competitiveness.

Europe is responding to these challenges, but the rate of change is uneven. Key markets, notably in services, are being opened to competition too slowly, and the presence of European companies in leading technologies and fast-growth markets is lagging behind. Societal values, institutions and public policies do not sufficiently encourage risk taking and structural change.

Globalisation and the emerging knowledge-based society

The world economy is undergoing dramatic change, with companies and markets everywhere becoming exposed to international competition. The benefits of internationalisation and competition are increasingly also recognised by developing countries – never before have the principles of the market economy been shared and applied so extensively in the world economy.

Information and Communication Technologies (ICT) have been a major driving force in globalisation, in two distinct ways. First, they make skills and know-how "portable". Tasks that were once the exclusive reserve of advanced industrial countries with elaborate and mature infrastructures can now be performed anywhere in the world. Second, ICT has overcome the barriers of distance and time for the exchange of information, the management of organisations, production lines, marketing and logistics. At the same time, transportation costs have also fallen dramatically.

Globalisation

Economic activity is becoming characterised by a close and intricate cross-border networking of commercial transactions, such that each country in the world is becoming linked to the others in a network of "spiders web" relationships. The modalities of interdependence are three-fold, namely "arm's-length" trade, foreign direct investment and inter-firm co-operative agreements.

The volume and scope of cross-border transactions have greatly increased: as a proportion of world Gross National Product (GNP) they have more than doubled since 1970.[1] The value of foreign production by multinationals, together with the contribution of cross-border alliances, now considerably exceeds that of trade.[2] The internal transactions of multinational companies now account for one-third of world trade.

Growing integration is a rich source of opportunities, facilitating the diffusion of technical change, allowing firms to operate more effectively and enabling countries to more fully exploit their comparative advantage.

At the same time, globalisation is associated with stronger competition and turbulence. Firms can no longer be protected and insulated: they must face the uncertainty resulting from the rapid development of innovative products and services that could destroy their current position.

It is no longer sufficient simply to develop lower cost, higher quality products of a similar nature: winning market share often requires changing the product, or service, or the underlying concept. The ICT domain offers outstanding examples of this. For over two decades now we have observed revolutionary changes, not only in hardware and software, but also in the nature of market competition in a way that leaves no incumbent safe.

The increased competition resulting from globalisation and the development of ICT is based on an ability to innovate and to respond rapidly to changing market demands, to the opportunities offered by technology, and to the progressive dismantling of barriers to entry. Industries and firms must continuously adjust their structure and organisation in order to remain competitive.

The changing nature of organisations

As the dividing lines between markets, companies, products and services become blurred, the changing environment and market structure have far-reaching implications for both company management and organisation.

Companies must be able to combine inputs from a range of sources to create attractive products and services. The "service" content of almost all products is increasing. This is reflected in the cost structures of products and corporations: value added tends to be in services, not materials.[3]

As a result, the core task of firms has become an ongoing reconfiguration and integration of competencies. Companies must be proactive in acquiring knowledge and in sharing, retaining, managing, updating and exploiting that knowledge.

In this context, single-activity, autonomous and hierarchy-oriented firms have become the exception rather than the rule. Successful firms are those that are part of a web of inter-firm co-operative alliances, have a decentralised management structure, distribute responsibility widely, and are able to obtain flexibility and a high level of skills from their staff.

These changes favour the development of small and medium-sized firms since they make it possible for SMEs to operate on a global scale in a way that was unthinkable only ten years ago. SMEs represent the backbone of the European economy, accounting for more than 70 per cent of employment. If these firms can be mobilised and massively involved in the new game, they offer great promise of growth and jobs.

The European economy under stress

Europe's productive base reposes on high-quality human and physical assets. Its workers are well-educated and European companies benefit from an accumulated experience of industrial prowess. The network of public infrastructure is extensive. Scientific research is up to the highest standards in the world in many fields, and can rely on outstanding educational and research institutions.

These strengths are enhanced by the very size of the European economic system. The European Union represents 30 per cent of global GDP, and its 370 million consumers enjoy among the highest average per capita incomes in the world. European firms are present worldwide and the EU continues to attract large foreign investments. The internal market provides a strong basis for firms to expand and adapt to the demands of global competition.

However, European productivity still lags behind that of its main competitors, and European firms encounter difficulties in innovating and expanding in fast-growth markets. Average unemployment rate is close to 11 per cent with large differences among Member States – while some countries are again creating jobs at a brisk pace (the United Kingdom, the Netherlands, Ireland and Finland are good examples), others are still experiencing an increase in their already high unemployment rates. Large numbers of our younger citizens face dismal prospects in the labour market, and a significant share of the workforce suffers long-term structural unemployment.

Losing ground in fast-growth markets

Europe has been losing share in world export markets. In 1995, Europe accounted for 19.4 per cent of total world exports, compared with 21.1 per cent in 1990. While to a certain extent this is simply a reflection of growing output and GDP in developing countries, it cannot be entirely discounted as irrelevant, since Europe is losing ground notably in fast-growth markets and technologies.

The EU has been penalised by its low presence in the Asian NIC and Latin American markets which, over the past few years, have experienced the highest growth in demand and imports. Foreign direct investment in fast-growth economies has also lagged behind that of the United States and Japan.

The EU has also demonstrated poor trade performance in sectors such as electronic data processing, consumer electronics and instrument engineering, where many of the new IT technologies find their application. Since 1990, Europe's share of the worldwide IT market has declined from 35 to 28 per cent.[4] Similarly, some of the sectors in which Europe has traditionally been strong (*e.g.* chemicals-pharmaceuticals, engineering, certain basic industries, etc.) are facing growing competitive pressure from non-OECD countries.

Slow pace of innovation

Although European scientific research is up to the highest standards in the world, it seems that European firms have difficulties transforming R&D into commercially viable innovations and new products.

European companies apparently obtain lower returns than US companies on R&D investment, measured in terms of their ability to leverage R&D into patents and to leverage patents into products for the global market. The international diffusion rate of patents generated in Europe is only two-thirds that of the United States. [5]

Innovation entails more than simply applying existing technologies: the nature of technological change depends on where it is implemented. If the ground is fertile, more plants and fruits will spring up.

The core of innovation is management and organisation. European companies are not moving as rapidly as their US counterparts in the adoption of ICT in management and organisation. Too many companies seem to regard ICT as an element of cost, to be cut back as soon as business confidence slows down, rather than as a source of empowerment. Few companies have undertaken the organisational decisions required for full exploitation of ICT.

Furthermore, many European companies still appear overweight and more hierarchy-oriented than their American competitors. Integration within and between companies still seems to be directed more to vertical integration than to networking or strategic alliances.

High costs and rigidity

The effectiveness of new production technologies and organisations depends on how quickly the basic structures and institutions of society can adapt. In all likelihood the poor adaptability of society provides an important explanation for the limited effect of new production technologies on productivity.

In Europe, pervasive rigidities and distortions hamper the functioning of markets, increase costs and prevent innovative responses. New technologies will not be fully reflected in productivity growth until companies have undergone thorough reorganisation and societal constraints have been removed.

Labour costs in many key sectors in Europe are some 30 to 50 per cent higher than in the United States. Flexibility in labour management is restricted by sector-wide wage bargaining, by restrictions on working hours governed by collective agreements and by highly intrusive employment protection legislation.

Prices for key services, such as energy, communications and transport, remain high in Europe owing to barriers to entry and restrictive regulations. With accelerating progress in liberalisation elsewhere, the gap between Europe and its major competitors has been widening.

These rigidities are far more significant and more discriminatory for SMEs, whose smaller structures give less room for compensatory resources. Such obstacles especially hamper the development of new forms of services, lead to inefficiency and stifle innovation.

An industrial policy to provide a better regulatory environment...

Against this background, European industrial policy aims to create a favourable environment for innovation and growth with market-based policies designed to remove barriers to entry, foster competition and flexibility, diffuse information, encourage investment in knowledge and risk taking.

The general principles for European industrial policy in an open and competitive environment were laid down in 1990 and 1994 in two Commission Communications to the Council and Parliament.[6] It was clearly stated that the primary responsibility for innovation and upgrading productive structures rests with the private sector. However, public policy can play an important role in providing a supportive environment. It can also assist in overcoming information and co-ordination failures in private behaviour.

Productivity, innovation, and the diffusion of technology are promoted through horizontal policies that benefit all industries, large companies and SMEs alike, rather than targeting specific technologies, sectors or national champions.

Completing the European regulatory framework

In an increasingly interdependent world, rigid rules and institutions can do great damage to the economy's ability to meet competitive challenges, and thus ultimately to growth and job creation.

We must therefore endeavour to bring about a better and simpler regulatory environment, one that takes into account the needs of a competitive economy.

To this end, we are promoting a comprehensive review of legislation inside the Union, and we are launching a new Action Plan to complete the Internal Market and improve enforcement. Outside the Union, we are working with our main industrial partners to remove technical barriers to trade and investment and lay the foundations for a truly integrated global market-place.

The new Internal Market Action Plan

The Single Market remains a major objective and policy tool of the Union. The Commission's Communication on the Impact and Effectiveness of the Single Market, which presents the results of two years of research, shows that the efficiency and the trade performance of EU industry have improved, and that substantial restructuring has boosted productivity and quality.

However, the full potential benefits of the Single Market have not yet been realised. Three areas have been identified for policy action:

◊   Closing the gaps in legislation

As pointed out in the Commission's Communication "Putting Services to Work", the importance of services in all advanced economies is enormous. In the European Union, as elsewhere, services now account for more jobs than industry and agriculture combined. Nevertheless, the Single Market is less complete in the area of services than in that of products. A strategy for removing the remaining barriers to service provision will be one of the keys to realising the full economic potential of the Single Market.

◊   Simplifying legislation

There are too many detailed and complex rules in the Single Market as it stands today. The business community has repeatedly expressed its concern over the complexity of the regulatory framework, and the costs that such complexity imposes on industry. The key to the future competitiveness of the Union is to achieve maximum flexibility and choice within the Single Market. This holds even more for SMEs which are most damaged by the complexity of regulation.

◊   Confronting technological changes

Technological developments in ICT are creating new ways of doing business in the Single Market, as witnessed by the rapid development of electronic commerce. However, these developments also confront the Union with new challenges. We must preserve the integrity of the Single Market while providing the necessary safeguards for consumers and owners of intellectual property rights (IPR). At the same time, we must offer business the legal framework it needs to trade and work on-line.

For example, the ease and speed with which copyright laws can be violated on networks require that regulators adopt procedures to ensure swift enforcement and punishment for infringement of intellectual property rights.

Data protection, security encryption, on-line contract law and electronic signatures, IPR and protection against unwanted content are some of the areas that are becoming prominent on the policy agenda.

Standards

The European Union has a critical responsibility in relation to the timely development of high quality standards and technical specifications.

Standards and technical specifications are fundamental in determining the pace of innovation and the size of markets. An environment in which standards are harmonized within and outside the EU should be seen as a tool to open markets and increase competitiveness.

Among manufacturers, small and medium-sized enterprises have the most to gain from effective and open standardization. While multinational companies can absorb the costs of producing to national standards, SMEs often cannot and need the assurance of international standards to tackle the export market.

Europe has developed a transparent and independent standardization system that relies increasingly on industry and market incentives, the role of public policy being confined to that of ensuring openness, transparency and fair play.[7]

The international dimension

EU trade policy has shifted towards placing emphasis on market opening, as witnessed by the recent Communication on "A Market Access Strategy".

Opening markets

The European Union is fully committed to the multilateral trade system and the efforts of the World Trade Organisation (WTO) to promote integration on a global scale. In this context, regional and bilateral arrangements can offer useful stepping stones in the process of multilateral liberalisation. They make it feasible to advance into deeper integration on a regional basis when this is not possible on a global scale. And they make it conceivable to develop and try out solutions in new areas – regulatory, competition – where ready-made solutions are not available.

With trade barriers in most areas reduced to a minimum and with increased economic interdependence via the investment link, the international economic policy agenda has increasingly focused upon divergences among domestic institutions, regulations and administrations.

Managing system frictions

System frictions arise from the interaction of different market models or systems and the conflicts inherent in the different cultural legacies and approaches to public policy that underpin them.

The obstacles to trade and investment that arise from these differences in domestic regulatory frameworks are now taking centre-stage in negotiations to open markets among advanced countries. The essential and novel characteristic of these negotiations is that the focus will be on reconciling different internal regulatory and procedural systems rather than resolving tariff or border control issues.

The ultimate objective is that of ensuring full market access everywhere based on a single regulatory requirement (full harmonization).

The initial step would be to build a network of mutual recognition agreements whereby countries accept to grant market access based on one-stop-shop conformity assessment, while maintaining different standards and norms where appropriate.

In December 1995, at the EU-US summit in Madrid, the European Union and the United States adopted a "Transatlantic Agenda". This included the Trans-Atlantic Business Dialogue (TABD) as an important pillar. The TABD offers a unique formula, with the business community on both sides of the Atlantic taking the initiative of identifying regulatory obstacles to trade and investment, and governments trying to put in place recommendations in response to these concerns.

The TABD agenda covers the reduction or elimination of tariffs, and negotiated reduction in regulatory and other non-tariff barriers to trade.

Significant progress is being made in negotiating mutual recognition agreements. Common initiatives are being undertaken to promote harmonization and develop international institutions suitable for the task.

...and foster the advent of the information society

The future of Europe – and its place in the world economy – will depend on the speed and degree of success with which it exploits the opportunities resulting from new ICT and moves toward the information society.

Over the last two years, the creation of an information society in Europe has gradually moved to the top of the European union political agenda. The EU strategy for the information society is an integrated framework encompassing a number of policy areas, including telecommunications, research and development, innovation, competition, economic and social cohesion, audio-visual, culture and education.[8]

The advent of the knowledge-based society requires fundamental changes in attitude, behaviour and organisation. It demands that individuals, firms and policy makers adapt quickly to changing situations and re-examine their practices. Benchmarking is one way of getting everyone involved in continuous learning.

The Information Technologies Programme

Spreading the adoption of information and communication technologies is a key task of EU information strategy. The new Information Technologies Programme, launched in 1994 under the Union's Fourth Framework Programme for Research and Technological Development, represents an integrated programme of industrial R&D projects and take-up measures. Its aim is to contribute to the creation of an advanced skills base and help pave the way for the advent of the Information Society in Europe.

Since there is great uncertainty as to the directions that technology and society might take, the research programme for IT needs to follow, accommodate and stimulate, rather than command and direct.

A user- and market-oriented programme

The Information Technologies programme has abandoned the technology-driven approach of Community R&D of the 1980s and has introduced a user-oriented, market-focused approach that provides a solid platform for contributing to industrial competitiveness and building the Information Society in Europe.

In order to foster the user-supplier relationships that are crucial to innovation, the Information Technologies programme brings together industry, users, universities and research centres with a common research objective. Moreover, it integrates take-up measures such as pilot projects, best practices and awareness actions within the research activities.

Specific measures are envisaged to encourage SME participation in the programme, including exploratory awards and technical assistance in project formulation.

Flexible management

Our Research and Technology Programme has developed methods for flexible management to respond rapidly to industry's changing needs, to reduce the time taken to respond to changes in technologies and markets, and to enhance its ability to target and support new ideas.

To address this need, the IT programme is pioneering new approaches. It has introduced a rolling work programme, updated annually on the basis of extensive consultation with industrial users (via its Industrial Advisory Panels, which encompass all sectors of industry), and frequent calls for proposals.

As a result, 40 per cent of the participants in the IT programme are from user industries: from the pharmaceuticals sector, aircraft manufacturers, maritime industries, as well as small specialist companies. Around one-third of participants in the Information Technologies programme are SMEs.

Promoting continuous improvement and adaptation through benchmarking

In an increasingly interdependent world, individuals, firms and countries are competing with the best. Continuous improvement and adaptation are indispensable in order to guarantee that everyone stays in the race.

To this end the Commission Communication on "Benchmarking the Competitiveness of European Industry" proposed that benchmarking be utilised across-the-board in the economy and society to compare existing practices that determine economic success in key aspects and sectors.

A process for improvement

Benchmarking has two major features. First, in order to recognise best performance, it compares societal behaviour, business practices, market structures and public institutions across countries and regions, sectors and companies. Second, it uses reference to best performance as an instrument to identify directions for change and to maintain continuous pressure on all actors of the economy and society to move in that direction.

The first feature requires a willingness on the part of all actors to question existing practices. In this regard, benchmarking only works if it exposes weaknesses and inefficiencies. Therefore it is likely to encounter resistance and opposition initially. However, its benefits can be substantial – improved services for individuals and business alike, lower costs, more user-friendly administrations, better economic performance, more jobs and wealth creation. It would also contribute to the convergence of performance across the Union, thus reducing productivity dispersion and economic inequality.

The second feature requires a commitment to pursue changes. It is not sufficient to accept changes only if comparison shows a better way. A continual search for the best way of doing things must become a constant feature of the decision-making process.

There is no established method, formula or procedure for applying benchmarking. Many of the phenomena and processes that need to be addressed are difficult to measure. Thus it is important that any dogmatism be avoided and that ample room is left for experimentation and adaptation of the approach to well-founded constructive criticism. Openness and transparency of methods, procedures and target selection are also very significant in ensuring broad acceptance of the approach and results.

At all levels: firm, sector, framework conditions

In its new Communication on Benchmarking the Commission supports a flexible, multiple-layer approach to benchmarking. The Commission's objective is to promote the concept of benchmarking as widely as possible – that is, to encourage a multiplication of initiatives at different levels: companies, sectors, Member States, but also by other societal organisations.

The responsibility for undertaking specific initiatives will lie primarily with the various actors in the economy and society. Public powers can encourage and support, and sometimes help organise and finance initiatives, but it is not for them to run or manage all the experiments.

Company-level benchmarking is essentially about diffusion of best practice in management and organisation. It can cover every aspect of company activity: design, production, logistics, distribution and finance, and is of particular relevance to small and medium-sized enterprises. The Commission will encourage the constitution of a European network.

At the sectoral level, benchmarking focuses on the evaluation of the specific framework conditions required for sustaining competitiveness in a particular sector. A pilot programme has been undertaken with MITI for electronic suppliers. Other initiatives are being promoted by the chemicals industry and the car industry.

The benchmarking of framework conditions (cost of factors, infrastructures, qualifications, environment and innovation) is a means of assessing the success of public policy in promoting competitiveness. Potentially a broad range of variables can be targeted. Consistent with the analysis of the Communication on "Benchmarking the Competitiveness of European Industry", it would be advisable to focus on the following conditions: quality of legislation, innovation systems and functioning of markets.

The Commission will provide support for the development of adapted methodologies, the elaboration of qualitative databases and the diffusion of experience. But for the success of this benchmarking exercise, it is essential that the European Commission, European Member States, industry and other actors in society work closely together to build an environment open to change, where all actors strive continuously to improve their methods and skills.

Conclusion

Europe's economy suffers from high costs, rigidity and an insufficient pace of change to new products and services and new technologies; it also displays large-scale under-utilisation of its working-age population. These features are especially troublesome in view of the accelerating pace of change in the world, under the twin impulse of globalisation and rapidly spreading new technologies.

The development of a society based on knowledge requires an open and competitive environment favouring innovation. Europe's industrial policy aims at fostering such an environment with market-based policies that remove obstacles to change, encourage flexibility, spread information and know-how, and foster knowledge investment and risk-taking.

European industrial policy is mainly a co-ordination framework. Since implementation of required changes remains in the hands of Member States, enterprises and societal behaviour at all levels, only the commitment of these different actors will restore strong economies, growth and jobs.

Rather than being afraid of change, we should actively pursue the opportunities offered by the advent of a society based on high-quality industry and services, knowledge and innovation.

NOTES

1. In the United States, for example, the percentage of GNP accounted for by trade rose from 7 to 26 per cent between 1970 and 1990, while that accounted for by the stock of inward and outward direct investment increased from 89 to 156 per cent.

2. UNCTAD suggests that in 1993 the sales of the foreign affiliates of MNEs amounted to US$5.5 trillion compared with that of trade of goods and services of US$4.0 trillion.

3. In Europe and in the United States, services account for 60 per cent of total value added.

4. Over the same period, the American IT market has grown from a similar base size to represent about 41 per cent of the worldwide market in 1996.

5. Diffusion rate is defined as number of out-of-the-country patent applications per domestic patent application. In 1994 for ICT and other technology sectors, the European diffusion rate was 3.03 and the American rate 5.39 (OECD, *Main Science and Technology Indicators*).

6. Commission Communication on "Industrial Policy in an Open and Competitive Environment" (1990), and "An Industrial Competitiveness Policy for the European Union" (1994).

7. The European standardization system is composed of experts working independently of the European Commission.

8. The main documents of the Commission on the Information Society are: "Europe's Way Towards the Information Society" [COM(94)347], "Europe at the Forefront of the Global Information Society: An Action Plan" [COM(96)607], and the Green Paper, "People First, Living and Working in the European Information Society" (1996).

Chapter 11

HUMAN CAPITAL FORMATION AND INDUSTRIAL COMPETITIVENESS

by

Naohiro Yashiro
Sophia University, Tokyo

The implications of the borderless economy for industry

We are rapidly moving towards a borderless economy. With the increasing liberalisation of international trade in goods and services, labour and capital – two major factors in production – can move more freely across national borders. This is because an increase in imports of labour-intensive products from developing countries is the same as importing low-cost labour, putting a downward pressure on domestic wages. Also, imports of land-intensive farming products would stimulate a shift in the use of the land away from farming to offices or housing – thus the land space can be "imported" from abroad. With the globalisation of industrial activities, the range of trading has expanded enormously.

Moreover, the impact of movements of international capital and in particular of foreign direct investment (FDI), will be even larger than that of free trade. Although foreign indirect investment (FDI) covers only movements of capital, it in fact represents movements of firm ownership. A country's acceptance of multinational firms implies that it imports not only foreign capital, but a combination of high-technologies and management skills, and a sales network abroad. Exports through the intra-firm trading network, which might otherwise have taken a long time, are facilitated through the development of such "foreign domestic markets". The borderless economy gives multinational companies more freedom to choose the country in which they wish to locate their activities.

Some of the implications of a borderless economy include:

◊ International competition between firms is becoming more intense. Firms in traditional industries, which used to compete only with other domestic firms, now have to compete with foreign firms with completely different strategies. Where foreign firms used to produce overseas, they now produce next door, employing workers with the same skills and using the same production networks, thus aggravating the effects of this phenomenon.

◊ Competition among domestic firms is stimulated. Firms with similar technologies and sales networks can gain an advantage over their domestic competitors by shifting the labour-intensive production process to overseas factories.

◊ Competition increasingly takes place not only between companies, but also between nations. The OECD countries have less and less room in which to determine their own domestic institutions or business trading practices. Countries with relatively high domestic trade barriers or insufficient social infrastructures and inferior market conditions face the risk that private capital, from both foreign and domestic sources, may rapidly leave the country. For example, Japan's liberalisation of its domestic financial markets was accelerated partly out of fear of capital flights to the Euro-market, which has virtually no regulations.

The increasing globalisation of economic activities used to be referred to as "new colonialism" *i.e.* the economic invasion of under-developed economies by the industrialised countries. Today, it is rather the OECD countries that worry about the decline in employment which is a consequence of the increasing globalisation of economic activities. The popular argument is that imports of labour-intensive manufactured products from developing countries may substitute for low-skilled labour in industrial countries, thereby increasing unemployment or causing wage differences in the domestic labour market to widen. This "ironic reversal" (Bhagwati) is characteristic of the current international economic situation.

Employment – a major issue

The number of people unemployed has continuously increased in Europe. Unemployment is a major factor encouraging countries to rely on protectionism, in the form of both tariff and non-tariff barriers against imports. A major characteristic of unemployment in Europe is jobless growth, *i.e.* GDP growth without employment growth. Various structural rigidities related to excessive intervention by the public sector in the labour market – such as minimum wages, restrictions on lay-offs, and/or strong union pressures – persist, inducing major firms to encourage labour-saving technologies and reduce employment opportunities.

While, in the United States, the number of people in employment has significantly increased, and the rate of unemployment has remained relatively low, quality of employment, in terms of high skills and wages, is not necessarily sufficient. The per capita income of the average worker has scarcely increased over the last decades and income disparity has widened. Lack of on-the-job training in firms is one of the major factors underlying this situation. With the increasing globalisation of economic activities, these low-skilled jobs are threatened by increased imports from developing countries.

European policies to combat unemployment have not been successful. Encouraging the early retirement of older workers in order to create job opportunities for the youth has failed due to the associated increases in social costs imposed on employers, which discourage employment in general. An increase in public-sector employment has also been hindered by a growing fiscal deficit. Public training programmes are not effective because they often lag behind business needs, resulting in a mis-match in job skills. Public-sector policy initiatives aimed at reducing the supply of labour and increasing labour demand have been unsuccessful.

Human-capital formation

Human capital is the key to creating high-quality employment opportunities. The OECD countries still have a comparative advantage over the Newly Industrialising Economies in the human capital-intensive production of goods and services. How to maintain this comparative advantage is particularly important in attempting to increase industrial competitiveness in a knowledge-based economy.

Human-capital formation can be financed either by individuals or by the firm. Individual initiatives, supported by academic infrastructures, are more prevalent in the United States, while firm-level initiatives dominate in Japan. Skills in most white-collar jobs tend to be financed individually, while blue-collar skills are more likely to be financed by firms. The different types of human-capital formation in the United States and Japan are closely related to their comparative advantage in services and manufacturing, respectively.

Those skills which are financed by individuals and supplied in the market tend to be general to all firms, while the skills financed within firms are those more specific to a particular firm, *i.e.* skills which are not easily transferable to other firms. Firm-specific human capital has an advantage in matching demand and supply for a worker's skills. This is because, compared with skills formed in the market, on-the-job training is provided in the workplace where the skills are actually used, there is thus less danger of mis-matching.

Japanese employment practices, based on long-term employment security, seniority-based wages and firm-specific labour unions, are not necessarily related specifically to Japanese culture, as is often advocated by sociologists. Instead, they provide an efficient mechanism for creating firmspecific human-capital formation within the firm, as well as stable industrial relations:

◊ The scheme represents a joint investment between the employer and the employees, with both parties sharing the risks. The employee pays part of the costs of human-capital formation by accepting lower wages at the beginning of his career, and re-captures the return in later year in terms of higher wages. Continuous investment in human capital over the life-cycle creates a steep age-wage profile. This sharp age-wage profile is a prominent feature of Japanese employment (Figure 1).

◊ Joint investment in the worker's human capital by both firm and employee is reflected in their long-term profit-sharing behaviour. As the employee invests a major portion of his life-time earnings in the firm, and the return is in the form of higher earnings at the age of 40-50, the employees' major interest is the growth of the firm, as is the shareholders'. Harmonious industrial relations with neither serious strikes nor objections to the introduction of labour-saving technologies are a natural consequence of this joint profit maximisation.

◊ The risks of human-capital investment and the commitment to long-term employment can be partially offset by wage flexibility. Bonus payments account for about one-quarter of annual earnings; this fluctuates over the business cycle. In addition, labour unions accept wage reductions in real terms in the event of recessions or large external shocks – thus contributing to the flexibility of earnings over the business cycle.

Skills are formed within the firm through frequent job rotations. An employee entering the firm is assigned to less-skilled jobs. After a few years, when his productivity has reached its peak, he is assigned to jobs requiring more skills. With a sequence of such job rotations, an employee's productivity over his life-time is an envelope curve of individual skill formation (Figure 2). Frequent job rotation and the resulting continuous growth in a worker's skills is a major factor underlying the steep wage profile. Also, these wide-ranging job rotations are supported by firm-based labour union membership. If the Japanese labour unions were occupation-based, as are their European counterparts, such job rotations would be difficult to implement.

Figure 1. International comparison of wage profiles in manufacturing

① Male production workers

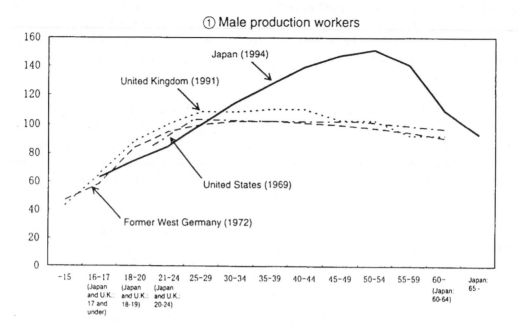

② Male clerical, administrative and technical workers

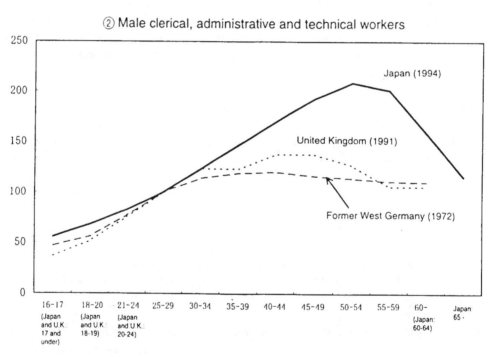

1. Indexed to 25-29 years = 100.
2. Wages shown are regular earnings in Japan; hourly earnings for production workers and monthly earnings for clerical, administrative and technical workers in former West Germany; and weekly earnings in the United States.
Source: Basic Survey on Wage Structure (Ministry of Labour), Structure of Earnings in Industry (EC), Current Population Survey (US Department of Commerce) and New Earnings Survey [UK Departments for Education and Employment (DFEE)].

Figure 2. Job rotations and on-the-job training

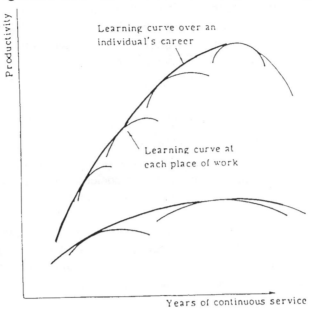

Directions for change

The strong demand for firm-specific human-capital formation by Japanese firms was induced by the high rate of economic growth. The higher the economic growth, the greater the expected returns from investments, and the more firms are incited to invest. This is common to investment in both physical and human capital. However, average economic growth in Japan has been declining over time (Figure 3), and, with the maturity of the Japanese economy, the high rate of investment in both physical and human capital of the past will not be sustainable in the coming years.

Figure 3. Real economic growth rates
Average growth and standard deviation

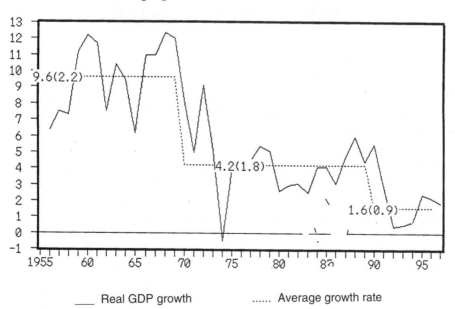

_____ Real GDP growth   ...... Average growth rate

Source: National accounts.

129

Moreover, Japan is facing a rapid ageing of its population. The share of the elderly will reach over 25 per cent in the year 2025, while the active population age will continue to fall. There is a vicious circle between low economic growth and investment. Insufficient investment in physical and human capital is a cause, as well as a consequence, of the low level of economic and productivity growth. A major issue for Japan is how to maintain a high-skilled workforce in the coming ageing society.

The role of government

There are various ways for government to play a role in stimulating human-capital formation. Policies need to be directed away from tax incentives or subsidies to firms, and towards policies promoting the efficient utilisation of human capital in society. Strong policy initiatives need to be directed towards removing existing obstacles hindering the efficient utilisation of human resources:

◊ Early retirement, particularly of skilled workers, is a common feature of many OECD countries. A reversal of this trend is necessary to improve overall productivity and reduce the costs to the economy of taking care of an increasing number of pensioners. The transmission of their skills to the following generation is also important.

◊ Lowering minimum wages to an appropriate level reflecting market equilibrium is important in encouraging firms to hire youth and invest in their human capital. In addition, a reduction of too-generous unemployment benefits is necessary in order to encourage young workers to accept jobs which involve self-investment in skills.

◊ Using tax incentives to encourage the introduction of profit-sharing, rather than fixed wages – this would also help to improve industrial relations, avoiding destructive strikes.

In many European countries, growth in industrial productivity or output per employed worker is relatively high. It is "social productivity" *i.e.* output per working age population, which is generally lower in Europe, particularly compared with that in Japan (Figure 4). Although employed workers in Europe work efficiently, they have to support a large non-working population, for example, the unemployed or those on early retirement schemes. In the United States, on the contrary, growth in social productivity is higher than that of the productivity of the employed popultion, mainly because of the high workforce participation of the population.

In summary, a strong orientation towards investment, both in physical and human capital, is needed in order to improve labour productivity and increase industrial competitiveness in the OECD countries. Increased industrial productivity – which could be achieved by laying off workers – is not the only target; social productivity is also important. The reform of the social security system is a key to improving industrial competitiveness by cutting the costs borne by society.

The rapid catching-up of the Newly Industrialising Economies, and in particular those of East Asia, is a major factor in the loss of OECD competitiveness in labour-intensive and low-technology-based capital-intensive production. The economic activities of the industrialised countries are becoming increasingly knowledge-based through efficient human-capital formation.

Figure 4. Output per working-age person and per employed worker, 1980-95

Annual average growth rates

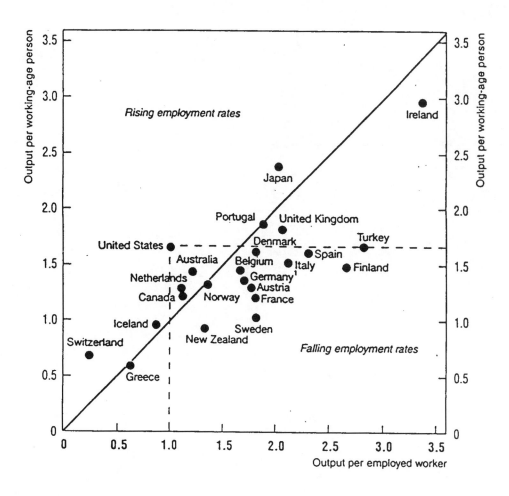

1. Western Germany.
Source: OECD.

Part III

The National Agenda – Increasing Interaction between Macroeconomic and Structural Policy

Chapter 12

MACROECONOMIC AND STRUCTURAL POLICY IN THE KNOWLEDGE-BASED ECONOMY: NATIONAL POLICY CHALLENGES

by

Luc Soete
Director, MERIT, University of Maastricht

Introduction

A number of recent OECD reports[1] have emphasized the fundamental transformation many economies are currently going through and which is closely associated with the use of knowledge. As the OECD (1996*b*) report on *Technology, Productivity and Job Creation* states:

"Today, knowledge in all its forms plays a crucial role in economic processes. Intangible investment is growing much more rapidly than physical investment. Individuals with more knowledge get better paid jobs, firms with more knowledge are winners on markets and nations endowed with more knowledge are more productive." (p. 12)

The growing consensus on the importance of knowledge for industrial competitiveness is closely related to the rapid technological change in the cluster of new information and communication technologies (ICTs) and the resulting dramatic decline in the price of information processing; the technological "digital convergence" between communication and computer technology; and, last but not least, the rapid growth in international electronic networking.

A number of authors (David and Foray, 1995; Abramowitz and David, 1996; Foray and Lundvall, 1996) have described the impact of ICT on the process of knowledge accumulation as a process of "codification"[2] of knowledge, reducing costs of knowledge acquisition and diffusion. Elsewhere I have argued that as a consequence of this increased potential for international codification and transferability, the new information and communication technologies can to some extent be considered as the first truly "global" technology (Soete, 1996). The ability of ICTs to codify information and knowledge over both distance and time brings about more global access. Knowledge, including economic knowledge, is become available world-wide. While the local competencies to access or use such knowledge will vary widely, the access potential is there. In other words, ICTs bring to the forefront the potential for catching-up, based on the economic transparency of advantages, while at the same time stressing the crucial "tacit" and other competence elements in the capacity to access international codified knowledge.

In this paper, I describe some of the main microeconomic, "structural" policy challenges associated with this process, particularly as it appears to have affected European economies. There is at least an impression that policy makers in Europe appear to be somewhat bewildered by the rapidity of both the new policy challenges they are increasingly confronted with and the diminishing room for manoeuvre for traditional macroeconomic and budgetary policy making. Obviously, the list below is non-exhaustive.

The particular importance of skills and knowledge accumulation

It is crucial to realise that ICTs are in essence technologies that are complementary with investment in human resources and skills. In this way, they differ from previous major technological transformations. Most previous major new technology clusters were complementary with physical capital accumulation. Thus, "railroadification", for example, induced a major boom in investment in the essential material and capital-equipment inputs, leading to a strong upsurge in overall economic growth. Similarly, the mass consumption of motor cars, which "induced" demand for better roads, easily accessible motorways, and readily available petrol and car maintenance services, led to an upsurge of growth based both on the growth of final consumption and the many intermediate demands for materials and capital equipment.

Unlike previous technology clusters, the new ICTs appear not to have such major linkages to intermediate demand for *physical, material* goods and capital equipment. It is difficult to see how the increased demand for computers, mobile phones, optical fibres or Internet connections, would lead to a major growth impulse following the "induced" demand for plastics in computers and optical fibres or iron oxide in semiconductors. Despite the heavy capital investments required for some of these products (*e.g.* semiconductors), the material, physical capital accumulation is no longer the essential *"complementary asset"* of these sets of new technologies. Rather, since the knowledge on how to use information typically depends on one's skill level and "tacit" knowledge, the new complementary asset to the growth and use of new ICTs is investment in human, immaterial capital.

I would consequently argue that the transformation of the emerging information society into a true "knowledge society" calls in the first instance for a major effort by both the public and private sectors in the essential *"complementary assets"*: training, education and lifelong learning. Unfortunately, in Europe in particular, a number of disincentives appear increasingly to operate with respect to traditional education and human resource investment:

◊ First, there is the simple feature of the greying of Europe's working population. As the OECD has emphasized many times, a gap is emerging between the rate of renewal of the working population – some 2 per cent per annum – and the rate of knowledge acquisition in society at large – some 7 per cent per annum. Without additional training and learning during working life, in ten years' time 80 per cent of new knowledge acquisition will be concentrated in only 20 per cent of Europe's labour force. As a recent European Green Paper put it: "The workforce is ageing and the technology is getting younger." Acquiring knowledge and skills is therefore no longer limited to school-aged children, but involves all groups in society: youngsters, middle-aged and older people, people with jobs as well as the unemployed.

◊ Second, knowledge acquisition increasingly is no longer a simple incremental accumulation process. In many information handling and processing areas such as, for example, software engineering, the rate of obsolescence of knowledge is high. Knowledge acquired only ten years' ago but not maintained has often lost much of its value. This explains why the unemployment of people with qualifications – but with outdated skills – has become a European characteristic of the 1990s.

◊ Third, the increasing trend towards "external" labour-market flexibility, with greater mobility and transparency in labour markets, has undoubtedly made firms wary of investing in human resources if those investments are likely to benefit, in the first instance, other competing firms. The incentive to invest in general-purpose knowledge and human resources has declined in many of Europe's largest firms. Typically companies with a high labour turnover tend to invest little in human resources.

◊ Fourth, the fiscal consolidation set in motion as part of the EMU convergence criteria has led many European countries to reduce their public spending on education. This reduction comes precisely at a time when, as argued above, such investments are being recognised as essential *complementary assets*" for future growth and competitiveness in the emerging "global information society".

Liberalisation: beyond telecommunications

The industrial transformation associated with the so-called "convergence" between the audio-visual, broadcasting and telecommunication sectors is characteristic of the current digital technological convergence between information and communication technologies. An essential role for governments as safeguarders of competitive forces is linked to creating the optimal conditions in which new investment, markets and services can flourish.

The digital convergence between technologies for broadcasting visual images (television) and for the transportation of data and voice messages (telephony) raises some fundamental regulatory problems. Typically, the creation, distribution and commercialisation of "information" involves many market failures, leading amongst others to market dominance and attempts at vertical integration between incumbents and new entrants across and in each of the various market segments: content creation (including publishing), service provision, distribution network and hardware equipment producers. Regulating such a complex and moving field is a difficult undertaking. The current telecommunication liberalisation process is, from this perspective, only the start of a far more fundamental liberalisation and reregulation process involving telecommunications, broadcasting and publishing. There are strong doubts as to whether the European Community regulatory approach and available regulatory instruments[3] are broad, capable and flexible enough to respond to the current and future technological challenges of inter-network competition.

Already today, there is a clear trend towards increased horizontal concentration among the various market segments mentioned above encompassing the entire territory of the EU. To tackle these, as well as many other potential issues of market-power abuse associated with the current broad convergence between audio-visual sectors and telecommunications, there is, it seems to me, a need for the transfer of regulatory power to the Community level. Dealing with 15 national regulators, getting them to agree, dealing with dispute settlements, etc., is no longer appropriate.

Public information services: a new engine for European growth?

To simply limit the role of the public sector to an "economic" enabling role is, in my view, to grossly underestimate the role and importance of public agencies and services as information providers and information processors in a multitude of economic, social and policy areas. The wide variety of public information services provides a number of opportunities for information-led growth, whereby such services might become the "killer applications" for new, demand-led growth, allowing the public sector to take the lead as *content provider* and opening up new market opportunities for private partnerships in the development, distribution and maintenance of new information systems.

At the same time, the public sector can help to guarantee comprehensive and reliable information which has a high level of accessibility, user friendliness and affordability. Public services could, in other words, be viewed as one of the most promising engines of new demand growth in Europe for the following reasons:

◊ First, by the simple fact alluded to above, that public administration, whether at a national or local level, is first and foremost an information service, often involving many private and public information features. This raises important questions about privacy, access and democratic control.

◊ Second, because the physical and human-capital investments in such activities are often substantial, they provide interesting opportunities for improved connectivity, standards setting, etc. Public administration might, in other words, take the lead in the Information Society given the high risks involved in investing in new, interactive information systems, and opening up new market opportunities for private partnerships in the development, execution and maintenance of new information systems. Pilot projects could bring to the forefront the many organisational bottlenecks, and enable diversity at the local administration level. Such pilot projects, in the courtyard of government so to say, are likely to reveal more immediate solutions and insights into some of the practical organisational and local problems associated with the use of ICTs. Again, this does not necessarily imply that these services must be provided by public authorities. Rather, the initiative should come from the authorities and involve, wherever possible, new emerging partnerships between public administrations and private firms.

◊ Third, many public services such as social services, immigration, police, libraries and many other local services, are bound by the geographical limits of the country, region or town in which they are situated. Clearly, European, cross border interconnectivity of such services is one of the greatest bottlenecks to intra-European mobility of workers and citizens. At the same time, it is one of the most promising areas for European public procurement and new policy initiatives.

The provision of such "public" services could be viewed, in other words, as a possible engine for new, local, information-led, employment-intensive demand growth creating, on the one hand, the minimum efficient scale for some of the new, upgraded, affordable information and communication infrastructures while, on the other hand, paving the way for the emergence of more market-driven "private" services. Such an ICT-driven process of local employment creation corresponds in many ways to the "electronic" version of the personal-services-led *"emplois de proximité"* process in operation in many EU countries. However, in contrast to such personal-services-subsidised employment creation, the proposed "electronic" version suggested here is likely to provide more significant learning and reskilling opportunities.

Assisting organisational change

The full potential of the new ICTs cannot be realised if firms concentrate on technological factors only. Despite considerable investment in ICT hardware, many European companies have been unable to significantly improve their competitive position because of skill shortages and inadequate work organisation. Efficiency and the ability to innovate cannot be improved through isolated modifications to work organisation. To be successful, elements of a flexible work organisation such as staff versatility, training, flexible hours, new pay systems, more team work and flatter hierarchies, must be embedded in the broader structures of the firm. Any changes, including the introduction of new ICTs, are only sensible if they are consistent with the overall situation and conditions of a firm.

With the new ICTs, communication can take place in "real" time and over vast distances. Somewhat paradoxically, however, the importance of person-to-person communication requiring physical proximity has not necessarily declined in the working world. Rather the contrary. New approaches to management stress the importance of inter-personal communication while the decentralisation of responsibilities has increased the need for direct communication.

Virtually all companies are reviewing their range of activities and transferring certain activities to outside suppliers. There are several reasons why firms choose to outsource: some companies form strategic alliances; some concentrate on core activities; and some exploit cost-differences between in-house and external production. Outsourcing is undoubtedly a major growth factor for the new, specialised firms with a highly specialised workforce. Other suppliers, however, have been downgraded to mere suppliers of parts. Competition from low-wage countries will in these cases seriously threaten the viability of such organisations. Small and medium-sized suppliers are under particular pressure, and will only survive if they develop expertise as partners in the production and development of new products and services. Such strategic expertise can be developed through co-operative relationships with other firms thus allowing them to free themselves from "electronic hierarchies" by building up their own networks.

Such organisational and technological innovation by SMEs is highly dependent on support within the region, through for example, training or technology transfer centres. In particular, it is essential that public policy concentrate on helping SMEs in their restructuring efforts.

Reorganising time

One of the most dramatic features of the current ICTs is their enormous potential for the rapid transfer of digital information. This opens up many new opportunities for more flexible production and quicker responses to changes in demand. In some service sectors the speed of response has become the essential ingredient of economic value.[4] In other sectors, interactivity, facilitated by digital communication, has created new trading opportunities. At the same time, human capital has to be developed. Workers need more time for retraining. "Time" is becoming an essential new production factor.

In sectors dealing with the production, transportation and distribution of material goods, new ICTs allow for a reduction in the time/storage dimension between production and consumption. Many of the most distinctive characteristics of the new ICTs are related directly to the potential of the new technology to link-up networks of component and material suppliers, thus allowing for reductions in storage and production time costs. At the same time, certain activities can be outsourced to places far removed from the assembly or final point of production. In transport and logistics, the new technologies facilitate more efficient usage and flexibility in the delivery and transport of goods. In distribution, the increased flexibility associated with the new technologies allows a closer integration of inventories with demand, thus reducing the firm's storage and inventory costs.

In contrast to some of the traditional sectors involved in the production and distribution of material goods, many service activities are characterised by the simultaneity of production and consumption. It is this simultaneity feature which has generally limited productivity improvements in such activities. As argued above, ICTs, almost by definition, will allow for the increased tradeability of service activities. By introducing a time/storage dimension, information technology will enable the separation of production from consumption. It is this latter feature which is behind the enormous new potential for the tradeability of communication and entertainment services reflected in the growth of multimedia. The fact that the "consumption" of such services can take place at a different time than the production allows these services to be much more widely distributed.

However, contrary to the traditional "time-saving" nature of the sort of capital embodied in new manufacturing technologies, the postponed consumption of such services will become "time consuming". In other words, the new demand generated by ICTs does not only allow more immediate communication and quick responses and interactions, it can also require consumers to spend more time.

From this perspective it is essential to re-evaluate the debate on the reduction of working time. The focus should shift away from issues related to the distribution of work and instead concentrate on the increased time required to consume new ICT goods and services, including training and reskilling. Despite the relative material affluence of our societies and the availability of numerous time-saving household equipment, there is still, in most households, a dramatic shortage of time for "non-work" activities.

However, the new ICTs do not only tend to restructure the old, traditional forms of production; they also call into question the accepted conventions of place and time of work. The nature of work and its role are likely to undergo major change. Although the nature and extent of these changes will vary markedly from place to place, the general dimensions are an increase in part-time work, an increase in the unpredictability of working hours, an increase in casual forms of work (temporary or fixed-term contracts, etc.), and a decline in the expectation of a career for life.

On many dimensions the increased use of ICTs both increases the salience of these trends and provides scope for new policies to improve the integration of one's working life into the rest of one's life. For instance, the increasingly rapid rate of obsolescence of existing skills is undoubtedly endangering the employability of older workers and might increase their unemployment rate. Those who have interruptions in their careers – usually women – are finding it increasingly difficult to keep abreast of rapidly changing skill requirements and often end up in peripheral jobs. An economy that is increasingly based on high-quality products and services cannot afford to have an increasing proportion of its workforce in peripheral and atypical jobs. If this occurs then human capital is being unnecessarily wasted and social cohesion will be reduced. Lifelong, flexible working can increase the opportunities for learning to preserve employability and facilitate the reconciliation of work and family.

NOTES

1. See, amongst others, OECD (1996*a*), *Employment and Growth in the Knowledge-based Economy,* Paris, and OECD (1996*b*), *Technology, Productivity and Job Creation,* Paris.

2. "It is a process of reduction and conversion that greatly facilitates the transmission, verification, storage and reproduction of knowledge" (David and Foray, 1995).

3. Directives based on Article 90(3) EC. Once the exclusive and special rights which Article 90(3) directives are designed to deal with have been removed, traditional competition policy provisions (Articles 85 and 86) will have to be relied upon.

4. The speed of reaction for a firm like Reuters is said to be within the time slot of 6 seconds.

REFERENCES

ABRAMOWITZ, M. and P. DAVID (1996), "Technological Change and the Rise of Intangible Investments: The US Economy's Growth-path in the Twentieth Century", in *Employment and Growth in the Knowledge-based Economy*, OECD, Paris.

DAVID, P. and D. FORAY (1995), "Accessing and Expanding the Science and Technology Knowlege Base", *STI Review*, No. 16, Special Issue on Innovation and Standards, OECD, Paris.

FORAY, D. and B.Å. LUNDVALL (1996), "The Knowledge-based Economy: From the Economics of Knowledge to the Learning Economy", in *Employment and Growth in the Knowledge-based Economy*, OECD, Paris.

OECD (1996*a*), *Employment and Growth in the Knowledge-based Economy*, Paris.

OECD (1996*b*), *Technology, Productivity and Job Creation*, Paris.

SOETE, L. (1996), Globalisation, Employment and the Knowledge-based Economy", *Employment and Growth in the Knowledge-based Economy*, OECD, Paris.

Chapter 13

STRUCTURAL ECONOMIC POLICY IN AN INTEGRATED WORLD

by

Everett M. Ehrlich
Under Secretary for Economic Affairs, US Department of Commerce

The relationship between conventional macroeconomic stabilisation policies, on the one hand, and structural economic policy, on the other, is not an abstract one. Nor can it be seen in an historical context.

All of the advanced regions of the economy today face the same circumstances. In each, the tools of stabilisation policy have been set in a long-term direction. In Europe, fiscal policy consists of a race to the Maastricht criteria, a race that is often at odds with the concepts and outcomes that made fiscal policy prominent in the first place. But Europe has decided that fiscal policy, like Odysseus, may be best left tied to a mast if it is to avoid temptation. National monetary policy is soon to be no more, although it is even now out of reach as a countercyclical tool.

The same situation exists in the United States. To a great extent. There is a political consensus that the fiscal deficit would best be eliminated by 2002. The substantive consensus agrees. Only the details remain to be determined, and even here the differences are not great. US monetary policy is also probably now, more than ever, the subject of consensus. Such a consensus is easy when the economy is growing without price pressure and when the central bank's authorities have a hot hand, as Chairman Greenspan does now.

Our macroeconomic thinking, therefore, has gone from the long term to the short term. We are coming to see the most important aspect of our national budgets not as the stimulus they provide, but the kinds of spending they foster, their composition. And, more importantly, we are all coming to accept that the most important aspect of monetary policy is to stabilise the economy by preventing inflation and recession in the long run, not correcting for them in the short run. The more success we have at the former, the less we will need to pursue the latter.

The relationship between structural and stabilisation policies is also affected by recent changes in the economy that appear to emphasize the first and de-emphasize the second. The business cycle may no longer be as cyclical as it once was. The digital revolution has allowed modern economies to better manage their assets. The United States, for example, has seen an ongoing improvement in its level of manufacturing inventories, and there is reason to believe that similar improvements may occur in retailing. This better asset management may taker some volatility out of the cycle. So might greater integration through trade, which allows foreign demand to serve as an automatic stabiliser during downturns and foreign supply to discipline prices (and wages) during upturns.

143

Conversely, epochal technological change makes structural policies more important, almost as a truism. It means great compositional change and market adjustment. It demands a different set of skills on the part of the labour force. It forces a review of our regulatory stance. It realigns economic regions. And it requires different physical and institutional infrastructure – from the broadband networks that make up the information "superhighway" to standards for data communications. If we believe that the shift to an information-intense economy really is an important phenomenon, then the rising importance of structural policy relative to stabilisation policy is both undeniable and unsurprising.

The most striking example of the use of stabilisation policy as a substitute for structural reform is the recent experience of Japan. In 1991, Japan's fiscal surplus stood at 2.9 per cent of GDP. Five years later, its deficit accounted for 4.1 per cent of GDP, a shift of 8 per cent. By comparison, during its worst days of fiscal abuse, the US deficit shifted by only 4.5 per cent (from 1.6 per cent in 1979 to a peak of 6.1 per cent in 1983). There is obviously no remaining room for fiscal stimulus in Japan.

Nor is there any room for monetary policy to work. Three-month passbook savers in Japan now earn an interest rate of 0.5 per cent. The liquidity trap in Japan has teeth. In fact, the low – if not absent – return to savers in Japan is probably acting to weaken the yen and undermine international confidence in the Japanese equity market rather than help to boost it.

Why didn't it work? The problem, as I see it, is that the stimulus fell on an economy unprepared to expand. The banking sector, riddled with troubled assets, was unprepared to lend, and the corporate sector, following the overexpansion of the previous decade, was unprepared to borrow. The workforce was experiencing a decline in the value of its real estate and equity assets and was entertaining its first thoughts of job instability. The problem was not low demand, but structural obstacles to the creation of demand.

In short, Japan has tried every policy cure except the one that will work – structural reform. Moreover, many of the structural reforms that have long been advocated by analyses of the Japanese economy would be exceptionally helpful if they accompanied some of the policy retreat that Japan must now undergo. Opening Japan's markets, for example, would allow prices to fall towards international levels and increase real consumer purchasing power, even in the face of the tax increases planned to close up the budget deficit. Greater competition in financial markets might ease some of the discomfort that might arise if Japan is forced to use interest rates to support the yen.

In fact, those policies would be just as effective, if not more so, than the stabilisation policies they would accompany. More open markets, by boosting real consumer incomes and increasing the value of consumer savings, might spur domestic demand, thus spurring growth. Greater competition in financial markets might attract capital into Japan, strengthening the yen.

The lessons of Japan's recent history, therefore, are inescapable:

◊ there comes a point at which stabilisation policy cannot substitute for structural policy or overcome structural impediments;

◊ structural policy makes the work of stabilisation policy easier; and

◊ structural policy can achieve stabilisation policy goals.

Were we to review comparable circumstances regarding structural impediments to growth in Europe, particularly those regarding labour markets, we would probably reach very similar conclusions. And the same might also be said of the United States. The most formidable structural problem we face, I believe, is the long-term stagnation of real wages. Competent macroeconomic policy over the past several years has created the first meaningful sings of improvement in real US wages in a long time. But the slow progress we're making demonstrates that growth alone cannot obliterate structural features of the economy. This is why the administration has chosen to make education and training the central aspect of its economic policy and recent budget submission.

When Ricardo first wrote about trade, he wrote about a world in which goods were mobile but factors were not. Today, we live in a world in which almost every factor is mobile. If it cannot be transplanted directly, as might a blueprint dispatched via fax or management skills imparted by foreign investment, then it can be incorporated via partnership, alliances, joint ventures or any of the other techniques by which modern corporations extend and complement their ability to create value.

If the web of plug-and-play corporations that now dominates the world economy can deliver virtually any resource to any place, then what distinguishes one economic location from another? What are the remaining determinants of economic competitiveness?

The answer, and the guiding framework for structural policies, is that in a globally linked, information-intense, factor-mobile world, the determinants of economic competitiveness are related to the "economic setting" created by the interaction of public-sector policies and business decision making. That is, our economies will grow as well as the behaviour of our companies allows.

That suggests to me that the goal of structural policy is to improve this "economic setting". This broad objective includes a wide variety of policy areas. Our economies' regulatory initiatives are of obvious importance. Our labour market policies, including the relative weight we assign to tomorrow's jobs compared to today's, are part of this system as well. So are the ways in which we promote skill development in both adult workers and our children.

But I wish to focus on a few other areas. The first is technology policy. Innovation is a hard objective to pursue, and even harder to "buy". However, given its very high rate of return, it is likely that well-designed innovation programmes, involving sound technical criteria, cost sharing, and broad potential social returns, will make good use of public moneys. The case for diffusion policies is even stronger. It strikes me as extraordinarily likely that a dollar competently spent on diffusing good technological practice to our firms will earn a very high return. I say this in view of the evidence collected in the United States and other nations from longitudinal data on plants and firms, which suggests that a relatively small number of "heroic" firms or plants account for a substantial share of the gross job creation in the economy. Moreover, the same research demonstrates that most of the economy's advances in productivity occur not because of general improvement in all plants or firms, but because high-productivity plants out compete low-productivity ones, gaining market share from them even as they create employment.

All of our economies reserve a special place for small business, and too often the place we reserve for it is more "special" than the small businesses themselves. Rather than think about how to create larger numbers of small businesses, we might think about how to make more of the existing ones successful. Diffusion policy goes directly to this objective.

A second area that should be considered part of structural policy is the quality of the decision making produced by our governments. I mean this in a sense larger than their simply making good macroeconomic policy or liberating their telecommunication sectors for competition.

For example, is the entirety of economic policy consistent? Do we provide tax benefits for R&D but then deploy other tax features (such as foreign tax credit limitations) that work in the opposite direction? Do we examine all expenditures for export promotion and determine their relative worth? Or, for that matter, do we subsidise exports and then deploy farm policies that discourage them by guaranteeing a return in our domestic markets? Are our data collection efforts dispersed in an unco-ordinated fashion using inconsistent methodologies?

Second, is government competent? The administrative aspects of government alone occupy a large share of GDP. Are they effective? Are the boundaries of government involvement correctly defined? Is outsourcing used when appropriate? Do the rules for government hiring lead to the right balance between developing expertise and institutional memory in the government, on the one hand, and avoiding entrenched bureaucracies, on the other?

Third, what is the decision-making process? This is an important issue in all of our nations. Does the system produce political latitude, does it make decisions quickly, does it make the right number and level of decisions (or does it overburden itself with too much to do)? This may sound like standard "good government" rhetoric, but it is not. Indeed, the first of the advanced economies to address forthrightly its major structural economic problems – be it deregulation in Japan, the role of entitlement expenditures and health care in the United States or the need for more entrepreneurship and labour market fluidity in Europe – will probably realise substantial gains – perhaps at the short-term expense of the others.

A third and final area that deserves mention is openness, in trade, investment and corporate governance. Openness in itself is an important national economic asset. In a globally integrated economy, autarchy policies are doomed to fail. In a narrow way, this proposition is visible in trade flows. Our nations turn imports into exports, from componentry that is integrated into computer systems to equipment that produces US media and firm entertainment.

But, in a broader sense, openness is a vital precondition to building our firms' competitiveness. The corporate manager of this information age is the one who can define what her or his firm is good at doing, wrap his company's boundaries tightly around those abilities, and then find skills and abilities elsewhere in the world that complement and lever his own. Technology's ability to "dis-integrate" our firms means that the vertical value-creating chains that once resided inside our organisations will be reassembled as global networks of production. All of our companies need to search for their place in this network. Only an open environment, one that allows trade, investment and that promotes governance focused on adaptation and change, can promote this objective.

Part IV

Intangible Assets

EVALUATING THE IMPORTANCE OF INTANGIBLES: HOW ARE THEY MANAGED AND ACCOUNTED FOR, AND HOW DO THEY CONTRIBUTE TO GROWTH AND EMPLOYMENT?

by

Ulf Johanson

Associate Professor, PhD, Personnel Economics Institute, School of Business, Stockholm University

General aim

The general aim of this project is to provide insight into the process of transforming intangibles into increased wealth. How are they managed and accounted for, and how do they contribute to growth and employment?

The project is limited to the following four types of studies.

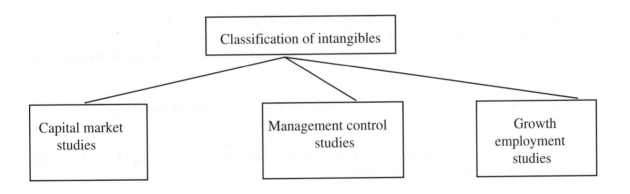

Core partners in the project are the Netherlands, Finland, Spain and Sweden. Norway will probably join as an affiliated partner. All studies are carried out in all countries. Theory will be generated from a comparison of the findings across the various countries.

So far, the project has benefited from the support of the OECD, the Swedish Ministry of Trade and Industry, the Research Council of Norway, and the Swedish Union for Academic Professionals (Saco). It has much in common with the suggested analyses presented in the preliminary report from the OECD meeting held in Hull, Canada, in December 1996.[1]

Rationale for undertaking the project – its general relevance

Objective 5 of the European Commission's White Paper *Teaching and Learning - Towards the Learning Society,* states: "treat capital investment and investment in training on an equal basis". In addition, the Commission had made an earlier proposition that arrangements should be introduced to make it possible for companies to enter some of their investments in training on their balance sheets.[2] In September 1996 a thematic conference on Objective 5 of the White Paper was arranged by the Commission in Brussels. The following questions were addressed at that conference:

1. What are the consequences of not addressing this issue from the point of view of promoting investment in human resources and intangible investments in general?

2. What indicators could be developed to improve the evaluation of the impact of human resources on the performance of a company?

3. What models of human resource accounting or reporting could be put forward that would be acceptable to accountants, investors, company managers and trade-unionists?

4. Should information on human resources be made available on the balance sheet or should it be in the form of supplementary information in the company's annual report or in addition to the annual report?

There are indications that failure to address this issue has created an inefficient allocation of resources (Question 1).[3] Furthermore, there is a risk that the superior transparency of tangible *vs.* intangible assets attracts capital investments – increasing rather than decreasing unemployment.

Many ideas and models concerning indicators (Question 2) have been suggested, but too little is known about the effects of these models on decision making and action (Questions 3 and 4).

Over the last few years, the OECD has also been discussing the transparency of investments in human resources and other intangibles. In 1996 and 1997, the subject was given special attention at three OECD conferences. In one of the workshops, held in Ottawa, December 1996, the following questions were discussed:

1. What evidence exists of a shift in the relative importance of tangible and intangible assets?

2. How strong is the demand for more and better information on intangibles, both within enterprises and external to them?

3. Among the various forms of intangible assets and capabilities, where is the greatest potential for improved information?

4. What different approaches to measurement and disclosing information on intangibles have been tried, and what are their respective strengths and weaknesses?

5. What steps might be taken by enterprises, labour, public authorities and bodies such as professional and business associations, to improve investment decisions?

———

Although the data do indicate a shift in the relative importance of intangibles (Question 1), and in spite of the fact that a number of approaches have attempted to address the issue of accounting for intangibles (Question 4),[4] even in these areas too little information is available to provide answers to the other questions.

Taking together the questions raised by the EC and the OECD, it is obvious that further research is necessary before introducing measures concerning: *i)* including investments in training on balance sheets; or *ii)* the disclosure of information on human resources and other intangible assets. However, before suggesting a programme of research, I would first like to considerably broaden the current perspective.

The overall research problem

It would appear that we will move into the new century with more off-balance-sheet phenomena than was the case in the past; mainly as a result of new financial instruments.[5] We are also entering a new era with far more organisations specialising in service and consulting;[6] it has become commonplace to refer to these firms as "network" or "virtual" or "imaginary" organisations.[7] Their strategic resources, production processes and products are of a human, structural[8] or hybrid nature.[9]

Thus, the genesis and spread of new ideas play an ever increasing role, not only in industries such as biotechnology, pharmaceuticals, health care, software and telecommunications, but also in more traditional manufacturing firms. These latter continue to enhance their wealth in areas such as design, logistics, marketing and management.

Although organisational theory and research on "virtual" or "imaginary" organisations have started to develop a language designed to perceive and recognise the meaning of these new phenomena, from an accounting point of view they are almost invisible. All the elements in the value creation chain (resources, production process and products) are filled with invisible phenomena (events and states). Although some progress has been made through research on goodwill, brand and human resource accounting, accounting in general has not yet succeeded in grasping this *invisible reality*.

On the contrary, the annual statement has become a *visible illusion*[10] in the sense that the figures are accurate but do not make any functional sense.[11] Evidence of the phenomenon of visible illusion resides in the growing discrepancy between the market and book values of listed companies (see below). Other evidence is the possible abnormal return on investments in knowledge-based companies (see below). Johnson and Kaplan[12] express a similar visible illusion in management accounting that can be be interpreted as accounting nonsense. The authors refer to this illusion as "relevance lost". It seems that today's accounting system has lost part of its rhetorical dimension[13].

Even if invisible reality could be reflected in accounting, could it be audited? The audit explosion[14] in quantity can be challenged by the debate of audit functions or the "revenues" of auditing. If these invisible features become more important for organisational success, then, by definition, auditing solely the visible illusion restricts its reputed functions.

Even if most of this invisible reality does not show up in the accounting, it is dealt with at the company level. Locating and mapping intangibles is probably an important building block for any company aspiring to create value for its shareholders, employees and other stakeholders. However, intangibles are scattered, difficult to find and prone to leave; they reside in the peoples' heads, in obscure notebooks, on computer discs and in vast networks. Best practice can be helpful in steering a course to where to look for such assets.

How are important intangibles identified and defined? How can invisible realities be accounted for, controlled and audited? How does visualisation through accounting, auditing and management control affect organisational efficiency and social order? What is the importance of intangibles in the creation of value added, growth and employment?

The four types of study

Capital market studies

Between 1975-92 accounted goodwill for companies listed on the Stockholm stock exchange grew from less than Skr 1 billion to Skr 37 billion (*i.e.* from 1 per cent of total stock exchange value to more than 7 per cent).[15]. The difference between market and book values also increased substantially during the ten-year-period from 1985 to 1994, as can be seen from Figure 1.

Figure 1. The difference between market and book values among Swedish companies on the Swedish stock exchange, 1985-94

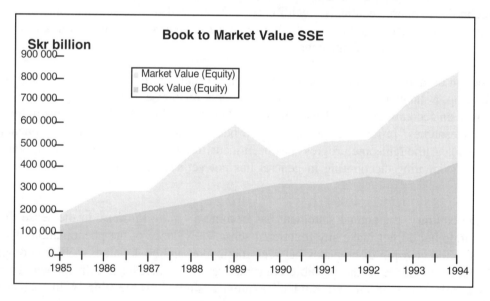

During the period 1975-82, book value was higher than market value.

If the companies are ranked according to their dependency on human resources,[16] and if the highest decile (knowledge-based firms) is compared with the lowest decile (capital-intensive firms), then a significant difference is revealed. This means that investments in human resources represent a significantly higher value to the capital market today than was the case ten years' ago. It is also an indication that one reason for the increasing difference between market and book values is the growing importance of human capital.

A recent study,[17] showed that the return on a stock portfolio of knowledge-based firms at the Stockholm stock exchange was significantly higher than that on a portfolio based on firms with a higher dependency on tangible assets.

Figure 2. Comparison between the most and the least human-capital-dependent companies on the Swedish stock exchange in relation to the difference in market and book values, 1985-94

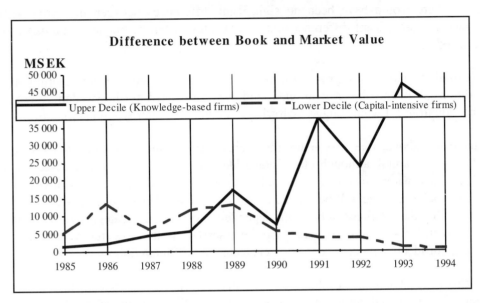

Figure 3. Comparison of rates of return on different portfolios with respect to dependency on human capital

Cumulative risk-adjusted rate of return

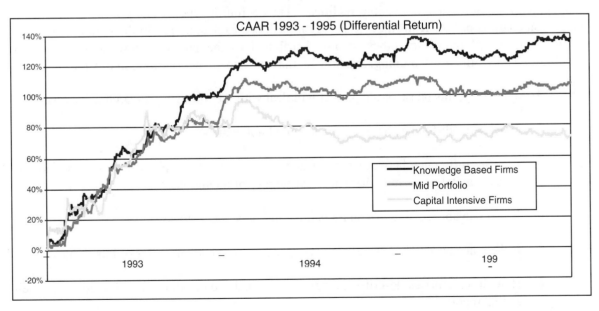

Companies were ranked according to their dependency on human resources. The daily risk-adjusted return was compared with the daily stock market index from 1993 to 1995. Figure 3 shows the cumulative average return for each portfolio. There was no evidence to show that investors perceived knowledge-based firms as involving more risk than firms with a higher dependency on tangible assets.

I would suggest that, if investors had performed a more accurate valuation of investments in human resources, there would have been no significant differences between the three portfolios. However, the fact that significant differences exist, indicates that investments in human resources were underestimated.

These findings indicate the growing importance of, and the need for, information on human capital. In addition, all of the above-mentioned studies were carried out in Sweden[18]. What is the situation in other countries? I would suggest carrying out comparative cross-country studies.

As indicated above, one reason for the increasing difference between market and book values might be human capital, although other intangibles, such as structure capital, R&D capital or market capital, are explanatory factors which could account for the difference. To investigate this, companies on the stock exchange will be ranked according to their dependency on a certain category of intangibles. Finally, the relationship between dependency on a certain category of intangibles and the difference between market and book values will be assessed. In the case studies described below, operational criteria for identifying dependency on each category of intangibles will be examined.

It is also suggested that the study of abnormal return on investments in human-capital-dependent companies be carried out as comparative studies in different countries. As a complement to this analysis, similar studies will also be performed, taking into account other categories of intangibles.

As outlined above, one of the aims of this research programme is to increase our knowledge of how enterprises account for invisible realities. Thus a fourth type of study is desirable. This would be an analysis of how firms that are listed on the stock exchange inform the public about their intangibles in annual reports or other reports distributed to the public. How do they classify intangibles, *e.g.* investments in training, and how do they describe their contribution to value added?

To summarise, this phase of the project will deal with the following research questions:

◊   What is the difference between market and book values?

◊   Can the difference between market and book values be explained by dependency on human capital or on any other specific category of intangibles?

◊   Is there an abnormal return on human-capital-dependent stocks?

◊   Is there an abnormal return on stocks dependent on other categories of intangibles?

◊   How do enterprises describe intangibles and their contribution to value added in their annual reports?

Management control studies

The main reason for improving financial accounting for capital-market purposes is to establish conditions for more efficient capital allocation. However, if accounting information is to be reliable from an investor's point of view, it has to be founded on a valid and reliable accounting for management control. This raises the second research problem of this project, namely accounting for management control of the invisible. How do enterprises control the invisible? What is the nature of the invisible? How can it be identified and classified? How is it described and valued? How are investment procedures treated?

An indication of the growing importance of intangibles in the management control process is the increasing number of concepts aspiring to make a contribution, *e.g.* balanced score card, human resource accounting, utility analysis, intellectual capital, monitoring of intangible assets. None of these concepts, however, is universally accepted – each has its advocates and antagonists.

Several indications of the need for new tools in the management control process may be found in evaluative studies on the implementation of human resource costing and accounting (HRCA)[19] in Swedish organisations. In five studies,[20] representing seven cases, about 100 financial, line and personnel managers were interviewed concerning their reactions to the implementation of HRCA. The results indicate that attitudes to HRCA were positive across the studies. Managers perceive that HRCA has an important goal to attain. It is obvious from most of these cases that the discovery of hidden costs, incomes and values acts as a very strong incentive to use HRCA in the future.

In one of the studies[21] about 700 hundred quotations, describing individual and organisational learning processes, were collected. The quotations indicate that the failure to address the issue of HRCA has resulted in an inefficient allocation of resources. There seem to have been underinvestments in human resources. However, according to managers, focusing on the issue of HRCA will bring about a change in resource allocation.

In this project the idea is to map best business practice. How do firms measure, present and establish outcomes[22] for intangibles, *e.g.* competence development? We suggest that 5-7 enterprises, known for dealing with intangibles in an interesting way, be selected from each country. Preferably these firms should represent different categories of a theoretically developed classification of intangibles.[23] For example:

Country	Category 1	Category 2	Category 3	Etc.
Finland	Company F1	Company F2	Company F3	
Netherlands	Company H1	Company H2	Company H3	
Spain	Company E1	Company E2	Company E3	
Sweden	Company S1	Company S2	Company S3	

This means that the selection of companies cannot be accomplished until a theoretically based classification has been made. A number of specific questions must be examined. For example: How are investment procedures treated? How do firms account for the invisible? How is the benefit obtained from investments in intangibles described? In what way do intangibles create value added for the firm?

Data collection will be carried out through interviews and literature studies. A theory on management control of intangibles will be generated through a comparison of different enterprises, categories and countries.

From the case studies, the following results, with implications for other research projects in this programme, will be obtained: *i)* empirical data on the classification of intangibles; *ii)* operational criteria for identifying dependency on a particular category; and *iii)* a hypothesis on the importance of competence development and other intangibles for growth and employment.

To summarise, the following research questions will be treated in this section of the project:

◊ How do the selected firms classify their intangibles?

◊ How do the selected firms treat intangibles in their management control process?

◊ What operational criteria exist in the selected firms to help identify dependency on a particular category?

◊ What are the hypotheses that can be generated for the selected firms regarding the importance of intangibles for growth and employment?

Growth and employment studies

The greatest share of the productivity improvement which took place in Sweden between 1980 and 1995 is concentrated in the 30 per cent of all workplaces in the business sector which can be classified as knowledge-intense. Productivity growth in these branches has been three times as high as for the rest of the economy. Meanwhile, the majority of the 90 000 new jobs created in the economy during 1994 and 1995 were in these sectors.

The purpose of this study is to investigate the causes and effects of the invisible assets of a company on its investments, growth and employment. Can intangibles help to avoid diminishing returns on investments? Is there a link between investments in intangibles and investments in tangible assets? Can investments in intangibles enhance innovativeness, and how can the spillover of knowledge across individuals and firms be stimulated? Can intangibles increase growth and employment?

Hypotheses on the importance of intangibles will be put forward in the management control studies. These hypotheses will then be tested at the macro level on two different groups of firms. The first group consists of the 1 800 fastest growing companies in Sweden, and the second is a reference group of 700 work locations, representing 70 per cent of all Swedish work locations in the business sector.

Research question:

◊ What are the effects of intangibles on *i)* investments, *ii)* growth, and *iii)* employment?

Classification of intangibles

Intangibles will be classified from a study of the literature and through logical deduction. This classification will serve as the basis for selecting enterprises for the management control studies. The theoretical conclusions will be compared with empirical data on how firms classify intangibles from a management control perspective. Finally, annual reports will be studied to analyse the external presentation and classification of intangibles. The idea is to develop a classification system that promotes understanding and communication.

Different stakeholders (*e.g.* company management, investors, creditors, and policy-making bodies such as governments) must have an input into the development of the classification system. This implies that their opinions must be taken into account.

The research question may therefore be posed as follows:

◊ How could intangibles be classified in order to promote understanding and control for external as well as internal purposes?

Timetable

The project is planned to start in July 1997. Literature surveys and the theoretical part of the classification study will start at the end of the summer. Empirical work concerning the management control studies will be started at the end of 1997 and terminated during spring 1998. The capital market and the growth and employment studies could begin in spring 1998. Preliminary findings could be available at the end of 1998. Final reports, including policy implications generated from the research findings, will be available in autumn 1999.

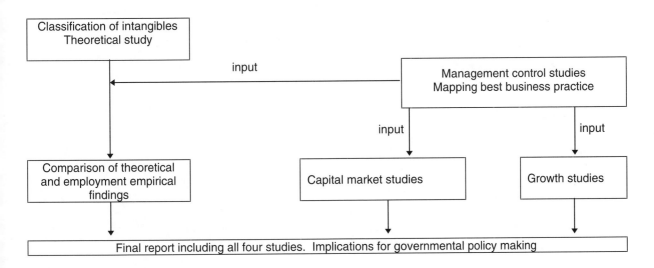

Outcomes, benefits and diffusion of results

The consequences of this project could be far-reaching:

◊ At the *individual level,* the possibility of relating task qualification and individual competence to organisational outcome might increase.

◊ At the *organisational level,* the management of invisibles can affect organisational efficiency. New or alternative investment opportunities will emerge. The project can demonstrate to what extent and how investment in intangibles can be reinforced.

◊ At the *national level,* the intention is to create a foundation for governmental policy making in the field of investments in intangibles in general.

The results of the project will be published as reports. At the end of the project, the intention is to collect all the reports in a book.

Project management

The project is co-ordinated by a matrix organisation. Individual studies are managed by research leaders, one of whom acts as national co-ordinator. Each type of study is also co-ordinated internationally by a functional co-ordinator. The overall co-ordination of the project is carried out from Sweden.

NOTES

1.   The fact that studies carried out earlier by Baruch Lev and Ernst & Young (reported at the Hull meeting), are not mentioned here does not imply that we think they are not desirable.

2.   European Commission, *An Industrial Competitiveness Policy for the European Union*, [COM(1994)319final].

3.   Johanson, U. (1996), Speech at the White Paper Thematic Conference, Objective 5 in Brussels, September.

4.   Johanson, U. (1996), *Increasing the Transparency of Investments in Intangibles,* Speech for workshop 6 at the OECD conference in Ottawa, December.

5.   That this is the case for Swedish companies is shown by Rundfelt, R., *Tendenser i börsföretagens årsredovisningar (Tendencies in the Annual Reports of Companies on the Swedish Stock Exchange)* 1991, 1992, 1993, 1994, Stockholms Fondbörs & Bokföringsnämnden, Stockholm.

6.   According to the Federal Statistics Bureau in Sweden, between 1964-90 this sector had grown from 49 to 64 per cent of Swedish GDP.

7.   As an expression of this type of organisational research with accounting implications, see Hedberg, B. *et al.* (1995), *Imaginära organisationer (Imaginary Organisations)* Liber Hermods, Stockholm.

8.   The term "structure assets" denotes the book value of the structural investments made; see Konrad (1988), *Den osynliga balansräkningen (The Invisible Balance Sheet),* Affärsvärlden, Stockholm.

9.   Here a "hybrid asset" denotes some sort of combination of real, financial and intangible assets.

10.   Gombridge Art and Illusion.

11.   On organising and sensemaking, see Weick, K (1995), *Sensemaking in Organisations,* Sage, London; and Salzer, M. (1994), *Identity across Borders. A Study in the IKEA-world,* Linköping University, Sweden.

12.   Johnson, H.T. and R.S. Kaplan (1987), *Relevance Lost: The Rise and Fall of Management Accounting,* Harvard Business School Press, Boston.

13.   Czarniawska-Joerges (1993), "The Leading Rhetoric of Economics is the Rhetoric of Numbers", p. 91.

14.   Power, M. (1994), *The Audit Explosion,* Demos, London.

15.   Gröjer, J.E. (1993), *Redovisa anställda på balansräkningen! (Statement of the Value of Employees on the Balance Sheet),* Labora Press, Stockholm.

16. The ranking has been obtained by using the following selection ratio:

Selection ratio = $A_i/(N_i/W_i)$
where A_i is the average wage, N_i is the proportion of non-wage costs, and W_i is the proportion of wage costs for firm i.
The proportion of non-wage costs divided with the proportion of wage costs shows the human resource intensity of the company while the average wage is supposed to reflect the value of the production from the human resources to the company.

17. Hansson, B. (1996), *Personnel Investments and Abnormal Return. Knowledge-based Firms and Human Resource Accounting,* Work in Progress, Personnel Economics Institute, School of Business, Stockholm University.

18. Studies on the difference between market and book values have, according to the 1996 OECD Hull report, also been carried out in the United States and the Netherlands.

19. Human Resource Costing and Accounting (HRCA) tries to highlight the costs and income related to human resources. The concept of HRCA comprises both human resource accounting (HRA) and cost/benefit analyses of human resources.

20. Johanson, U. (1997), *Why Human Resource Costing and Accounting Does not Work,* Work in progress. Personnel Economics Institute, School of Business, Stockholm University.

21. Johanson, U. and M. Nilson (1995), *Personalekonomi och organisatoriskt lärande (Human Resource Costing and Accounting and Organisational Learning),* Personnel Economics Institute 1995:1, School of Business, Stockholm University.

22. Quotation from the 1996 OECD Hull report.

23. The following classification is used in the Hull report for the same illustrative reason: R&D innovation, Software, Human capital, Organisational capital and Marketing.

Chapter 15

ECONOMICS OF THE WORKING ENVIRONMENT AND HUMAN RESOURCE ACCOUNTING

by

Heikki Rouhesmaa
Ministry of Labour, Finland

Introduction

Since the 1960s, determining the financial value of staff has attracted considerable attention, particularly in the United States. To this end, staff is seen as "human capital" that includes the knowledge, experience and skills of the individual employees and their financial value to the company, as well as the investments made in the development of human resources. From a wider perspective, human capital also includes the psychological energy and motivation of the staff, which, together with the other assets listed above, can be harnessed by the organisation for a certain period of time in order to produce goods and services.

A debate on the economic impact of the working environment was initiated in the Nordic countries in the 1980s. According to the theory, successful corporate operations are determined by the standard of working conditions, which will affect the company's profits both directly and indirectly by reducing absenteeism and staff turnover. Other factors affecting a firm's productivity are the skills and level of education of its personnel. While the tangible framework for the working environment is provided by its physical characteristics, the actual contents are created by the organisation and the individuals working in it.

The impact of the working environment on corporate activities can be clearly shown by means of a few simple indicators. The most important of these are absenteeism, staff turnover and training, which can be easily measured in terms of numbers. Environmental factors can thus be given specific monetary values that help to illustrate the financial impact of the working environment on corporate performance.

The concept of the economics of the working environment was introduced on a broader front by the Working Conditions Committee's 1991, in which it underlined the importance of developing programmes for influencing decision making to promote policies favourable to the working environment. Furthermore, it was pointed out that there was a need to devise simple calculation models to help companies improve their ability to monitor the financial impact of the working environment. At the same time, the idea of publishing a balance sheet on human resources in order to increase awareness of the working environment, both within the organisation and outside it, by was put forward.

Human resources

The personnel is generally regarded as the most important asset of a company. Human resources consist of the quantitative and qualitative characteristics of the staff. How efficiently these resources can be used very much depends on the working environment and organisation. The table below shows the different components of human resources.

Table 1. Human resources

Quantitative input by personnel	Working environment and organisation	Qualitative input by personnel
Number of personnel	Physical and mental strain caused by work	Work capacity
Theoretical working hours	Job satisfaction	Professional skills
Absenteeism, holidays	Content of tasks	Work experience
Overtime	Co-operation and communication	Training and staff development
Staff turnover		Staff turnover

The capacity of the organisation depends on the *quantitative* and *qualitative* input of the personnel.

However, organisational resources are not simply a sum total of quantitative and qualitative inputs. *The working environment and the organisation* determine how efficiently the human resources can be used. If the organisation works efficiently, its performance exceeds the collective combined input of the staff. However, the organisation may also restrict individual activity to the extent that all synergy benefits are lost and the organisation is inefficient in making use of its personnel.

To ensure the rational use and development of human resources, it is necessary to establish a monitoring system that gives a detailed and comprehensive picture of the personnel. Mathematical models make it possible to reliably define the cost of various activities. Areas that can be measured include recruitment, absenteeism, training and staff turnover.

Human resource investments are the outlays needed to develop the personnel, giving rise to short-term procurement, development and allocation costs. Such investments are made in order to improve the professional qualifications of the staff and to enhance work performance – leading to increased organisational profits. Thus, the input-output approach is the cornerstone of human resource calculations. Personnel costs are indispensable inputs that enable the organisation to work and produce results.

For the success of any organisation, it is necessary that the personnel work efficiently for the good of the whole. Since the staff is a productive factor and contains a large number of the elements necessary for economic success, special attention must be paid to organisational management and personnel investments. Only an appropriate incentive management can ensure good results. Economic calculations concerning staff provide an efficient tool for management and make it possible to forecast, follow-up and evaluate any measures adopted. Statistics based on these calculations can be complied into a personnel balance sheet.

Balance sheet on human resources

The Working Conditions Committee expressed the need to develop a personnel balance sheet. A number of organisations have already drawn up such balance sheets. A working party set up by the Ministry of Finance has developed a framework model for personnel balance sheets to be used by governmental organisations.

The purpose of the balance sheet on human resources is to give shareholders, management, personnel officers and the staff itself information on current trends in the volume and structure of human resources, the use of working hours, costs, work skills and training, the state of the personnel, remuneration, efficiency and service capacity.

If correctly applied, personnel balance sheets will become a valuable part of the management's information system that is worth developing and investing in. Personnel balance sheets are equally important for the staff because they underline the importance of investing and developing the personnel and looking after its well-being.

The Working Party on Personnel Accounting has proposed a framework model that includes the following components:

◊ number and structure of personnel;

◊ demand for and supply of personnel;

◊ use of working hours;

◊ sick leave;

◊ training;

◊ requirements, work performance and performance-based compensation plans;

◊ labour costs;

◊ staff turnover;

◊ economic parameters;

◊ job satisfaction;

◊ client satisfaction;

◊ personnel replacement costs.

The idea is that the organisation selects suitable items from the list and prepares a personnel balance sheet on human resources based on the data collected. The data must be gathered using the same methods for several years to reflect changes in the operations of the organisation and the correlation between personnel issues and such changes.

In the following model, personnel inputs have been divided into quantitative and qualitative inputs in accordance with the division of human resources discussed above (Table 2). Elements describing the state of the working environment and level of personnel investments are included. In addition, indicators illustrating the efficiency of the personnel are also provided.

Table 2. Model for a balance sheet on human resources

Personnel inputs		1995	1994	1993
Quantitative				
• personnel	no.			
- total working hours	- h			
- absence due to sickness	- h			
- absence due to accidents	- h			
- annual holidays	- h			
- other statutory leaves	- h			
• hours worked	- h			
• hours worked/total working hours	%			
• total wage cost	FIM			
• indirect employee costs	FIM			
• wages paid for hours worked	FIM			
• wages paid for hours worked/total wage cost	%			
Qualitative				
• age distribution				
• gender distribution				
• level of education	index			
• period of service	years			
Working environment and organisation				
• work capacity	index			
• workplace atmosphere	index			
• cost of staff turnover	FIM			
• cost of sick leave	FIM			
• cost of accidents	FIM			
Investments in personnel				
• occupational health services	FIM			
• training and development	FIM			
Outputs		1995	1994	1993
Efficiency of personnel				
Productivity	performance/inputs			
Financial performance	performance/costs			

Chapter 16

HUMAN RESOURCE ACCOUNTING AND REPORTING

by

Professor Willem Dercksen
KPMG Economic Research & Policy Consulting, The Netherlands

Introduction

Roughly speaking, there are two kinds of intangibles. First, knowledge and procedures owned by companies – their tacit knowledge. Examples are copyrights, patents, computer software, networks, databases and organisational structures. The second kind of intangible concerns the human capital of a company. In this contribution, I will mainly confine myself to the second kind of intangible – the human resources of a company.

The topic of human-resource accounting and reporting within enterprises is becoming increasingly important. The European economies are in a period of transition. Mass production is being replaced by modes of production which are tailored to the needs of individual customers. Concepts such as just-in-time production, core business, flat organisational structures and human resource management are recognised as being of utmost importance in maintaining or increasing competitiveness. Moreover, we are in the middle of an ICT revolution. However, the potential impact of communication and information technologies on modes of economic production is difficult to assess. In our emerging knowledge-based economies, fewer and fewer workers can survive in their working lives in the absence of the ability and the willingness to learn. Ability and willingness are crucial for both the employability of workers and the success of their companies. Companies must invest in the training and employability of their employees in order to remain competitive. In many European countries, companies' training costs account for an average of 2-3 per cent of the wage bill. In the high-tech and business service sectors this percentage is much higher. In this context, the question of whether it is possible to account for human resources on company balance sheets is gaining renewed interest.

In this chapter I would like to address four questions pertaining to Human Resource Accounting and Reporting (HRA&R):

◊ How important is HRA&R?

◊ What are the main objections against accounting for human resources in balance sheets?

◊ Do alternatives exist?

◊   Is there a future for HRA&R?

I would like to add that this chapter draws on the results of a study carried out by KPMG Economic Research & Policy Consulting for the Dutch Ministry of Education, Culture and Sciences.[1] In that study, we addressed, *inter alia*, the four questions posed above.

How important is HRA&R

One indication of the relevance of HRA&R might be found in the difference between the market and book values of companies. The ratio of market to book value is known as the Q-ratio. For American companies the Q-ratio is about 1.7. For Swedish companies the ratio is close to 2.0 and for Dutch companies it is 2.1. The difference between the market and book values indicates the hidden value of a company's intangibles: its *tacit knowledge* and its *human resources*. Human-resource *accounting* might improve our knowledge of these hidden values. When the results of the accounting exercise are made available to the external stakeholders of a company, human-resource *reporting* might contribute to a better functioning of capital markets.

A second argument for HRA&R is the emergence of the knowledge-based economy. Human-resource accounting could help companies to improve the effective and efficient use of knowledge and human resources. This is of special relevance to knowledge-based companies. Or to put it simply: if these firms knew what they knew, they would be three times more effective. Human-resource reporting might contribute to a process of learning from each other.

Consequently, there are two main functions of HRA&R. HR accounting could contribute to the better functioning of companies and, when the reports are published, also to the better functioning of capital markets.

Objections

The second question regards the objections to the inclusion of human resources on balance sheets. The human resources of a company are sometimes called its "assets". However, a serious auditor will object to this label, because human resources do not meet the characteristics of an asset. Three of the characteristics of an asset are:

◊   the capacity to generate future earnings;

◊   measurability;

◊   ownership.

All three of these characteristics raise problems in relation to human resources. Firstly, it is not always possible to tell in advance whether investments in human resources will generate future earnings. Secondly, the value of human resources is difficult to measure. And thirdly, in a market economy employees are not slaves: they are free to resign.

These objections imply that it is not possible to account for the value of *all* the human resources of a company on the balance sheet. In my opinion, however, it is possible to include *some* investments in human resources on balance sheets. For instance, I do not see any objection to including investments in specific, expensive training programmes, where the contribution of those training programmes to the results of the company are obvious and where there is a contractual agreement that employees will refund these costs if they resign within a specified period.

Alternatives

Fortunately there are also alternatives to including human resources on the balance sheet. In our study we distinguished three types of HRA&R, which also have counterparts in the business environment. Each alternative is relevant for a different category of stakeholder. Stakeholders are: shareholders, management, clients and consumers, employees, social partners and governments. The alternatives are:

◊ standardized human resource management;

◊ effect studies on training programmes;

◊ satellite balance sheets.

Standardized human resource management is particularly relevant for internal stakeholders: management and employees. It might be described as a structured way of dealing with human resources and as a justification of the mutual responsibility of management and employees in the employment relationship. An example of standardized human resource management is the use of Business Score Cards and Individual Score Cards. Business Score Cards may help to detect the performance of a company; Individual Score Cards may help to detect an individual's contribution to the performance of the company, as well as the individual targets to improve this contribution. KPMG Netherlands has recently introduced score cards to improve and standardize human resource management.

Effect studies on training expenditures are especially relevant for management. Effect studies look at the costs as well as the monetary benefits of training. Several companies have developed methods to find out whether investments in training are profitable. These studies may improve decision making on training expenditures. Interesting methods are bing developed by Albert†Heijn, a large retailer in the Netherlands, and AEG in Germany. In the Albert Heijn study, productivity gains are measured by surveys and subsequently valued in monetary terms. In the AEG study, a number of costs and benefits of the dual training system were measured.

Satellite balance sheets – annexes to the annual report – are another method of reporting on investments in, and the allocation of, human resources. These satellite balance sheets primarily address external stakeholders: the capital market and consumers. Furthermore, they are also relevant for the other (internal and external) stakeholders of the company. Examples of the few companies publishing a satellite balance sheet are Skandia AFS in Sweden and KEMA in the Netherlands. One of the problems of these annexes is that companies are free to select the issues on which they want to provide information and the methods used to collect the information. Or, to put it another way, the companies are counting what counts – but not everything that counts – and they do so in their own way. In contrast with financial performance reports, there is no independent auditor to guarantee the objectivity of annexes on human resources.

The future of HRA&R

The final question I would like to address is what the future might bring with regard to HRA&R. I will restrict this question to public reports on the human resources of companies. Of course, no one can predict the future. However, I do not think that we can foresee companies publishing objective reports on their intangibles which are also validated by external auditors. Technically speaking, it would be feasible to develop a format for human-resource indicators. Technically speaking, it would also be feasible for an external auditor to review the human-resource information provided by a company. But, why would companies publish this kind of information? Some might do so in order to attract new capital, to impress clients or consumers, or to improve their public image. But most companies would probably be hesitant about publishing sensitive information.

From a political point of view there are no strong arguments to enforce the publication of human-resource indicators. Drawing on the two main functions of HRA&R, one could say that a better functioning of capital markets is attractive from an economic perspective. However, such an argument is not very strong since capital can usually survive without public intervention. The second function of HRA&R is a better functioning of companies. However, this does not imply that the reports should be made available to external stakeholders.

Nevertheless, there does seem to be a way out: in my opinion it would be useful to experiment with disclosure of human-resource information by way of a human-resource database, drawing on voluntary participation by companies. I think I am correct in saying that the Swedish professor Ulf Johanson has already taken such an initiative. The idea is that companies provide information on their human-resource indicators to an independent agency managing the database. The agency publishes only average outcomes which cannot be traced to individual companies. Furthermore, the agency could inform participating companies as to differences between their human-resource indicators and the averages in their branch of industry. In this way, the agency would provide feedback to participating companies on their own performance. The feedback would be confidential and would act as an incentive for companies to participate in the database. The first function of the database would be to provide companies with relevant benchmarks. In addition, companies could publish the information if they so wish. Secondly, the database would provide vital information to governments and social partners on average developments in human-resource investments.

Conclusion

In many industries, human resources have become the key factor in economic production. Unfortunately, my main conclusion is that it is not feasible to include *all* human resources on company balance sheets. Nevertheless, it is feasible to cover *some* investments in human resources. Investments in training can be included where a contract exists between a company and an employee, specifying that training costs must be reimbursed in the case the employee resigns within a specified period. Furthermore, alternatives to including human resources on the balance sheet exist: standardized human resource management, effect studies on training expenditures and satellite balance sheets. Each of these alternatives may be relevant to different categories of stakeholders in a company.

Finally, I think it would be worthwhile to experiment with human-resource databases drawing on the voluntary participation of companies. These databases could provide standardized, and possibly externally validated, information on the human resources of companies. However, somebody has to take the initiative of starting such an experiment – obvious candidates being national governments or international institutions such as the European Commission or the OECD.

NOTE

1. KPMG Economic Research & Policy Consulting (KPMG Bureau voor Economische Argumentatie), *Kennis in balans*, Max Goote Kenniscentrum, Amsterdam, July 1996.

Part V

Knowledge Infrastructures and Flows

Chapter 17

KNOWLEDGE FLOWS IN NATIONAL INNOVATION SYSTEMS

by

Jean Guinet
Directorate for Science, Technology and Industry, OECD, Paris

Tracking flows of knowledge in national innovation systems

The OECD is currently undertaking the second phase of a project on "Knowledge Flows in National Innovation Systems". This project aims at developing a conceptual framework and quantitative indicators for analysing the processes of knowledge creation, distribution and use in national systems of innovations. It seeks to map and to compare knowledge flows in national innovation systems with a view to helping policy makers meet the new challenges brought about by the emergence of a globalised knowledge-based economy.

Currently, the work is being carried out along two tracks. First, in-depth thematic work in so-called "focus groups", analyses key features of innovation systems with regard to: the (internal) characteristics of innovative firms; the types of collaborations used by innovative firms; the clustering of innovative industries; the interplay of different institutions in the process of innovation (especially at the interface of public and private institutions); and the specific problems of catching-up economies. The second track consists of "horizontal work" which aims at producing an internationally comparable quantitative picture of the specificities of different national innovation systems.

The preliminary findings can be summarised as follows:

◊   There is a clear trend towards higher knowledge intensity in all economic sectors, and there are indications that higher knowledge intensity leads to better performance at the firm, sectoral and aggregate levels.

◊   The private sector still innovates primarily through internal R&D (at least in manufacturing), although the importance of other intangible investments and the use of external resources (*i.e.* public sector, international sources) is slowly increasing.

◊   Flows of tacit knowledge (*e.g.* personnel mobility and informal interactions) have an important positive effect on innovation performance, and particularly on the ability of firms to detect, adapt, adopt and use new knowledge and technologies.

◊ International flows of knowledge are still mainly embodied in traded equipment, goods and materials, but the internationalisation of innovation networks is accelerating, expanding the range of types of knowledge exchanged and modes of knowledge transmission.

◊ In most countries there exist "clusters" in which firms interact through dense knowledge networks and which show above-average performance in terms of international competitiveness, growth and employment. These clusters are not always high-technology or R&D-intensive (*e.g.* the forest cluster in Finland, the aquaculture cluster in Norway, or the cut-flowers cluster in the Netherlands), but they are always knowledge-intensive when one takes into account the intensity of knowledge interactions among the actors.

◊ While there is a growing incidence and variety of collaborations between industry and the public research sector (universities and publicly funded research institutes), these do not generally appear to have a significant impact on the innovative performance of firms in most sectors.

◊ In many countries this reflects mismatches between private firms' needs and the public knowledge infrastructure, which remains underutilised, except when successful programmes of public-private partnership catalyse more productive relationships.

◊ By contrast, inter-firm research collaborations are increasing, with positive impacts on innovative performance.

Facilitating flows of knowledge to increase economic performance – the role of government

Fruitful interactions between the different components of an innovation system can be hampered by a number of factors:

◊ conflicting incentive structures (cultures) of partners (*e.g.* university *vs.* industry);

◊ market failures which may hamper access by firms, especially smaller ones, to information, technology and know-how, or may weaken or distort firms' incentives to invest in technology or absorptive capacity (*e.g.* high transaction costs, lack of competition stimuli);

◊ co-ordination failures whereby agents fail to recognise their complementary needs and assets;

◊ lack of managerial competencies reducing the understanding of the role of technology and innovation in competitive strategy, and of the benefits of collaborative strategy of knowledge acquisition.

◊ financial markets unable to assess firms' investment in interactive learning (*e.g.* underdevelopment of specialised venture capital);

◊ last but not least, lack of human resources on which to build capabilities to absorb external knowledge.

Policy responses to these market and systemic failures can be categorised as follows:

◊ framework conditions (macroeconomic stability to help strategic investment decisions; labour market policy to facilitate mobility of S&T personnel; or competition policy to increase propensity to innovate while allowing co-operative behavior in building and using the knowledge base);

◊ infrastructural policies to fill gaps in the knowledge base (*e.g.* support to basic research or to the development of infratechnologies), and make the public infrastructure more responsive to evolving business needs and motivations (*e.g.* IPRs for university research);

◊ catalytic actions to stimulate inter-firm co-operation and public/private partnerships in the development of generic technologies (*e.g.* the so-called Advanced Technology programmes);

◊ technology diffusion policies to correct market failures in knowledge transactions due to supply or demand factors.

Best practices in technology diffusion policies

Recent OECD work on technology diffusion policies illustrates the need to envisage their efficiency in the broader framework of an overall policy strategy to facilitate flows of knowledge and other interactions between the different components of an innovation system. It points also to the following trends regarding their objectives and instruments and identifies some principles of "best practice":

◊ There is an overall shift from traditional supply-side diffusion measures toward policies that reflect a more interactive model of innovation and recognise innovation and diffusion as a interdependent processes. This translates into greater role for demand-driven programmes, network-building initiatives, measures to upgrade the technology diffusion infrastructure and improve its relevance for and accessibility by smaller firms.

◊ The nature of the knowledge being diffused is changing. Greater attention must be given to diffusing "soft organisational technologies" of technical and quality management (*e.g.* ISO certification) as well as "hard technologies" of communication and information management (*e.g.* Internet and electronic commerce).

◊ There is a need to clarify and hierarchise the main policy objectives (*e.g.* build the overall innovative capacity of firms, improve the general technology receptor capacity of firms, encourage the adoption of specific technologies). This is necessary to achieve greater coherence between programmes with different targets (specific technologies, sectors, institutions or regions) and offering different diffusion services (*e.g.* technical assistance, information, training).

◊   In order to achieve maximum leverage, technology diffusion policies must build on existing interrelationships in national innovation systems, especially networks within which firms collaborate and exchange tacit knowledge.

◊   Public programmes must contribute to create an "appetite for change" among firms and stimulate demand for technological services, but avoid creating dependency and crowding out private initiatives in the provision of such services.

◊   While acting locally, near clusters of innovative firms, government must assess its action globally, since the economy-wide effects of technology diffusion policies depend on dense linkages between these clusters at national and international levels.

◊   Technology diffusion policies mostly address the needs of the highly heterogeneous population of SMEs, from high-tech start-ups to non-innovative firms in mature industries or traditional services. Their interactions with other policies in achieving their own goals or in contributing to other policy objectives are quite specific to the type of firms considered.

This latter idea can be illustrated by considering the role of technology diffusion policies in the promotion of new technology-based firms (NTBFs), which has become a priority objective in the majority of OECD countries.

Figure 1 shows that realising the potential contribution of new technology-based firms to economic growth and job creation depends on a number of conditions: the existence of business opportunities, an entrepreneurial culture, a supportive business and technical infrastructure, and the availability of and access to key resources. At first sight these are the same factors of success as for SMEs in general. However a closer look suggests that they are partly specific to new technology-based firms (*e.g.* the nature of the supportive infrastructure or financial needs, and the particular importance of the entrepreneurial drive in activities characterised by high risks in exploring uncharted territories).

Technology diffusion policies (shaded area in Figure 1) need first to be tailored to the particular needs of NTBFs. In doing so governments should be guided by two overriding considerations:

◊   In many activities technology-based firms do not create themselves new knowledge through formal R&D activities, but rather test on the market new ways of combining existing technical solutions. In other words, they are all knowledge-intensive but not always R&D-intensive and need easy access to external sources of ideas and talents. Spin-outs of technology, personnel and business opportunities from large firms' R&D efforts are important in this respect. In addition, the more diversified is the research portfolio of universities and other non-business organisations the more it is a good springboard for NTBFs in a wide spectrum of activities.

◊   NTBFs agglomerate within regional or local clusters of knowledge-intensive activities. This territorial dimension makes more important the choice and co-ordination between different levels of conception and implementation of technology diffusion policy measures.

Figure 1. Promoting new technology-based firms

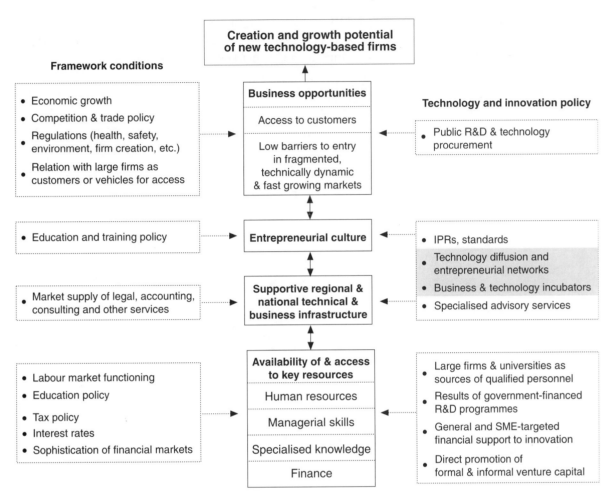

Source: OECD Secretariat

Second, the efficiency of technology diffusion policies in promoting NTBFs depends on a number of conditions subject to government influence. The left part of Figure 1 lists the relevant areas where government should check the adequacy of current policies, provided that:

◊ NTBFs have already to cope with an exceptional level of technical and commercial risks and they may be consequently more vulnerable than other firms to the additional uncertainties that government action may create in their tax, regulatory or macroeconomic environment.

◊ Rewards expected by the entrepreneurs and their financiers should be proportionate to the risks they take. Framework conditions should not impact unfavorably on this risk/reward ratio (*e.g.* tax system discriminating against capital gains, high interest rates) but should provide mechanisms for rewarding investment in NTBFs (*e.g.* efficient secondary stock markets).

◊ Flexibility in seizing market opportunities and developing innovative responses is a characteristic of successful NTBFs which rests primarily on their individual managerial and organisational skills but depends also on external factors, such as the mobility of human resources and the good functioning of markets of specialised services.

Chapter 18

THE EFFECTIVENESS OF THE DIFFUSION-ORIENTED TECHNOLOGY POLICY OF SWITZERLAND – THE CASE OF ADVANCED MANUFACTURING TECHNOLOGIES (AMT)

by

Dr. Heinz Hollenstein
Swiss Federal Institute of Technology, Zurich[1]

The characteristics of technology policy of Switzerland

The main feature of Swiss technology policy at the federal level resides in the low weight placed on direct measures for fostering innovation in the economy. Swiss policy is instead oriented towards creating a favourable environment for the introduction of new products and production techniques, irrespective of whether such innovations repose on developments internal to the firm or on the adoption of novelties generated by other firms or institutions.

According to this policy orientation the public authorities are responsible for implementing legal and institutional regulations favouring a high innovation performance of the business sector. Property rights, the tax system, the foreign trade regime and many other framework conditions are designed accordingly. Some shortcomings, related in particular to competition policy and regulations for public utilities, have been recently corrected or will be overcome in the near future, although in some fields only to a certain extent. In addition the government supports innovation through high levels of investment in public infrastructure such as education and research, transport, telecommunications, etc. However, R&D remains primarily the responsibility of the individual firm, which is reflected by a public share in R&D expenditures of below one-third, *i.e.* much less than in most other industrialised countries. In recent years, a series of technology-oriented R&D programmes in specific technology fields such as optoelectronics, material sciences, biotechnology, etc., have been implemented which may be characterised as "oriented research in the pre-competitive stage"; these measures are part of the aim of supplying the business sector with high-quality infrastructure.[2]

This framework-oriented policy is supplemented by specific measures to encourage co-operation between public research and private enterprise through joint projects between these two partners. In addition, policy initiatives exist to support rapid diffusion of basic technologies which are seen to be relevant for a broad spectrum of industrial activities. Two examples of these "action programmes" are "Advanced Manufacturing Technologies" (AMT) and "Microelectronics", which offer firms information and training services as well as subsidies for consultancy and development projects; the latter are in many cases based on joint ventures between firms or between firms and research institutions. The duration of these programmes is restricted to a couple of years, *i.e.* the policy concept is to give initial support for activities posing a challenge for many firms and most industries. These measures repose on the hypothesis that significant bottlenecks exist in the early phase of diffusion; secondly, and in a more general perspective, it is assumed that intensively linking a firm's knowledge base to external know-how is a key factor in securing high innovation performance – a proposition proved to be correct in the Swiss case (see Arvanitis and Hollenstein, 1994 and 1996*a*). An additional characteristic of these programmes, which seems relevant in the context of this workshop, is the assumption that the successfull introduction of these technologies depends on an approach which takes account of human, technical and organisational factors and restrictions [termed the "MTO approach" ("Mensch-Technik-Organisation") in Switzerland].

In the following I would like to present some information on a larger research project which is being carried out by our Institute, whose specific objective is to evaluate the effectiveness of these two diffusion-oriented "action programmes". This work is embedded in a more general objective and framework of analysis; that is, a thorough empirical investigation of the diffusion process both at the descriptive (diffusion profiles across firms and over time) and the explanatory level (testing of various theories of technological diffusion). For several reasons this chapter concentrates on the programme to promote the diffusion of AMT.

Objectives and methodology of our research

The project is empirical in nature, and has a descriptive as well as an explanatory dimension. At the descriptive level the main focus is on the following questions:

◊ How many firms are using (or are planning to use) one or more of the 19 individual AMT elements distinguished in this study (see Table 1 for an overview of the individual technologies)?

◊ How intensive is the use of these technologies, *i.e.* what is the degree of firm-internal diffusion of AMT?

◊ Are the individual technologies linked (or planned to be linked) to form an integrated manufacturing system? What degree of integration has been or will be reached in the near future?

◊ What is the time path of diffusion of individual technologies as well as their integration?

◊ What have been the firms' objectives in introducing AMT at the process as well as at the product level, and are there specific factors forcing a firm to adopt these technologies?

◊ What have been the main bottlenecks and impediments affecting the decision to (not) adopt AMT or impinging negatively during the introductory phase?

◊ What has been the impact of the application of AMT on the firm's productivity and competitiveness, the level and (qualification) structure of employment as well as the organisation of production?

◊ How efficient has public assistance been in its different forms (schooling and information services as well as consultancy and development projects) according to the firms' assessments?

At the explanatory level the analysis aims primarily at an empirical modelling of the adoption decision by testing several theoretical (in some aspects competing, in others complementary) hypotheses. To this end various bivariate and multivariate estimation procedures such as probit models with adoption/non-adoption of AMT as the dependent variable, count data models for AMT intensity as the variable to be explained, and hazard models for the explanation of the point in time of AMT adoption will be applied (for a review of the state of the theoretical, methodological and empirical knowledge in this field, see Karshenas and Stoneman, 1995). The main explanatory variables, catching both demand- and supply-side factors, proposed by one or more of the four basic diffusion models distinguished in the literature (epidemic, rank, stock and order models) are related to:

◊ *the technology market*: transparency; uncertainty related to the effectiveness of the technology; information costs; general range of application (technological opportunities); market concentration; expected (price) of the technology;

◊ *product market*: demand perspectives; intensity of price and non-price competition; market concentration;

◊ *general firm characteristics*: firm and plant size; age of the firm; type of ownership; capacity to use external knowledge sources in general;

◊ *adoption-specific firm characteristics*: know-how in the field of AMT; firm-specific potential for the application of this technology depending on the type of products and production processes; compatibility of AMT with the existing physical, human and knowledge capital as well as the organisational and managerial structures inducing AMT-specific adjustment costs;

◊ *technology policy*: specific subsidies and/or broader-based policy measures to favour the adoption of AMT.

Many of these variables are not directly observable. However, measures related to specific bottlenecks/obstacles to AMT adoption, the objectives pursued in introducing such technologies, the factors enforcing the adoption of AMT and information referring to a firm's characteristics in general as well as to its innovative activities, may represent the underlying "latent variables" to a sufficient degree.[3] Such data have been collected by means of the third "Swiss Innovation Survey" conducted by our Institute in autumn 1996. This exercise yielded data for about 2 200 firms from the private business sector, about half of which belonged to the manufacturing sector. Because only manufacturing firms with more than 20 employees were asked to answer the questions on AMT and because some did not reply to all of the corresponding questions, we finally dispose of information for somewhat more than 600 firms, 36 per cent of which belong to the machinery sector; that is, mechanical and electrical engineering, vehicles, electronics, instruments and the watch industry.

From a policy perspective, special attention has to be devoted to obstacles to the diffusion of AMT. In particular there is a need to define, first, those bottlenecks which may be influenced by policy measures and, secondly, those to be removed from a welfare point of view. In addition, we will analyse whether firms taking part in the AMT promotion programme are more keen to adopt and link these technologies than non-subsidised firms with similar structural characteristics. Based on this type of analyses, the effectiveness of the Swiss programme of action to promote the diffusion of AMT will be evaluated (for methodological considerations, see Arvanitis and Hollenstein, 1997).

Table 1. Percentage of firms using or planning to use Advanced Manufacturing Technologies (AMT)

Type of advanced manufacturing technology	Machinery sector* (N = 238)		Other manufacturing (N = 368)		All manufacturing (N = 606)		United States** (estimate)	Denmark
	1996	1999	1996	1999	1996	1999	1996	1994
CAD/CAE	82.8	85.7	52.4	57.3	64.4	68.5	65.8	55
CAD/CAM	58.8	65.5	39.7	45.4	47.2	53.3	-	28
Rapid Prototyping, Simulation	15.5	21	7.1	10.3	10.4	14.5	-	-
Digital firm data representation	60.5	71.8	52.2	72.8	55.4	72.4	-	-
CAP	62.6	72.3	53.5	69.6	57.1	70.6	-	-
CNC/CND machines	68.1	68.9	51.6	54.9	58.1	60.4	51.3	43
Materials working laser	19.7	23.9	6.8	9	11.9	14.9	9.7	-
Pick and place robots	26.9	30.3	24.7	28	25.6	28.9	14.7	17***
More complex robots	14.3	16	14.4	16	14.4	16	10.3	17***
Flexible manufacturing cells (FMC)	19.3	26.1	13.6	18.8	15.8	21.6	19.6***	-
Flexible manufacturing systems (FMS)	19.3	25.2	11.4	17.1	14.5	20.3	19.6***	6
Storage/retrieval System (AS/RS)	36.1	44.1	32.2	43.5	34.3	43.7	5.4	
Guided Vehicle Systems (AGVS)	7.6	8.8	17.7	22.6	13.7	17.2	2.4	21
CAQ on material	34.9	47.5	17.2	43.2	30.2	44.9	16.6	36**
CAQ on final product	36.1	46.6	29.1	46.5	31.8	46.5	20.2	36**
LAN for technical data	53.4	63.4	32.9	45.7	40.9	52.6	41.1	-
LAN for factory use	40.8	53.8	31	46.2	34.8	49.2	36.4	-
PPS	67.2	77.2	54.9	72	59.7	74.3	-	-
Supplier/customer network	20.6	37.4	17.7	43.8	18.8	41.3	31.5	-

1. Mechanical and electrical engineering, vehicles, electronics, instruments and watches.
2. The data for the United States are for the machinery sector as defined for the Swiss case, complemented by the metalworking industry
3. Aggregate information exists only for FMC and FMS in the US case and for robots as well as CAQ for Denmark.
Source: US Bureau of the Census (1994), Danish Ministry of Business and Industry (1996) and unpublished (provisional) data from the Swiss Innovations Survey 1996.

The empirical results of both the descriptive and the explicative analysis will be compared to those of similar work for other countries. Because for each firm the year of adoption of each AMT element is known, we can produce comparative results for every reference year used in other country studies.[4] We would expect Swiss industry to feature among the leading users of AMT. In addition, we wonder whether the bottlenecks to introducing AMT vary across countries, which would imply different policy needs.

First empirical results

At this point in time we can only present preliminary results at the descriptive level. These are based on highly aggregated analysis which does not take account of differences in industry and firm size, which are highly important for a final evaluation.

Diffusion of AMT in Swiss industry reached a high degree in 1996 (see Table 1). No less than 84 per cent of the firms in our sample use one of the 19 AMT elements listed in the table. However, diffusion differs significantly among the individual elements of the technology, with CAD/CAE, PPS, CNC/CND, CAP at the top end, and storage/retrieval systems and CAQ as well as LANs in the middle range. The other technologies are less often used, partly reflecting their early stage of development (*e.g.* rapid prototyping, simulation), partly because they are follow-up developments to other AMT elements (*e.g.* FMC *vs.* CNC). The diffusion of almost all AMT elements is higher in the machinery sector than in the rest of manufacturing – although even in the latter sector the adoption rate is high. Data for the United States, which are comparable for most of the AMT elements distinguished in this study, and for Denmark (as an example of recent study on the topic), whose comparability is somewhat more restricted, seem to confirm that the diffusion of this technology in Switzerland is very high indeed. In addition, Table 1 shows that the adoption of AMT will grow strongly over the next three years. Among the technologies with the highest levels of growth, *i.e.* the largest difference in percentage points between 1996 and 1999, are some AMT elements "just taking off" (*e.g.* intercompany networks) and others starting from an intermediate level of diffusion (such as LANs and CAQ); however, even some of the technologies used already by a large share of firms will again diffuse quite strongly (*e.g.* CAP or PPS). On the other hand, there will be little additional use for some "old technologies" with a high degree of diffusion in 1996 (*e.g.* CNC or CAD/CAE) or for very new ones (*e.g.* simulation); however, the latter will spread quite rapidly if we look at the growth rate of adoption rather than the difference in percentage points.

A more precise picture of the extent to which the production system of a firm is based on AMT is given in Figure 1*a, b, c* showing the intensity of use of AMT. Almost two-thirds of firms use between three and nine AMT elements, and one-quarter apply ten or more such technologies. The median use of 7.3 AMT elements seems very high indeed. In the machinery sector the median is even higher (8.8 technologies), and roughly one-third of firms in this sector use more than ten AMT elements. These data show that, in many firms, production is "computerised" to a very significant extent.

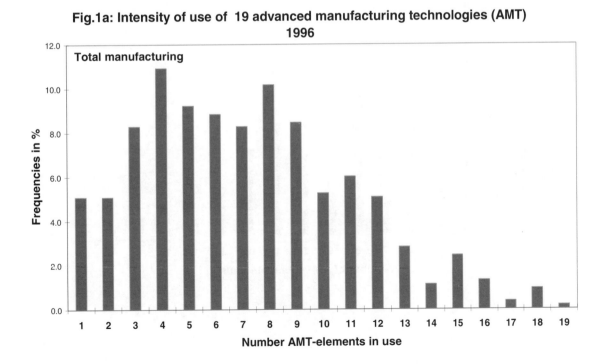

Fig.1a: Intensity of use of 19 advanced manufacturing technologies (AMT) 1996

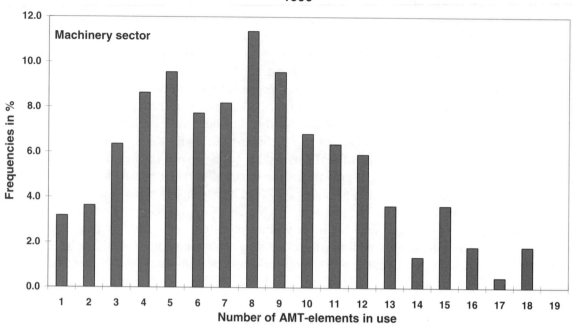

Fig.1b: Intensity of use of 19 advanced manufacturing technologies (AMT) 1996

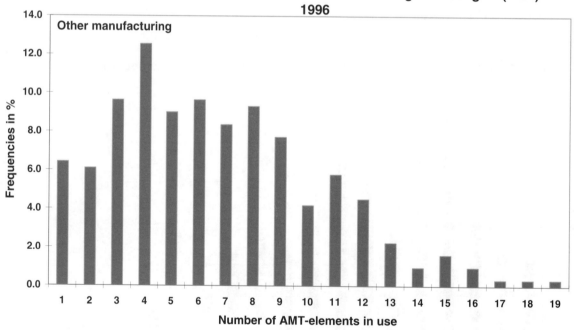

Fig.1c: Intensity of use of advanced manufacturing technologies (AMT) 1996

Another characteristic of the diffusion of AMT is the linking of its elements. According to Figure 2a, b, c the integration of Swiss manufacturing based on information technology reached a moderate level in 1996 with a median of 2.6 out of ten links,[5] with 15 per cent of firms showing an integration of five or more elements. Within three years the degree of integration will increase substantially. The share of firms with five or more out of ten possible links will almost double, and the median will increase to 3.6 links. This development is even more accentuated in the machinery sector; in 1999 one-third of firms in this sector will be characterised by five or more AMT links, with 11 per cent exhibiting a full integration of all ten elements – the median will rise to 4.1. Although not easy to evaluate in the absence of an international comparison, it would be surprising if Swiss industry did not figure among the top performers on this count. According to Figure 3a, b, c, which shows the types of AMT links, the integration between CAD, CAP, CAM and PPS is most frequent, a pattern which would seem even more pronounced in 1999. Within the planning period the integration of the "economic" (PPS) and the "technological" (CAD, CAP, CAM, CAQ) side of production is growing rapidly and will become an essential ingredient of manufacturing in Switzerland.

Fig. 2a: Intensity of integration between selected advanced manufacturing technologies (AMT)

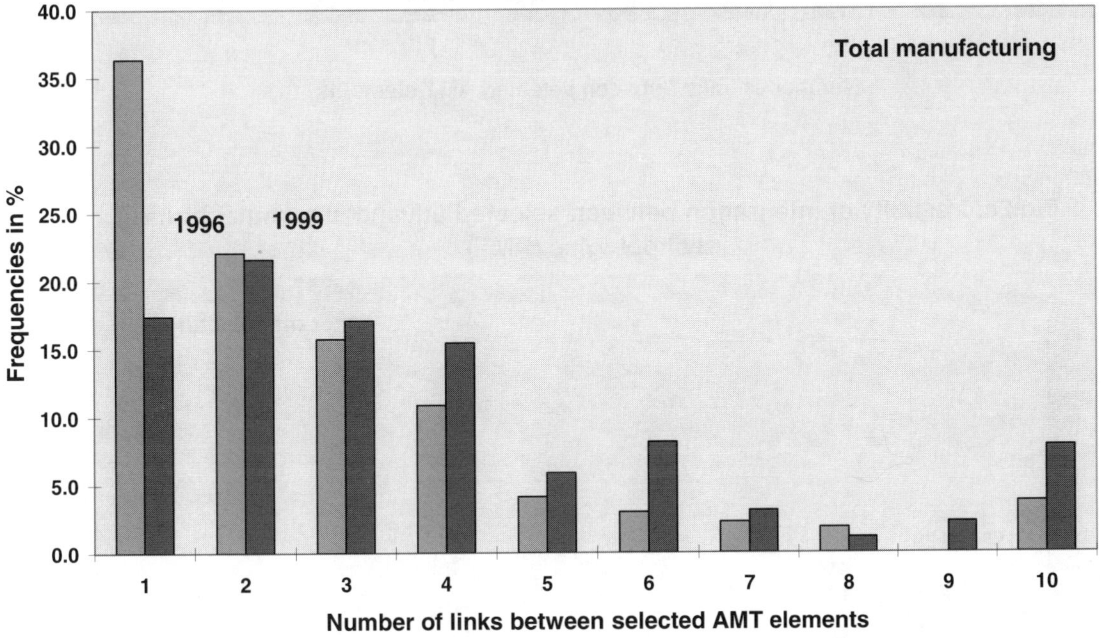

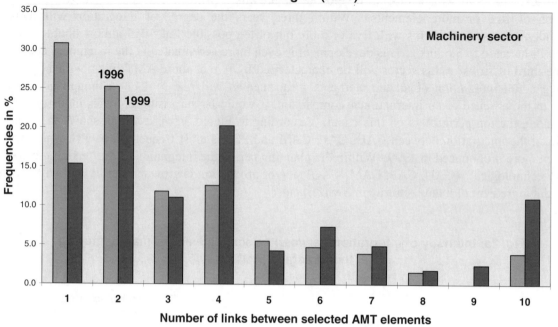

Fig.2b: Intensity of integration between selected advanced manufacturing technologies (AMT)

Machinery sector

1996
1999

Frequencies in %

Number of links between selected AMT elements

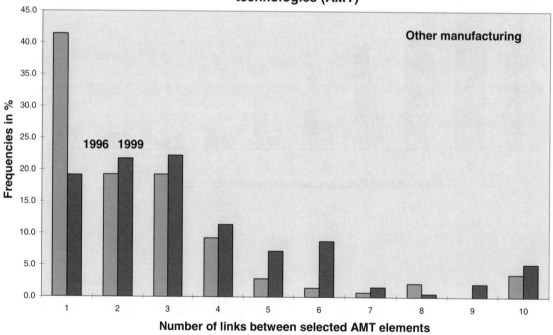

Fig.2c: Intensity of integration between selected advanced manufachturing technologies (AMT)

Other manufacturing

1996 1999

Frequencies in %

Number of links between selected AMT elements

Fig.3a: Links between advanced manufacturing technologies (AMT)

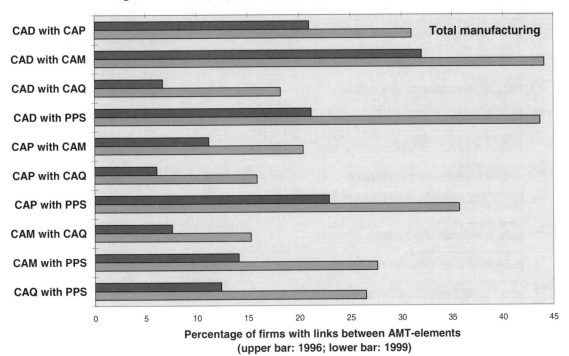

Percentage of firms with links between AMT-elements
(upper bar: 1996; lower bar: 1999)

Fig.3b: Links between advanced manufacturing technologies (AMT)

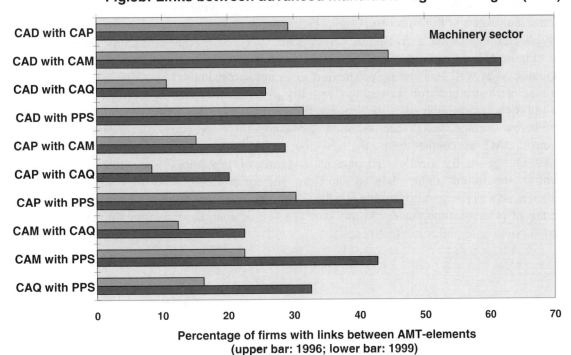

Percentage of firms with links between AMT-elements
(upper bar: 1996; lower bar: 1999)

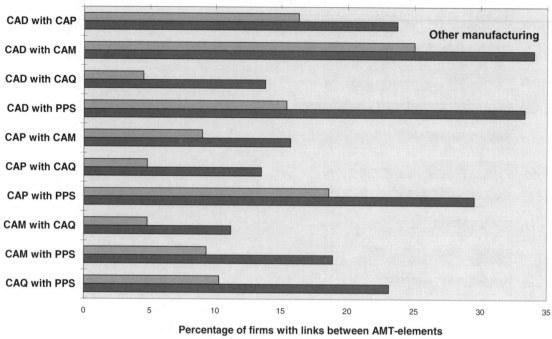

Fig.3c: Links between advanced manufacturing technologies (AMT)

Percentage of firms with links between AMT-elements
(upper bar: 1996; lower bar: 1999)

The data on the objectives and determinants (factors enforcing the adoption) as well as the obstacles to introduction of AMT, give some insight into the underlying forces of the diffusion process as well as some indications with respect to policy. Figure 4*a, b* shows a selection of firms' assessments of 26 objectives/determinants on a five-point Likert scale.[6] Three groups of factors seem to be most important (Figure 4*a*). Cost reduction in general, and with respect to all types of inputs (labour, machinery, stocks) as well as lowering production time, not surprisingly, ranks first. Secondly, AMT is seen as a suitable instrument for increasing flexibility in production and on the market. Third, it is a means to improve organisation of work – again firms are looking for more flexibility. According to Figure 4*b*, below-average scores are reported for competitive pressure (decreasing market share, introduction of AMT by competitors); the adoption of AMT thus seems to represent a response to a fundamental change in the firm's environment in terms of technology and globalised competition (investment in the future) rather than to short-run and specific problems of competition. In this perspective it is no surprise that favourable conditions for financing and public support for the adoption of AMT are not of primary importance. At this (early) stage of analysis, the latter finding should not be interpreted as pointing to policy ineffectiveness.

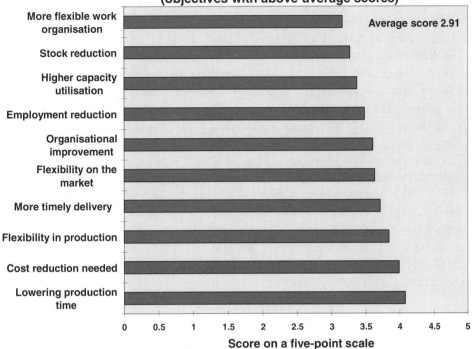

Fig.4a: Assessment of selected objectives related to the introduction of AMT (objectives with above-average scores)

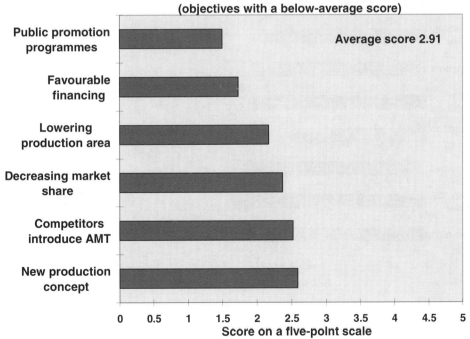

Fig.4b: Assessment of selected objectives related to the introduction of AMT
(objectives with a below-average score)

Among the obstacles to the introduction or further development of AMT (Figure 5a, b) - the corresponding assessments pertain to adopting as well as to non-adopting firms - two groups of factors predominate (Figure 5a). One problem stems from the large amount of investment required. Because, in many cases, the introduction of AMT is a fundamental change, the investment may be large compared, for example, to the capital stock or the cash flow. This problem, which may be somewhat overestimated because it also reflects the unfavourable economic situation of the last few years, is more pronounced for smaller than for larger firms. Secondly, the price of AMT in the widest sense of the word, *i.e.* including, in addition to the "pure" price of the technology and the corresponding software, also uncertainty with respect to the performance of AMT as well as information problems/costs, seems in many instances to be (too) high. A further prominent obstacle is incompatibility with the product range; in this case, not adopting AMT seems to be no disadvantage as long as a firm's product programme remains promising. Rather surprisingly, deficiencies with respect to (highly) qualified manpower (engineers, technicians, computer specialists, other qualified labour) as well as quantity and price of training (development of AMT-specific knowledge) are not seen to be a major bottleneck (Figure 5b). However, this assessment might (partly) reflect the current imbalance on the labour market.[7] Finally, we note that organisational problems are not a widespread impediment to the adoption of AMT; in view of the high importance of organisational flexibility as an objective of the introduction of AMT this result may indicate that the organisational change required is manageable.

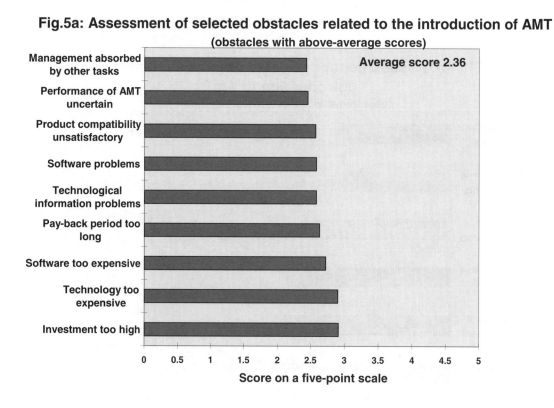

Fig.5a: Assessment of selected obstacles related to the introduction of AMT
(obstacles with above-average scores)

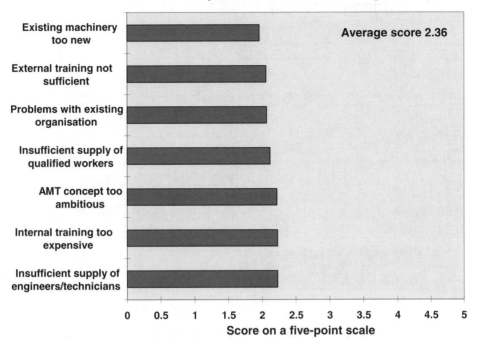

Fig.5b: Assessment of selected obstacles related to the introduction of AMT
(obstacles with a below-average scores)

From a policy perspective, the impact of the introduction of AMT on variables such as productivity, competitiveness and employment is of primary importance. At this stage, we are able to give some indication of the employment effects (Figure 6). According to the firms' assessments the level of employment decreases somewhat as a consequence of adopting AMT. However, this result has to be taken with caution because, first, the data refer to a recession period which has been accompanied, at the same time, by high rationalisation investments and a large reduction in employment; therefore it is very difficult to filter out the "pure" AMT effect. Secondly, an assessment of the impact of AMT adoption on employment levels takes little account of the (positive) employment effects in the longer run resulting from improved productivity and competitiveness. More reliable are the results with respect to the changing structure of demand for different levels of qualification: Adoption of AMT seems to have a substantial negative impact on the demand for workers with low qualifications. On the contrary, whereas there is a slight, but hardly significant, increase in demand for employees with university degrees, the medium skill range benefits from the introduction of these technologies, in particular those at the higher end.

Fig.6: Employment effects of the introduction of manufacturing

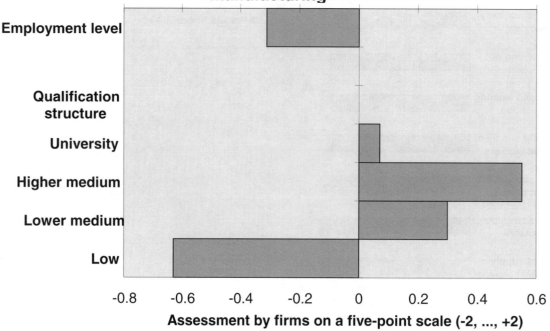

Assessment by firms on a five-point scale (-2, ..., +2)

As far as the impact of the government's measures to promote AMT is concerned, only very provisional results can be presented. Table 2 shows how firms taking part in one or more of the programme's elements assess their impact on the introduction or further development of AMT. Information and training seem to have the most positive effect, whereas development projects get the lowest rating. This result, however, has to be qualified. The positive impact is definitely higher for small than for larger firms and most pronounced in the case of R&D projects, which are active in AMT anyway and for whom the subsidy is small compared to their investment budget. This difference according to firm size affects the relative performance of the three elements of government action because SMEs are involved in training activities and – to an even more pronounced extent – consultancy projects more often than large enterprises (subsidised R&D projects in the field of AMT are carried out primarily by small and by very large firms). To evaluate these policy measures in a reliable way further analysis is needed, in the first place a model-based investigation of differences in adoption behaviour between subsidised and other firms (a description of the evaluation method to be used is given in Arvanitis and Hollenstein, 1997).

Table 2. Impact of the government's programme to promote AMT

Percentage of firms

| | Firms' assessment on a five-point scale | | | | | |
| | 1 | 2 | 3 | 4 | 5 | |
Type of promotion	Very low				Very high	Average score
Information/training	7.9	21.1	42.0	21.1	7.9	3.00
Consultancy project	11.1	40.0	26.7	13.3	8.9	2.69
Development project	31.1	31.1	23.1	13.1	1.6	2.23

Policy implications

At this stage of the research it would be unwise to draw definite conclusions with respect to the effectiveness of the government's programme to promote rapid diffusion of AMT. Nevertheless some policy implications may be identified based on the employment effects of the adoption of AMT, as well as some general reflections. This research, as well as our work over the last few years related to firms' innovation performance and its determinants (see, for example, Arvanitis and Hollenstein, 1996*a*) as well as its impact on productivity (Arvanitis and Hollenstein, 1996*b*), show that – apart from creating a competitive environment for the business sector – human-capital formation is the most important field for policy measures in this matter.

Compared to other highly developed countries, human-capital endowment in Switzerland is characterised by a rather weak position at the top (university-level) as well as at the bottom (low-skill) end of the distribution of employment by qualifications, whereas the intermediate level, reaching from apprenticeship up to non-university technicians (and comparable) qualifications, is highly developed. This distribution is distinctly different, for example, from that of the US economy which has a much larger top and bottom part of the distribution. The diffusion of AMT, as has been shown in the previous section, will lead to a shift in the demand for labour qualifications primarily from the low to the intermediate level, in particular to the upper part of the middle range. This direction of change, which in a similar though less pronounced way is also characteristic of other technologies and economic activities (*e.g* the banking sector), represents a challenge for Swiss educational policy which has been recognised by policy makers, who have initiated a reform of the educational system to strengthen the upper-intermediate skill level. More specifically, polytechnical schools (and similar institutions, for example, for business economists), if they fulfill certain standards, are being up-graded. In addition, in order to increase the intake of such schools, an A-level certificate with a vocational orientation has been introduced; the latter may also be seen as a measure to shift the educational mix of 16-20 year olds from general education to more practical curricula which are considered to be more productive. In addition, a reform of the apprenticeship system is underway; a major objective of this reform is to enhance flexibility by, first, reducing the degree of specialisation, *i.e* significantly lowering the number of officially recognised occupations, and, secondly, increasing to some extent the general skill content of training (*e.g.* more abstract problem-solving capabilities); an example of this approach is the recently launched scheme of vocational training to be supplied by employers in the machinery sector (a reduction from more than 50 to some 15 basic occupations). However, while the necessary policy measures at the intermediate skill level are on track, the up-grading of the capabilities of persons with low or no qualifications, many of whom are unemployed and impeded by language problems, is more difficult. To this end, the government has intensified active measures of labour-market policy in the framework of a revision of the unemployment insurance implemented at the beginning of 1997.

In sum, we advocate keeping the framework-oriented policy design. In the Swiss case, improvements are necessary to induce more competition in the non-traded goods sector and to upgrade the stock of human capital. As far as the lower part of the distribution of qualifications is concerned, investment in training needs to be supplemented by more specific measures to avoid marginalisation of this section of the population. In addition, there is a case for public promotion of technologies with a wide potential of application in order to reduce uncertainty and the corresponding information costs. The Swiss government has taken or is taking policy initiatives pointing in the right direction in each of these fields. An assessment of the results of these measures is, however, not yet feasible.

Conclusions

Our research is still at a very early stage; most of the work outlined above has yet to be carrried out, at the descriptive and at the explicative level as well as with respect to policy. The available data set for Switzerland will allow interesting work to be carried out at all three levels. In addition, cross-country comparisons will be highly relevant from both a scientific and a policy perspective. Such comparisons are necessary to assess, for example, the country-specific degree of diffusion because there is no absolute yardstick. At the explicative level comparative work (if the theoretical framework and the data at hand are sufficiently similar) would facilitate the identification of robust relationships, because country-specific regularities could prove to be simply specific characteristics of the sample used in the single-country framework. As far as policy is concerned, I am not sure whether international comparisons will allow the identification of best practice policies; perhaps a more realistic objective for such an exercise would be to identify policies which, given the specific history and institutional framework of a country, point in the right direction.

NOTES

1. The research reported on in this chapter was supported by the Swiss Federal Ministry of Economic Affairs.

2. Swiss research institutions and firms also participate intensively in the various EU research programmes.

3. An example of this type of approach is given in Fritsch (1991), although he does not use the data to produce econometric estimates.

4. For a summary of such studies referring to the late 1980s, see Northcott and Vickery (1993, 1995); references for two more recent studies are given in Table 1.

5. The questionnaire distinguishes 19 AMT elements but only ten possible links between four groups of AMT; in this perspective technologies such as CAQ on material and CAQ on final products are seen as belonging to one group; the same holds, for example, for various AMT elements related to production on the factory floor (material working laser, robots, CNC/CND, FMC, FMS, AS/FS, AGVS).

6. Because the correlation between many of these variables is high, a further step of analysis will be devoted to the condensation of the information by use of a factor analysis. The same holds for the obstacles to diffusion.

7. Some evidence in this respect is the rather pronounced change in the assessment regarding the availability of R&D personnel as an obstacle to innovation between 1990 and 1993 (Arvanitis *et al.,* 1995).

REFERENCES

ARVANITIS, S. and H. HOLLENSTEIN (1994), "Demand and Supply Factors in Explaining the Innovative Activity of Swiss Manufacturing Firms. An Analysis Based on Input-Output- and Market-oriented Innovation Indicators", *Economics of Innovation and New Technology*, No. 3, pp. 15-30.

ARVANITIS, S. and H. HOLLENSTEIN (1996a), "Industrial Innovation in Switzerland: A Model-based Analysis with Survey Data", in A. Kleinknecht (ed.), *Determinants of Innovation and Diffusion. The Message from New Indicators*, Macmillan, London.

ARVANITIS, S. and H. HOLLENSTEIN (1996b), "Firm Performance, Innovation and Technological Spillovers: A Cross-section Analysis with Swiss Firm Data", paper presented to the 6th Conference of the International Joseph A. Schumpeter Society, 3-5 June, Stockholm.

ARVANITIS, S. and H. HOLLENSTEIN (1997), "Evaluating the Promotion of Advanced Manufacturing Technologies (AMT) by Swiss Government Using Micro-level Survey Data: Some Methodological Considerations", paper presented to the International Conference on "Policy Evaluation in Innovation and Technology" organised by the OECD, 26-27 June, Paris.

ARVANITIS, S., H. HOLLENSTEIN and S. LENZ (1995), "Innovationsaktivitäten in der Schweizer Industrie. Eine Analyse der Ergebnisse der Innovationserhebung 1993", *Studienreihe Strukturberichterstattung*, hrsg. vom Bundesamt für Konjunkturfragen, Bern.

DANISH MINISTRY OF BUSINESS AND INDUSTRY (1996), "Technological and Organizational Change and Labour Demand", June.

FRITSCH (1991), "Die Übernahme neuer Techniken durch Industriebetriebe. Empirische Bedunfe und Schlussfolgerungen für die weitere Forschung", *IFO-Studien*, No. 37, pp. 1-18.

KARSHENAS, M. and P. STONEMAN (1995), "Technological Diffusion", in P. Stoneman (ed.), *Handbook of the Economics of Innovation and Technological Change*, Blackwell, Oxford.

NORTHCOTT, J. and G. VICKERY (1993), "Surveys of the Diffusion of Microelectronics and Advanced Manufacturing Technology", *STI Review (Special Issue on Microelectronics and Advanced Manufacturing Technologies)*, No. 12, pp. 7-36, OECD, Paris.

NORTHCOTT, J. and G. VICKERY (1995), "Diffusion of Microelectronics and Advanced Manufacturing Technology: A Review of National Surveys", *Economics of Innovation and New Technology*, No. 3, pp. 253-275.

US BUREAU OF THE CENSUS (1994), *Manufacturing Technology: Prevalence and Plans for Use 1993*, Washington, DC.

Part VI

Enterprises and Social Responsibility

Chapter 19

THE SOCIAL RESPONSIBILITY OF ENTERPRISES: A NEW ROLE FOR GOVERNMENTS?

by

Stefan C. Wolter
Chief Economist
Federal Office for Industry and Labour, Switzerland

The new environment of the 1990s

The social responsibility of enterprises in a globalised world

Globalisation is a word which stands for different things, but one thing that is certain is that globalisation has made enterprises more independent of state intervention in the shaping of their business policies. Their considerable freedom in the geographical disposition of their activities[1] allows firms to escape rigidities and constraints which had earlier forced them to participate actively (and financially) in the societies in which they were located. In the era of globalisation, enterprises' social obligations to their employees – and also to the societies in which they are active – seem to have lost importance. In the globalised world enterprises have also become the driving force of social change, to which governments often adapt only with difficulty. In the following two sections, enterprises' behaviour will be examined with regard to their social responsibility towards their employees.

Against the background of the changes which I will describe, governments of practically all OECD Member countries face complex challenges. Increased interdependence, both political and economic, makes going it alone ever more impossible, thereby increasing the need for common, unitary strategies in all OECD countries to deal with enterprises' new behaviour.

Shareholders vs. stakeholders

In addition to the global changes mentioned above, enterprises, in Europe in particular, are under additional cost pressures from a none-too-positive economic environment. This pressure is yet another factor forcing enterprises to re-think their social responsibilities – which in business terms represent a non-negligible cost factor. The temptation is particularly great to start off by cutting intangible investments, because this has an instantaneous impact on the cost side and a negative impact on returns only after a considerable time lag. In the short term, therefore, enterprises can optimise shareholder value at the expense of their stakeholders. The fact that this can endanger the basis for the sustainable growth of the enterprise is often neglected.

Among the first casualties of these cuts is investment in the human capital represented by the firm's employees. The costs of further training, once seen as one of the most worthwhile aspects of the enterprise's social responsibility, more and more often fall victim to short-term savings. As shown in the following news items, randomly selected from the international press, this behaviour can be seen in many European countries: "Germany, November 1996: in a survey, the majority of companies asked said that they predict an increasing demand for vocational training on the part of their companies." In another survey only a month later companies answered that during the last three years they had cut vocational training budgets on average by 20 per cent. "France, September 1996: a survey of French companies showed a majority of companies with stagnating training budgets, with 16 per cent of companies cutting budgets and only 11 per cent showing positive growth." One might add the reminder that 1996 was the European Year of Lifelong Learning.

Although it is well known, and surely by most enterpreneurs, that workforce skills and employee commitment to a company are of crucial importance in sustaining its competitive advantage, the problem of positive externalities for those who invest in the training of their workforce and consequently the high incentive to behave as a free-rider on others' investment leads to market failure in the provision of general and work-related education and training.[2]

Social responsibility for whom?

The world isn't just black and white. Of course most enterpreneurs see social responsibility as one of their strongest marketing tools in attracting good workers and keeping them. But social responsibility and the consequent low turnover of highly skilled employees goes hand-in-hand with less social responsibility towards the less highly-qualified. More and more companies are developing a two-tier society within their own workforce. The strategy tries to socialise or externalise costs that were formerly borne internally by most companies.

Employment contracts are an example which demonstrate enterpreneurs' (social) attitude towards their employees. Switzerland is a country in which employment contracts are not as a rule of limited duration, with only about 3 per cent of contracts being fixed-term. A recent survey showed that, among unemployed people, 8 per cent had fixed-term contracts before they became unemployed, and that, after they had found a new job, 22 per cent of the formerly unemployed were on fixed-term contracts. As soon as a contract ends and is not renewed, it falls to the state or the unemployment insurance system to bear the social responsibility for the less fortunate. These developments are not in any way specific to Switzerland, having been observed for many years now in our European neighbours.

The new role of government and the dangers of a two-tier society

"Employability" is replacing "employment stability"

What can governments do, if enterprises no longer have a social responsibility towards all their employees? The Swiss government is conscious of the fact that enterprises cannot be coerced, and that a coercive strategy would very quickly become counterproductive – it is better for an employee to have a temporary job than to have no job at all. This is why the Swiss government's initiatives are aimed not so much at employment stability, which could create a dangerous insider-outsider problem, but rather at promoting the employability of all its citizens through investment in human capital. Again, however, it is very difficult to communicate such a strategy and the government always runs the risk that its projects may be rejected by the insiders, who still represent the majority of voters.

Equity vs. incentives

In Switzerland, but certainly in other OECD countries too, one of the great challenges of our times is the change in the wage structure. By the social responsibility of the enterprise we often understand two things: on the one hand, the guaranteed job (employment stability); and, on the other, good or fair pay. Good pay is always very relative, which means that in general people see small differences in pay as fair and good. This creates a certain feeling of equity, and an entrepreneur who provides this feeling of equity is regarded as a social entrepreneur. Now, the problem that arises with this kind of social responsibility is that it establishes no incentives, or at least no financial incentives, for individual investment in human capital. These considerations can be illustrated through two graphs. Figure 1 shows the growth in pay that employees can achieve either by changing from one qualification level to another (4 being the lowest, 1 the highest) – which presupposes investments in human capital (white column); or, as shown by the black column, by remaining on the original qualification level but accumulating some 15 years of service. The wage structure for Switzerland (excluding the state sector!) shows that, with the exception of the change from level 2 to level 1 (Top management), the passive strategy of "abstinence" promises a greater growth in wages than the costly active strategy.

Figure 1. Switzerland: differences in salaries depending on length of service and change in level of qualification

Salaries in the private sector, 1994

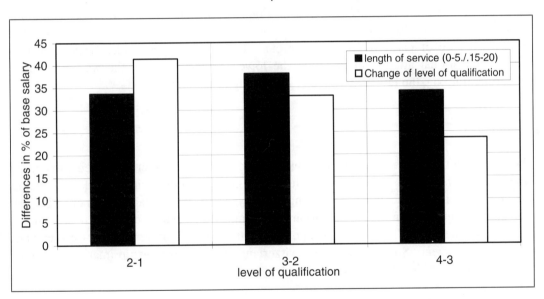

Figure 2. Switzerland: participation rate in continuous education depending on former level of education, 1996

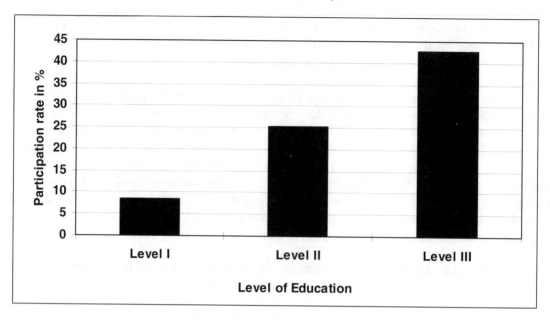

In Figure 2, which is the mirror image of Figure 1, we see the consequences of this wage structure, which presents little financial incentive for the less-qualified workforce to invest in their own human capital. The rate of participation in vocational further education is clearly dependent on the original level of educational attainment (1 being the lowest, 3 the highest), the well-educated taking advantage of further training, the less well-educated remaining passive.

"Make education pay"

The challenge that faces the social partners in all countries, together with their governments, is to reform their wage systems in such a way as to foster greater productivity and skills development, enhancing economic performance while rewarding employees in an equitable manner. The same is important for the trade unions: in their negotiations with employers, unions need to ensure that workers are not priced out of the labour market and (importantly) that their long-term careers are enhanced by rewarding skills development. So far, at least in Switzerland, unions have been primarily concerned with wage-agreements that reward length of service.

The OECD has established its strategy for reform of social insurance systems under the slogan "make work pay". At a time when employers complain of the shortage of appropriate qualifications and whole categories of the workforce do not participate in ongoing education and training, more than this will be required. The strategy needed by most OECD countries is to "make education pay". Demands on government should therefore be for a equal chance to participate in ongoing training, rather than for equal pay independent of what one is doing and how one is performing.

This idea is difficult to get across, but the socially responsible entrepreneur is not the one who pays equal salaries to everyone but rather the one who offers equal chances for education and pays according to individual qualifications and productivity. *Perhaps one sometimes needs more inequality in order to be truly social.* What is being claimed here is not completely new: in an article entitled, "Hang the Carrot Higher", the Nobel Prize winner Gary Becker recently wrote that sometimes more differentiation is needed to get the incentives right and to be socially responsible in a sustainable way.

Conclusions

In political economy we speak of the two possibilities of *voice* and *exit*. In a globalised world enterprises are increasingly adopting the second course. Their commitment to the society in which they work is lower now than it was ten or twenty years ago. Their social responsibility is focused on specific groups of highly productive employees.

All these developments certainly call for a new role for governments. Government has to abandon its paternalistic view of things, a purely legislative way of thinking. The effective rules of the game are no longer made by governments. People and enterprises don't just break them, they evade them. This is why government must realise that it is not simply the referee but rather a player in the game. The role of government will be to get the incentives right for all the players – companies and employees, not forgetting consumers – so that a fair game can be played.

Companies still depend on social stability

Despite the almost endless possibilities in a globalised world for enterprises to choose the economic and social framework in which to operate, they have not become any more independent of the actions of other actors. On the contrary, the increased division of labour between firms and countries has drastically increased the interdependence of all and thus the dependency of each. If industrial conflict breaks out in a faraway country, stopping production for days, weeks or even months, this generally affects not only one's competitors established there but also one's own suppliers or buyers, so that at some stage one's own production is endangered. Global, and not just local, stability has become much more decisive today, which again emphasizes the important role of governments and international organisations such as the OECD and the ILO.[3]

Social responsibility vs. self-responsibility: "The employee is dead – long live the life entrepreneur!"

More important than the social responsibility of the enterprise or of government is the strengthening of self-responsibility. Companies and governments have to establish incentives in such a way that self-responsibility is rewarded. The distinction between employers and employees is becoming more and more outdated. Everyone is the entrepreneur of his own life and the role of government is to provide equal access to all opportunities, a safety net for those who have failed and incentives to try again and again.

The decisive role of consumers

Over the last 20 years or so consumers have very effectively forced companies to show more responsibility in the use of natural resources. This movement had been accompanied by international action by governments setting minimal standards and preventing companies from evading national legislation. However, these developments were brought about not by governments but by the change in consumers' attitudes towards environmental problems.

Today there already exist examples demonstrating consumer awareness of social responsibility, for example special labels designating goods manufactured according to specified ethical and social standards in developing countries – and consumers are prepared to pay for this. Perhaps some day Greenpeace will have a sister organisation, "Socialpeace". The role of consumers in these developments is decisive, and the role of governments is to inform them and to support them, not to lead them.

In the end it will be up to consumers, and not governments, to discover that it is their work, their social environment which is at stake. The day consumers discover their social responsibility, the social responsibility of enterprises will come as a matter of course.

NOTES

1. See also Dunning, John (1997), *Reconfiguring the Boundaries of International Business Activity*, International Seminar on the Changing Nature of Firm, Stockholm, 19 February.

2. See also Booth, A.L. and D.J. Snower (1996), *Acquiring Skills - Market Failures, Their Symptoms and Policy Responses,* Cambridge University Press.

3. An example of how governments and international organisations can support the economic and social stability so important for enterprises is the ILO/Swiss Project on the Prevention and Resolution of Conflict and Promotion of Workplace Democracy in South Africa. South Africa is a country in which the economy suffers from severe labour conflicts. The Commission on Condition, Mediation and Arbitration, which the Project supports in terms of logistics, finance and know-how, has achieved a rate of arbitration of 80 per cent in approximately 40 000 labour conflicts during its first five months of activity.

Part VII

Intellectual Property Rights

Chapter 20

COLLECTIVE RESEARCH AND IPRs IN THE GLOBAL ENVIRONMENT

by

Georges Ferné
Directorate for Science, Technology and Industry, OECD, Paris

The variety and scope of international Research and Development (R&D) programmes and activities has rapidly become a major feature on the global scientific and technological scene. These activities range from structured and closely monitored efforts launched by governments (such as CERN) to informal groupings of researchers who join forces in areas of common interest, and increasingly include R&D alliances between firms. A number of factors converge to encourage these forms of collective research:

◊ the growing fixed costs of R&D;

◊ the easy divisibility of research efforts in important new areas (genome);

◊ the emergence of new research modes ("discovery in the context of application") that require strong interaction between long-term basic research and technological development;

◊ the availability of new communications channels and networks that provide access to distant databases and easy exchange of research-related data.

The resulting programmes raise a number of vital issues for their sponsors, but the question of the definition and distribution of Intellectual Property Rights (IPRs) comes to the fore when the expectation of R&D results prompts the decision to establish a group. Difficulties arise at the international level for a number of reasons:

◊ The existence of discrepancies between the national IPR systems that apply when scientists from different countries and different sectors are brought together.

◊ The many legal approaches that can be followed for the creation of research groups, such as mere R&D agreements and contracts, informal and temporary groupings, silent groupings, public or private limited liability companies, co-operative companies, general partnerships, associations or foundations, etc. Each of these legal frameworks entails varying risks, costs and benefits with respect to the exploitation of resulting IPRs.

◊ The new global electronic environment underpinning modern R&D efforts that avail themselves of public open networks such as the Internet increasingly affects the basis of IPR allocation.

Harmonization issues

The recent agreement on Trade-Related Aspects of Intellectual Property (TRIPs), under the aegis of the World Trade Organisation, has been an important step forward towards the global harmonization of IPR regimes. The agreement established minimum standards, in particular with respect to the scope of patentability, duration of patent protection and non-discrimination. It also provided a framework for enforcement procedures, including a multilateral dispute settlement mechanism.

Aside from the difficulties that may occur during the transition period until the TRIPs agreement is fully implemented, many important unresolved issues will continue to affect international co-operative research. While patents (and increasingly copyright) regimes have been the focus of interest in this connection, the fact that firms increasingly use the whole range of IPR instruments (including design, trade-marks and trade secrets) to protect their strategic interests also implies that differences in these areas may also increasingly affect the exploitation of research results emerging from international efforts. This being said, however, patent-related issues remain at the core of current concerns.

Examples of major issues still to be resolved include the following:

◊ While a majority of OECD countries apply the so-called "first to file" rule that assigns priority to the first applicant for a patent, other countries – notably the United States – apply a rule known as "first to invent", where priority will be assigned, in case of conflict, to the first inventor. In addition to the uncertainty that affects patents filed as a result of international collaborative efforts, the costs of patent filing and of litigation may be very high. Different national systems will also establish different dates for the beginning of the patent rights. Harmonization has been sought at the World Intellectual Property Organisation (WIPO) through negotiation of the Patent Law Treaty (PLT), but discussions are stalled.

◊ The existence in some countries of a "grace period" during which disclosure of an invention does not preclude the right to file for a patent. This difference is especially significant for academic participants in international collaborative research, because European scientists will feel disadvantaged, for example, in comparison to their US colleagues in terms of ability to publish their results. The differences may also become a source of conflict in countries where the grace period is not recognised.

◊ The scope of patentability still differs across countries, in particular with respect to living organisms and plant varieties, design of integrated circuits, or software.

At the same time, there are many expressions of concern about the costs of patenting, as a result of the broad variety of procedures implemented in different countries, of allegedly excessive official fees, of translation costs, of requirements for legal representation or of patent-related litigation. Industrial demands for a streamlining of the procedures at global level are increasing – most recently, for example, on the part of the International Chamber of Commerce. All these arguments tend to promote the notion of a "world patent" system.

Such a system would make it possible to address one of the difficulties currently facing international collaborative research efforts, namely the lack of a suitable instrument for the filing of collective patents that would probably remove many of the difficulties that currently face prospective partners when drawing up the framework and contractual arrangements for co-operation, and that take account of the potential IPRs to emerge from the work. These problems will be discussed in the next section.

In the meantime, some progress has been achieved towards greater homogeneity in the global patent system through regional arrangements under the European Patent Convention and the Patent Co-operation Treaty in Europe. Similar developments are taking place in the ASEAN and NAFTA areas.

Contractual diversity

The proliferation of international research undertakings is coupled with an even greater proliferation of contractual arrangements that affect IPRs. There is little evidence of an emerging "model" for the initial arrangements, to the extent that each collective research project involves an original definition of the rights and obligations of partners. The object is to address problems encountered or expected in specific circumstances and thus reflect a broad variety of contexts.

The complexity is all the greater where large programmes, such as EUREKA in Europe or Real World Computing in Japan, more or less allow individual sub-programmes to develop their own contractual arrangements within an overall framework that often allows for a great deal of flexibility.

In theory, and as long as one assumes that the object of a research agreement is to undertake research in order to deliver the expected product, these practices can be assessed as innovative approaches to the solution of specific problems and the need to implement trade-offs between the demands for rapid access to the necessary information, and to the knowledge-base, while safeguarding the rights of the participants in line with the resources they have invested.

In practice, the situation is rendered more complex because the research effort may not be the chief concern of some of the participants, who may be more attracted by other aspects, ranging from training of personnel to information gathering, and including broader strategic goals that call for co-operation between firms. At the same time, efforts that are not primarily launched in order to develop new opportunities for applications may well do so – and thus generate IPR distribution issues that were not anticipated.

Some of the major questions that have been raised about the international effectiveness of these contractual arrangements include:

◊ differences in the legal cultures of countries, that affect the extent to which contractual arrangements can or cannot be validated by the courts: in some European countries, for examples, judges may assess "the common intent of the parties" to go beyond the letter of the original contract;

◊ the collective ownership of IPRs by the partners or the sponsors, or the confidentiality of know-how and right to licence as a result of a research effort cannot be assumed – but must be defined *ex ante*: international differences in patenting, such as "first to invent/file" will obviously make a great difference if precautions have not been taken from the outset;

◊ the notion of "good faith" in the conclusion of contracts is not interpreted with the same scope everywhere – and yet it is vital when research efforts are based on knowledge provided by the different partners, each of which must assume that there has been full disclosure of rights that might affect the exploitation of results;

◊ the scope of the contract and expected product will need to be defined with great precision from the outset to avoid future conflicts and litigation – which is not always very easy with research and may lead to different interpretations if the case is submitted to different jurisdictions in different countries;

◊ collective ownership is often preferred by firms, but not readily accepted by many national patent systems;

◊ assignment of jurisdiction and arbitration clauses do not necessarily place all participants (such as academics or smaller firms) on an equal footing;

◊ participants may be drawn from very different settings (multinational firms, small firms, universities or government research establishments) and themselves may fall under different regulations with respect to their IPR entitlements (and those of their institution) under each of the relevant national regimes, thus leading to uncertainty with respect to the real nature of the partners involved and their ability to follow up on the results of the research;

◊ for the same institutional reasons, it is not always clear to what extent individual participants actually represent their institutions in a legal sense.

These are but a few examples of the kind of obstacles that might affect research projects and the successful exploitation of results, reflecting the absence of a coherent legal framework for international research.

Impacts of the electronic environment

More recently, a new global electronic environment for research has emerged, focusing attention on some of the major IPR issues that result from digitalisation. The intent here is not to discuss the major questions relating to copyright that have emerged in this context, but to bring to light three major consequences of the new milieu for the traditional IPR system as a whole.

First, the availability of new instruments for easy communication of data and information stimulates the spontaneous constitution of groups of researchers from different countries and institutional settings who are brought together by similar interests and may gradually shift from informal communication to co-operation without any formal arrangement. This is a source of concern for many organisations and represents a potential source of conflict once results emerge and the question of allocating IPRs must be addressed.

Second, confidentiality is compromised by the use of open public networks – such as the Internet – for scientific communications. Traditionally, communication of information between scientists is protected by a "confidentiality" clause. Open networks, however, are not secure at present To what extent does a simple electronic message represent disclosure of information that should have been protected? This type of question is yet to be addressed by most research organisations and has prompted demands for the creation of a new network that would be more directly geared to the needs of the scientists.

The third issue reflects the nature of electronic communication that can be archived. As a large – if not the largest – share of scientific communications today rely on available networks, the establishment of the history of new ideas is becoming increasingly conceivable. This would have obvious implications for the "first to invent/file" debate. At the same time, as mentioned above, the networks are not secure and the records could be tampered with. Yet the potential for the provision of electronic evidence exists – all the more so when the efforts of governments and the private sector converge to establish cryptography guidelines and thus enhance the security of the networks.

These examples are major challenges to the global IPR system and will need to be addressed in order to safeguard established principles, adjust the practice to the realities of research work and provide an overall environment that will take more directly into account the requirements of international research.

Impacts on international research

It is difficult, at this stage, to establish a clear-cut assessment of the implications of the existing international IPR environment for research efforts. A few questions, however, can be formulated for discussion and further exploration:

◊ Are there significant obstacles to private international research efforts resulting from discrepancies among national IPR regimes? Is there evidence of efforts *not* being launched because of the difficulty of finding satisfactory IPR arrangements, or because of the excessive costs expected?

◊ Are there potential actors in international collaborative research effort that are prevented from participating, due to statutory barriers (for example in the case of inter-governmental research bodies), to the legal complexity (as in the case of smaller firms), or to lack of institutional and private incentives (as in the case of academic scientists or government establishments)?

◊ Does the lack of a more coherent global IPR framework foster an excess of litigation, delays and other barriers to the exploitation of research results and technology diffusion?

◊ To what extent does the increasing use of electronic media for scientific communication represent a serious threat to the IPR system, and if so how could this problem be addressed?

◊ On the more positive side, are there models emerging from the proliferation of international research arrangements that could serve as examples of "best practice" in this area?

In the current context of globalisation, these questions are of the greatest relevance for the future of international R&D efforts and, by implication, the emerging global innovation system. Also, there is little doubt that new challenges will continue to emerge as a result of the combined forces of globalisation and technological change. Some of these changes might even modify our perspective on the notion of "appropriability" and extend the range of inventions and creations that deserve some form of protection. One may speculate, for example, on the ethical and economic rationale that might justify granting an IPR reward for the "invention" or the "design" of new services – an area where major innovative breakthroughs can be expected in the context of the emerging electronic commerce environment.

Chapter 21

TURNING RESEARCH INTO RESULTS

by

Professor John N. Adams
The Intellectual Property Institute, United Kingdom

Introduction

In principle, anyone is free to use anyone else's ideas, unless they are protected by some form of intellectual property right. The principal forms of intellectual property are patents, registered designs, trade-marks and copyright. Copyright, for example, protects this paper against unauthorised reproduction. In most countries of the world, the author of a literary work acquires copyright automatically by the act of creation, without the need for registration or other formality. This is not the case with other types of original works, such as inventions. Copyright can protect some kinds of invention, such as designs (and many countries have design registration systems), but for other kinds of invention the principal forms of protection are patents and trade secrets. Trade secrets are a very satisfactory form of protection if it is going to be impossible to discover the secret from analysis of the product. They are a good form of protection for those types of manufacturing processes which it is possible to keep secret, and for certain types of formulae which are difficult to ascertain by analysis, *e.g.* the secret syrup which goes into "Campari", or the mix of herbs which goes into "Drambuie". Trade secrets have the advantage that they potentially last forever (*e.g.* the "Drambuie" formula is supposed to go back to the early 18th century). Unfortunately, they do not protect against a competitor making the same invention independently, and then patenting it. The best you could hope for in this event is a limited right to continue use in the country of invention. There will be no rights internationally. Moreover, trade secrets are not a form of protection which is suitable for most inventions. These in general depend upon patents for their protection. The basic criteria for patentability are novelty (in most countries today tested against what has been made available to the public on a world-wide basis), inventive step, *i.e.* roughly that the invention represents a significant development of the prior art and industrial applicability. These criteria need to be borne in mind in relation to the following sections of this chapter.

Disclosure of the invention

The pressure on most researchers is to enhance their reputation with their peers by publishing the results of their research. It follows from the above, however, that to do so is potentially fatal to the subsequent secural of patent protection because when protection is sought, the invention will no longer satisfy the criterion of novelty. Research staff need to be firmly and clearly instructed (and ideally this is spelled out in their contracts of employment) that they *must not* disclose research results without authorisation. Disclosure may be permitted, for example, where the employer deliberately wishes to destroy patentability by competitors of technology it does not itself see much future in. Some countries, such as the United States, have what is called a "grace period" permitting patenting provided the application is filed within a period after the disclosure, which in the case of United States is 12 months. The United States, along with the Philippines, are the only jurisdictions of the world, however, to grant patents to the first to invent. The rest of the world grants to the first to file, and there are difficulties marrying a grace period to a first system – although Canada and Japan seem to have achieved this. In Europe, and most other parts of the world, there is no grace period, and any disclosure subject to minor exceptions will destroy patentability.

Identifying the invention

In most cases the person responsible for securing protection will be a patent agent or patent attorney, although some lawyers specialise in this field also. Their first job when a new piece of technology is brought to them will be to identify the subject matter which is protectable. This entails identifying what is novel about the technology having regard to the prior art as disclosed in published patent specifications and the technical literature – a difficult and time-consuming task. Having identified what is novel, they will then have to ask themselves whether it involves an inventive step and is capable of industrial application. Certain types of technology which pass all of these hurdles may, depending on the jurisdiction, be excluded from patentability. Computer programs are a common category. The part of the technology qualifying for patenting will form the subject matter of the principal claim of the patent. The basic theory of patents is that the state grants an exclusive right to the patentee in return for disclosure of the invention. This is done in a document called the "specification". The part of the specification which defines the extent of the exclusive right is called the "claims", and drafting these is a matter of considerable skill, as broad claims which extend to prior art are in principle invalid, and narrow ones which allow the invention to be "invented around" will confer too little protection.

Who made the invention and who owns it?

In the modern industrial world, inventions are not usually made by individuals, but by research teams. It is vital to identify who, in fact, was responsible for the patentable technology, and to ascertain who, if anyone, employed them. For example, if an invention is made in a university by a member of staff in the course of his or her employment, the invention will in principle belong to the university. But if it was made by a research student, it will not, unless there was some sort of contractual provision in his or her terms of work. If the research was paid for by an outside funding body, it may well be a term of the contract governing the funding of the research that patentable inventions resulting from it belong to the funding body. In many countries the relationship between the parties is entirely a matter of agreement, *i.e.* freedom of contract governs. In some countries, however, there may be employee inventor laws and the like which confer certain rights on the individual inventor. Leaving these aside, the arrangements under which any piece of research is undertaken can differ considerably. Companies may undertake joint research with a university department on the basis that any patentable outputs are owned jointly. They may simply pay for research students/fellows. Alternatively, they may embark on a collaboration. In all cases, the question of ownership should be settled by contract. If it is not, there can be considerable difficulties, occasionally resulting in expensive litigation between the parties to establish who owns what. What I said above relating to universities equally applies to joint and collaborative research between companies, but in this case care has to be taken that the relationship between the parties does not result in any infringement of antitrust laws. This is a matter requiring expert legal advice. Where the joint venture is between undertakings in different jurisdictions, not only must antitrust law be considered, but there is the additional complexity of potential conflict of laws and jurisdiction problems arising in relation to the contract. The contract can, in principle, contain choice of law and jurisdiction clauses, but these will have to be considered in relation to the domestic laws of the different jurisdictions involved. Again, this is a matter for legal experts.

The extent of protection required

Once the patentable piece of technology has been identified and its ownership established, it is then a question of deciding the extent of protection required, and how the patents once secured will be exploited. There is no such thing as a world-wide patent. Patents are national rights granted by national patent offices, though there are a number of arrangements such as the European Patent Convention which simplify the application process by permitting applications to be filed at a central office which will process them. What results, however, is a bundle of national rights. Securing patent protection is *very* expensive, in the order of £100 000 would usually be a minimum to cover the major countries in which protection would be wanted. Since any disclosure of an invention in principle destroys patentability, there would be a problem if the first publication of a patent occurred before other applications had been filed. This problem is dealt with by the Paris Convention. On first filing in a member state of that Convention the applicant acquires a "priority date", so that other applications can be filed in target member states within 12 months of the priority date. This makes possible a strategy for the impecunious applicant which is to file domestically, and to seek to licence before the priority period has run out. The risk is, of course, that the period will run out before the applicant persuades anyone that it is worth patenting his or her invention on a world-wide basis. The safer alternative, if this can be secured, is to disclose the invention to potential exploiters of it under letters of confidentiality. Most jurisdictions of the world recognise these and protect trade secrets disclosed under them.

Exploiting patents

A patent does not allow the patentee to exploit the invention which is its subject, but only to stop others from doing so. There may be an earlier patentee with a patent which inhibits exploitation, in which case the later patentee will need either to design around the earlier patent, try to have it declared invalid, or take a licence for the part of the earlier patent which would otherwise be infringed.

Subject to this, companies making inventions will usually have the option of exploiting them themselves by manufacturing products embodying them or, if the invention is outside of their core business, licensing others to do so. Sometimes a combination of the two will be adopted if the invention covered by the patent is both appropriate to the patentee's core business and capable of quite a different application by another company in a different field. For example, a pharmaceutical invention may have an agricultural application. In this case, returns are maximised if the unused aspect of the technology is licensed by the patentee. In general, the royalties and terms of the licence contract can be fixed by the parties, *i.e.* again, freedom of contract rules the day. However, in many jurisdictions, care has to be taken to ensure that the provisions comply with domestic antitrust laws. Typical things black-listed might be tie-ins of products when it is not strictly necessary that they should be acquired from the patentee for the proper exploitation of the invention. Such tie-ins foreclose other potential sources of supply. Cross-licensing between companies has to be watched exceptionally carefully.

Conclusion

The above is a very brief summary of a highly complex area. I hope, however, that it has highlighted some of the more important points.

Chapter 22

THE APPROPRIATION OF TECHNOLOGY: THE SITUATION IN FRENCH INDUSTRY

A FOUR-STAGE APPROACH: HOW TECHNOLOGY IS APPROPRIATED THROUGH TO INFRINGEMENT

by

Jean-Paul François
Ministère de l'Industrie, France

Introduction

In order to grasp and assess the extent of the problem represented by industrial infringement, especially to manufacturers, we have used a theoretical and statistical approach, starting with a description of the innovation process, and going on to evaluate the losses incurred by industry. These investigations provide information to the public authorities whose task it is to introduce legal and regulatory provisions to deal with the problem of infringement.

For France, this approach took the form of a number of statistical instruments based upon a series of three surveys carried out during the period 1990-94, and which resulted in the decisions reflected in the 1995 legislation.

Stage 1: the 1990 and 1993 innovation surveys

In the initial innovation survey carried out in 1990, industrial firms were questioned in a very conventional way about their sources of innovation. This exhaustive survey encompassed 22 000 firms – covering 85 per cent in terms of numbers and 95 per cent in terms of turnover – and involved more than 20 people. It provided a quantitative evaluation of the role played by external sources in innovation, notably the acquisition of industrial property rights. Patents and industrial property rights in general had previously been assessed as an output of invention (which is not the same as an output of innovation) by counting the number of applications filed. However, with the exception of cross-border movements in balance of payments studies, there had been no direct evaluation of the use made of intellectual property rights by firms as part of the innovation process.

The number of innovating firms using this type of source was evaluated at 28 per cent and 21 per cent, respectively, according to whether the firm filed the patent itself or acquired intellectual property rights held by others; these figures may be compared with the 85 and 63 per cent of firms, respectively, that had recourse to all internal sources (R&D, technical studies, and so on) and external sources (bought-in R&D, patents and licences, databanks, trade fairs and exhibitions, etc.). It is worth adding that 85 per cent of firms stated that they had acquired the technology via components or systems.

This raises the question of identifying the technology flows in which firms, as they deal with external sources, evade payment of royalties on intellectual property.

The second, 1993, innovation survey provided the first opportunity to extend the methodology by making an explicit distinction between the sources – the entities or organisations at the origin of the technology (for example, the firm itself, the group, universities, research centres, public laboratories, suppliers, etc.) – and the acquisition channels wherein purchases of intellectual property rights were supplemented by items arising, for example, from reverse engineering – which is really a form of imitation. In addition, these particular acquisition channels were examined in terms of their geographical origin, which relates to one of the questions about infringement.

The outcome of the survey indicates the degree to which this acquisition channel is used, with 40 per cent of firms reporting that they use reverse engineering, compared with about 20 per cent acquiring intellectual property rights in the proper manner (as in 1990).

This mode of acquisition comes just behind acquisition involving subcontracted or co-operative R&D, and relations with customers and suppliers – all of which are extremely informal.

This acquisition channel is in no way reprehensible in terms of our infringement study, but it does raise a large number of questions for a more thorough investigation – directly or indirectly – of the very nature of retro-designing, despite the fact that French firms are implicitly put in the position of potential counterfeiters rather than victims.

It should be noted that the countries of origin for retro-engineering are the major industrialised countries (France 28 per cent, European Union 23 per cent, the United States 10 per cent, Japan 7.2 per cent, and that it represents the most international mode of acquisition (see table below).

Means of acquisition of technology according to country of origin

Percentage of French innovating firms

	France	EU	Non-EU Europe	United States	Japan	Other	All
Subcontracted R&D	41.8	8.1	4.1	3.1	1.2	0.5	46.4
Co-operative R&D	46.3	12.5	2.0	2.9	1.0	0.6	52.7
The right to use the inventions of others	10.6	4.8	1.3	3.1	1.1	0.5	17.0
Analysis of competing products	28.3	23.0	6.8	9.9	7.2	1.6	40.0
Consultancy services, etc..	11.9	1.7	0.6	0.6	0.3	0.5	14.0
Purchase of systems	29.0	18.3	2.9	3.3	2.2	0.5	42.9
Recruitment of skilled workers	28.1	2.7	0.6	0.7	0.1	0.5	30.2
Communication with suppliers	44.8	20.7	3.9	4.0	2.0	1.0	51.1
Communication with customers	46.3	18.5	6.4	5.7	2.6	3.1	50.3
Purchase of another firm (or part of it)	8.7	2.0	0.7	0.8	0.0	0.4	11.6
Joint ventures or mergers	4.3	2.9	0.8	1.9	0.6	0.8	9.1
Exchanges of staff	3.6	1.5	0.2	0.6	0.1	0.3	6.2

Source: SESSI, 1994.

Stage 2: measuring the appropriation of technology

A further survey of industrial firms was carried out in 1993 with a view to clarifying the ways in which technology was appropriated, following the approach used by Professor Nelson in the so-called YALE survey. The questionnaire was sent to a representative sample of 2 600 French industrial firms employing more than 50 workers, who had responded to the SESSI "Innovation 1990" survey. All French firms with more than 1 000 employees were surveyed; the sampling rate was 1:2 for firms employing 500 to 1 000 people and 1:3 for those with between 50 and 500 employees. The response rate was very satisfactory, at 73 per cent in terms of numbers and over 96 per cent in terms of turnover. The reference period for which the firms were questioned covered the three years 1990-92. The French survey posed the following questions formulated in a way which directly targeted leaks of know-how:

To the best of your knowledge, were any of the important innovations developed by your firm over the last three years the subject of:

	Yes	No
-- infringement?		
-- industrial espionage?		

This question was supplemented by another concerning the effectiveness of the ways in which this knowledge was protected, depending upon whether it was orientated towards creating product or process innovations:

How effective are the following means of preventing or dissuading your competitors from imitating your new products and processes?

	Products					Processes				
	0	1	2	3	4	0	1	2	3	4
Patents										
Trade-marks										
Secrecy										

One question concerned the degree to which new products and processes could be imitated:

Are your new products and processes difficult to imitate or not worth imitating, owing to:

	Products					Processes				
	0	1	2	3	4	0	1	2	3	4
Their technical complexity										
Their frequent renewal										
The commercial benefit of being first on the market										

One question concerned the extent to which the firm controlled the dissemination of its know-how through scientific papers:

	Yes	No
Do your firm´s engineers have the right to disseminate non-confidential aspects of your new technologies (by publishing articles, conference papers, etc.?		

One question on the use of patents for protection:

During the last three years, have you:	Yes	No

lodged patent applications
    -- purely French
    -- European (possibly by PCT)
    -- American (possibly by PCT)
    -- Japanese (possibly by PCT)		

A question on the shortcomings of patents:

To what extent do patents have the following shortcomings as regards your firm's innovations?

	0	1	2	3	4
A patent is too expensive to obtain and maintain					
A patent is too expensive to defend					
Obtaining a patent does not prevent your competitors from imitating you					
A patent divulges too much information					

Finally, firms obtaining patents were questioned as follows:

	Yes	No
Do you have an industrial property section (either in your own firm or belonging to the group to which you belong) for obtaining and managing your patents?		

Do you file patents in order to:

	Products		Processes	
	Yes	No	Yes	No
Dissuade your competitors from imitating your inventions				
Prevent your competitors from accusing you of infringement				
Improve your position in negotiations with other firms having registered your discoveries				
Earn income (by licensing or transferring patents)				
Value or reward the work of your researchers				
Gain access to foreign markets where regulations require new technologies to be licenced to a national firm.				

Do you ever postpone filing a patent because you prefer a greater technological advance:

	Yes	No
For your product innovations?		
For your process innovations?		

Frequency of filing

	0-20	20-40	40-60	60-80	80-100
For what proportion of the new products your firm has introduced to the market did you file a patent application?					
For what proportion of new processes your firm has introduced to the market did you file a patent application?					

The main conclusions drawn from this survey are as follows (Th. Lehoucq, I. Kabla):

To secure protection from imitations...

Nearly 40 per cent of firms with innovative products or processes reported having suffered from infringement during the three years preceding the survey and 19 per cent from industrial espionage, the latter mainly affecting very large firms. Firms that only innovate as regards products are more frequently the victims of infringement (40 per cent) than those that only innovate in processes (26 per cent).

On the European market, the copying of new technologies developed by French firms is the main obstacle to the viability of innovations, even beating the constraints and standards of the country that stand against their new products. Firms are more disadvantaged by local constraints and standards on the American and Japanese markets, and indeed a discriminatory public purchasing policy in the United

States and Japan is particularly felt by very large firms. But in any event it is essential for the firm to develop a real technological protection strategy according to the nature of the new product or process.

... by patents or secrecy

A particular kind of protection predominates for each kind of innovation. Product innovations appear to be better protected by patents, process innovations by secrecy. Some 48 per cent of firms with innovative products regard filing a patent as highly effective for preventing or dissuading their competitors from imitating their innovations, while 38 per cent prefer secrecy, and 20 per cent rate the two approaches equally. Large firms in particular see filing a patent as highly effective. For firms employing less than 200 people, the res equally. Large firms in particular see filing a patent as highly effective in dissuading imitation. The patent also serves as an instrument in negotiation and for improving their position in co-operation with other firms, thanks to the legal registration of their discovery (53 per cent), but also as a means of protection against an infringement suit brought by a competing firm (49 per cent of firms). Only 21 per cent of patenting firms regard the patent on a product as a way of earning revenue, by transferring or licensing the patent.

Patents receive less support amongst firms that innovate in processes. Only 28 per cent regard patenting as highly effective. Since a new process is more easily concealed from the eyes of competitors than a new product already on the market, almost two out of three process-innovating firms regard secrecy as highly effective. This view is stronger the larger the firm, because larger firms are able to spend more on security. However, medium-sized firms, which are often subcontractors, are less well placed to protect themselves through secrecy. The pharmaceuticals industry is an exception; it is the only industry to regard both patents and maintaining secrecy as highly effective.

Of course patents and secrecy are not the only ways of protecting technological innovations. The complexity of an invention provides a natural barrier (particularly in the chemicals and pharmaceuticals industries, in aerospace and in the sectors of professional electrical and electronic equipment). The frequent replacement of products is another obstacle to imitation. Then again, being the first to market a new product is a powerful advantage for 59 per cent of product-innovating firms; this phenomenon can be seen throughout industry.

The strategy of technological protection is implemented in parallel with "technological watch". Despite the risk that strategic information will leak, firms are relatively open to the dissemination of those aspects of their new technologies they consider non-confidential: 45 per cent of innovating firms grant this freedom to their engineers, and the most innovative sectors are also those where firms disseminate the largest amount of non-confidential technological information. Thus innovative firms apparently consolidate their information through the dissemination of technologies via exchanges between engineers.

Only some innovations are patented

Among firms that file patents, 57 per cent report having done so for less than 20 per cent of the new products they have placed on the market over the last three years. Only 8 per cent of firms in the case of products, and 6 per cent in the case of processes, systematically have recourse to patenting (about 80 per cent of new products or processes). Very large firms, which employ over 2 000 people, stand out by making more systematic use of patenting for their innovations. The decision not to patent an innovation may have a variety of causes: a little under 30 per cent of patenting firms report having postponed filing a patent covering a product in order to acquire an even greater technological lead (37 per cent for process innovations). Also, the process of filing a patent gives rise to a relatively high degree of dissatisfaction. Some 57 per cent of innovating firms state that patents do not really prevent imitation, 43 per cent that they are too expensive to file and maintain, 39 per cent that they are too expensive to defend compared with the profit they hope to gain, and 38 per cent that patenting divulges too much information. In addition, competitors can sidestep the patent if they modify the invention they are imitating sufficiently to avoid being sued for infringement.

Relative effectiveness of patents and secrecy

Percentage of the number of innovative firms

	Patent highly effective	Secrecy highly effective
Product innovation	48.3	38.8
Process innovation	28.0	60.5

Source: SESSI 94.

Some elements of international comparison

In parallel with the French enquiry, MERIT (University of Maastricht) conducted a PACE survey of other European countries – centred solely on large firms – which looked into the filing of patents as an indicator of innovations (invention output) but also as a discloser of appropriation conditions, themselves influenced by the sectoral and dimensional structure of industry in different countries.

The main conclusions of this project, which was directed by Anthony Arundel, were as follows:

Evaluating the effectiveness of patents

As regards product innovations, more than 75 per cent of large European firms believe that patents are highly effective in protecting them against imitations. Only half believe the same about secrecy. Finally, one-third regard patents as definitely more effective than secrecy.

Conversely, firms regard secrecy as more effective in protecting their process innovations against imitation, with 50 per cent considering patents as highly effective, compared with two-thirds in favour of secrecy, and one-third regarding secrecy as more effective than patents.

After correcting for sectoral variations, German firms regard patents as most effective against imitation of their product innovations,. The judgement of French firms is more strongly contrasted in favour of patents compared with secrecy for protecting product innovations, and against imitation and in favour of secrecy compared with patents as regards process innovations.

Effectiveness of patents and of secrecy for innovations

Percentage of the number of innovating firms

	Product			Process		
	Patent[1]	Secrecy[1]	Patent more effective than secrecy	Patent[1]	Secrecy[1]	Secrecy more effective than patents
Germany	80	56	35	48	58	27
France	66	42	42	40	70	43
United Kingdom	72	63	23	49	67	32
Other countries	65	49	36	47	61	32
Total	71	52	35	46	64	34

1. Highly or very highly effective in preventing or dissuading imitation.
Source: MERIT.

Notwithstanding the above, the reasons for filing patents are mainly "protection against imitation, for both product and process innovations. Virtually all firms give this as a reason of medium or greater importance. Over 30 per cent regard it as the essential reason. In other words it is significantly more important than all the others".

The next two factors in terms of frequency of citation are not exclusively related to the passive protection approach but concern the possibility of hostile behaviour (leaks of know-how and infringement), establishing a legal anti-suit mechanism to avoid being accused of infringement by competitors, and as a weapon in negotiations in the event of legal action. After these concerns for avoiding lawsuits and establishing possibilities for negotiation, three other reasons of lesser importance are cited: earning income from licences, valuing or rewarding the work of researchers, and gaining access to foreign markets where regulations require new technologies to be licenced. As far as national differences are concerned, German firms mostly cite protection, British firms are more ready to file patents to avoid being sued for infringement, and French firms tend to be most ready to negotiate.

Reasons for filing patents for innovations

Percentage of the number of firms

	Product					
	To protect	To avoid lawsuits	To negotiate	To licence	To reward researchers	To access foreign markets
Germany	95	67	74	35	20	25
France	92	63	66	33	22	30
United Kingdom	96	76	69	41	18	18
Other countries	90	65	73	38	25	20
Total	93	67	61	36	22	24
	Processes					
	To protect	To avoid lawsuits	To negotiate	To licence	To reward researchers	To access foreign markets
Germany	77	53	59	30	18	21
France	82	55	64	30	21	27
United Kingdom	76	62	62	38	16	18
Other countries	75	59	60	34	20	17
Total	77	57	61	33	19	21

Note: Proportion of firms citing this reason as of medium or greater importance.
Source: MERIT.

One might question the significance of the drawbacks to patenting in the decision not to file a patent. Two deficiencies emerge: the ability of competitors to side-step the patent, and the amount of information that the process divulges. The reason for giving up a patent is only very rarely the cost of protection, except for British firms for whom the costs of the process are a somewhat stronger factor in not patenting than elsewhere. German firms are less sensitive to costs than any others.

Drawbacks to patenting

Percentage of the number of firms

	Application cost	Defense cost	Side-stepping	Divulging
Germany	21	08	54	60
United Kingdom	33	24	63	66
France	23	23	39	34

Note: Drawbacks regarded as important.
Source: MERIT.

Propensity to file patents

Large European firms vary much more in their patenting behaviour than in the views of patents they express. German firms stand out in particular by their propensity to file patents, which is much higher for each patenting system (national patent, European patent, American patent and Japanese patent); they patent a much greater proportion of their innovations, and file more patents. British firms on the average file fewer patents than the others. They also patent a slightly smaller proportion of their process innovations. French firms systematically patent a little less in the United States.

Number of patents filed

Percentage of firms having filed at least one patent

	National	European	American	Japanese
Germany	93	91	75	64
United Kingdom	86	77	74	58
France	65	83	65	51

Source: MERIT.

In considering which factors determine the propensity to patent, the latter is evaluated as:

◊ the proportion of innovations that are patented;

◊ the number of patents filed.

These two indicators are related in the following manner:

Number of patents filed = no. of innovations x proportion of innovations patented x no. of patents filed per innovation

The supporting variables are:

◊ the nationality of the firm;
◊ the sector;
◊ the R&D expenditure;
◊ the effectiveness protection of patents compared with secrecy;
◊ the reasons for filing;
◊ the shortcomings of patent protection.

This econometric analysis concludes that the main factors underlying the propensity to patent and/or the number of patents filed include the following:

◊ Extremely important factor: the effectiveness of the patent against copying, which incorporates the contrary impact of the effectiveness of secrecy but replaces it.

◊ Factors of intermediate importance in reasons for filing, including the use of the patent as a negotiating tool, which again raises the hostile environment where there is a dispute about copying or infringement (responding to an attack). Reported reasons for filing also include the need to earn income from licences and to gain access to foreign markets.

◊ Extremely important factor: sectoral effects, which also encompass the conditions in which technology is appropriated, and the ability – which varies from sector to sector – to retain the benefits of the innovation.

◊ National effects persist, even when corrected for the conditions in which technology is appropriated and for the sector, which could indicate greater efficiency of German research and, ultimately, according to the authors, cultural differences.

◊ Two other shortcomings of patents are also reported for their negative impact: the divulging of information and the side-stepping of patents, which we shall consider under the subject of infringement.

Stage 3: direct measurement of infringement

The investigation of technological appropriation reveals a considerable degree of sensitivity to infringement and industrial espionage.

An enquiry dedicated specifically to the direct measurement of infringement was carried out with the intention of covering all forms of the process. Conducted in the form of a poll, it also focused particularly on those firms that had reported specifically technological infringement in the appropriation survey, and on the luxury industries, which in France tend to polarise public opinion in too exclusive a manner.

Enquiry into infringement in the manufacturing industry: methodology

This enquiry was conducted as a telephone poll in the summer of 1994. It followed on from an earlier enquiry in 1993 concerned with technological protection. The enquiry covered all firms employing over 1 000 people: the polling rate was 1:2 for firms with 500 to 1 000 employees and 1:6 for those employing between 50 and 500 workers.

The questionnaire

Each firm was questioned on the following four topics:

◊ the type of infringement suffered:

- copying with identical appearance: crude or easily detectable by the consumer;
- copying with identical appearance: intelligent (detectable with difficulty or not detectable at all);
- copying not of identical appearance;

◊ origin of infringement suffered and markets affected;

◊ actions taken against counterfeiters (agreements, legal proceedings);

◊ evaluation of turnover lost directly (through the costs of legal measures, surveillance, etc.) and indirectly as loss of opportunity.

Note: the number of jobs lost was calculated by applying the percentage of sales through loss of opportunity to the workforce of each firm.

The main results of this enquiry were as follows (J.P. François, Th. Lehoucq).

Briefly, one in five French industrial firms employing 50 or more workers reported having suffered from infringement. According to these firms, nearly 30 000 jobs and nearly 3 per cent of turnover were lost each year through loss of opportunity. However, only 37 per cent of firms fight back by keeping markets actively under surveillance; half undertake legal proceedings or, less frequently, reach an agreement with the counterfeiters. The main victims are industries producing luxury goods and consumer durables. The French domestic market is most affected by these counterfeit products, of which three-quarters are produced outside France.

The adverse effects of infringement are particularly pernicious in France. In manufacturing industry proper, nearly 1 800 industrial firms employing 50 or more people report having been victim of infringement – with 25 billion francs of turnover lost every year. Large firms with a national and international reputation are particularly exposed.

The main victims: consumer goods, especially luxury items

In the consumer durables sector, 30 per cent of firms with more than 50 employees report that their products have been counterfeited, resulting in an actual loss of 2 per cent of turnover. Infringements mainly concern domestic electrical and other appliances (56 per cent of firms) and jewellery (65 per cent). The fact that these firms are large but few in number is the reason for these high proportions.

In the ordinary consumer goods sector, the extent of infringement appears significantly lower (20 per cent), but 3.5 per cent of turnover is lost. These industries are not very concentrated and it is primarily the major, internationally known firms that are affected, including the luxury goods industry, which is still the preferred terrain of counterfeiters. Of manufacturing firms in the luxury industry employing more than 50 people (totalling 36 000 employees and a turnover of 38 billion francs in 1993), 65 per cent report having been victim of infringement. All-in-all, damage represents 3.6 per cent of turnover with a loss of 1 000 jobs, however for certain well-known firms, losses can account for up to 25 per cent of turnover.

In total, copying affects 55 per cent of firms involved in producing soaps and cosmetics, 20 per cent in clothing. As regards routine consumer goods, a more serious form of infringement – which is a danger to public health – is the infringement of drugs, usually put on sale in developing countries, with results that are often dramatic: 21 per cent of French pharmaceutical firms have been affected and report a loss of 2.6 per cent of their turnover.

A more unexpected result is the proportion of firms suffering from infringement in capital goods (19 per cent) and semi-processed goods (18 per cent), representing losses of turnover of 2 and 3.2 per cent, respectively. As regards capital goods, the automobile industry (23 per cent of firms, mostly component suppliers) and the mechanical engineering industries are most affected, particularly machines for specific purposes (36 per cent of firms), agricultural machinery (40 per cent) and machine tools (40 per cent).

In the industries producing semi-processed goods, a few sectors suffer from infringement, either because certain firms are connected with the luxury goods industry (glassware, ceramics), or because they are situated upstream of highly exposed sectors (textiles, chemicals, rubber).

Counterfeit goods that deceive the consumer

The counterfeit world is not made up solely of tawdry items or crude copies. Nearly 90 per cent of firms suffering from infringement report copies of goods aimed at deceiving the consumer as to the product they are buying.

Only one-quarter of firms suffering from infringement are affected by crude copies of their products. This type of infringement does not really affect the authentic product as far as potential customers are concerned. There is no doubt that it spoils the image of the product, but it is the intelligent copy, rather than the crude copy, that damages the image and reputation of the firm by deceitfully imitating the product in terms of make, design and model.

Some 54 per cent of firms suffering from infringement are affected by intelligent copies of identical appearance. In this case the deception is difficult to detect and the consumer believes that he is buying the "real thing". Intelligent copies of identical appearance also lead to purchases of original products being replaced by purchases of counterfeit products by customers who are in the know, but who care less about quality than about appearance.

Copies that are not identical in appearance affect 42 per cent of firms. This type of infringement involves imitating packaging (products are sold, often in supermarkets, under a name very similar to that of a known brand); it also involves counterfeit production processes. Thus, this type of infringement tends to divert the consumer away from the authentic product. It also involves the fraudulent use of registered brand names and trade-marks for making products that do not figure in the range of the firm affected.

Infringement frequently involves only a single process. Some 83 per cent of firms affected report having suffered only a single form of infringement. Use of intelligent copies of identical appearance (39 per cent of firms) more particularly affects the spinning and weaving sectors, the rubber industry, and the manufacture of ceramic tiles and construction materials. Copies that are not of identical appearance (31 per cent) more specifically affect aircraft construction and electronic components. Crude copies of identical appearance (13 per cent of firms) affects woodworking, sheet-metal working and jewellery-goldsmithing. A few industrial sectors are under attack on all fronts: leather and footwear, optical equipment and clocks and watches, clothing and soaps and cosmetics.

Infringement of foreign origin mainly affects the French domestic market

According to firms' reports, two-thirds of counterfeit goods are imported from abroad. The European Union outside France is the main origin of counterfeit goods reported (34 per cent of responses), mainly countries from southern Europe (Italy: 14 per cent; Spain: 7 per cent). With France as the leading country of origin (33 per cent of answers), nearly two-thirds of counterfeit goods are reported as originating elsewhere in the Community, followed by South-East Asia (23 per cent), mainly Taiwan and China.

In terms of reduced turnover from lost opportunities, some 76 per cent of this can be seen as resulting from counterfeit goods made abroad, including the European Union outside France (a total of 30 per cent of turnover lost), South-East Asia (24 per cent), then the American continent (14 per cent). Counterfeit goods of French origin account for less than 24 per cent of lost turnover. In fact counterfeit goods of foreign origin are appreciably more destructive of turnover, since they mainly affect large firms and more substantial quantities of goods.

Counterfeit French products are sold on many markets, but it is mainly the French domestic market which is affected (75 per cent of answers), followed by the European Union (61 per cent) and the rest of the world (40 per cent). One-quarter of firms suffering from infringement and 45 per cent of firms in the luxury goods industry report that infringement occurs simultaneously in all three areas. These firms are, of course, mostly significant exporters. More generally, firms suffering from infringement tend to export more than the average: 43 per cent (compared with 28 per cent of all industrial firms employing over 50 people) export 25 per cent or more of their turnover.

Conversely, 15 per cent of firms affected by infringement report a solely French origin and destination for the counterfeit goods. These are often isolated cases that do not form part of organised infringement markets. Although some large firms occasionally fall victim, it is primarily small and medium-sized enterprises that suffer from these fraudulent operations. They include SMEs producing clothing, furniture and clandestine videos. As regards semi-processed goods, it tends to be processes that are counterfeited.

Keeping markets under surveillance to catch counterfeiters...

Fewer than 40 per cent of the firms that are victims of infringement maintain an organised system for keeping markets under surveillance in order to fight back against the perpetrators. However, large firms, which are more exposed to infringement and have greater financial resources, nearly always adopt surveillance systems (80 per cent of firms with more than 2 000 employees).

The sectors most actively involved in surveillance are, of course, routine consumer goods and consumer durables (including optical equipment: 80 per cent of firms; pharmacy: 72 per cent; manufacture of soaps and cosmetics: 72 per cent), but also chemicals (72 per cent), the automobile industry (76 per cent) and the luxury goods industry (70 per cent).

Firms use a variety of strategies to combat infringement: reaching an agreement with the counterfeiter can avoid a long and costly court case; legal proceedings in the national or international court are a more convincing weapon against more powerful counterfeiters. Since 1990, nearly half of firms suffering from infringement have used both of these instruments to fight back. However, in terms of the number of actions taken, three times more legal proceedings have been embarked upon than agreements reached with counterfeiters (4 500 court cases compared with 1 500 agreements). In fact very few firms stop at reaching an agreement or compromise with counterfeiters (12 per cent). However, 43 per cent of firms that are victims of infringement embark on legal action and nearly one-third opt solely for this means of counter-attack. These firms are naturally in the sectors under greatest threat, such as the luxury goods industry (87 per cent of firms take legal action and one-third are successful), consumer durables (50 per cent of firms affected by infringement), but also publishing, printing and reproduction (69 per cent). Two-thirds of legal proceedings are initiated almost systematically once infringement becomes known.

For many firms, legal action against infringement is practically impossible because the products are not always protected or cannot be patented (spinning and weaving). Also, despite the new GATT agreements which will serve as an international court in this field and will offer its member countries protection for brand names, certain countries such as China do not yet recognise international legislation and continue to openly manufacture counterfeit products which are nonetheless covered by legal protection. Notwithstanding this, the hesitations of French firms regarding ways of protecting intellectual property (patents, brand names, patterns) are frequently the cause of industry's inability to stem the flow of counterfeit versions of their products.

... additional cost: 0.8 per cent of turnover

It is very expensive for firms to protect themselves effectively against infringement. Overall, for all firms suffering from infringement, 0.8 per cent of turnover is lost in legal, surveillance and patent costs, and for certain firms in the luxury goods industry costs account for as much as 10 per cent of turnover. This loss is supplementary to that of loss of opportunity but, unlike the latter, creates jobs. These are new jobs – a sign of the times when technological protection and continuous surveillance of markets are an integral part of the industrial world.

Definitions

Infringement is a misdemeanour which involves infringing, in any form whatsoever, the various intellectual property rights as codified in French law by Law N° 92-597 of 1 July 1992 which groups the relevant provisions, for both literary and artistic property as well as industrial property.

As regards industrial property, the following are protected subject to prior registration:

Designs and patterns concerning any new plastic form, any industrial object which differs from its fellows either by a separate and recognisable configuration which confers a degree of novelty, or by one or more external effects giving it a specific and new appearance.

The patent is a title of ownership issued to the inventor in return for divulging his invention: it protects a new invention that lends itself to industrial application from a technological standpoint.

The manufacturing, trade or service mark is a symbol that lends itself to graphic representation used to distinguish the products or services of a physical or corporate person.

From the economic standpoint, infringement is a particularly reprehensible form of unfair competition.

For firms who are victims of infringement, there are two kinds of harmful effects:

◊ First, direct effects, where the counterfeit product is bought instead of the authentic product from the victim firm.

◊ Second, indirect effects, involving a more pernicious attack on the brand image.

While the traditional clientele for luxury products, for example, are less likely to purchase counterfeits owing to their inferior quality – although there are some more or less rational exceptions to this rule (the sneaking attraction of the ban, snobbery, a desire to preserve the originals by wearing copies, and so on) – they may be disgusted by the proliferation of imitations and simply stop buying the authentic products.

Accordingly the nature of infringement is analysed here from a combination of two standpoints:

◊ the appearance aspect which marks out products copied with an identical appearance, and which tends to concern the titles of ownership such as makes, designs and patterns;

◊ the aspect of being able to deceive the consumer which also concerns patents.

Share of enterprises suffering infringement by sector

Percentages

NAF 40	Percentage of goods counterfeited
Basic metals and metal products	9.7
Chemicals, rubber and plastics	20.6
Minerals	20.5
Pulp and paper	3.7
Electrical and electronic components	23.3
Textiles	36.7
Capital goods (mechanical)	19.3
Capital goods (electrical and electronic)	15.8
Motor manufacturing	22.5
Shipbuilding, aerospace and railways	17.7
Consumer durables	29.0
Clothing, leather-footwear, miscellaneous industries	22.1
Publishing, printing, reproduction	9.2
Pharmaceuticals, cosmetics	34.4
Total	19.2

Source: SESSI.

Methods used by firms to combat infringement

Percentage of firms affected by infringement

	Use of surveillance mechanism	Firms embarking on:	
		Agreements	Legal action
Semi-processed goods	30.5	23.7	34.7
Capital goods	35.0	27.5	40.3
Consumer durables	47.8	21.4	50.5
Routine consumer goods	47.9	27.3	58.9
of which luxury goods	67.6	41.0	87.3
Industry	37.0	25.2	42.8

Source: SESSI.

Agreements and legal action

Percentage of firms involved

NAF 40	Agreements (%)	Legal action (%)
Basic metals and metal products	13.7	40.4
Chemicals, rubber and plastics	24.5	39.1
Minerals	33.4	39.1
Pulp and paper	43.3	34.7
Electrical and electronic components	27.0	46.8
Textiles	20.0	20.3
Capital goods (mechanical)	25.9	39.1
Capital goods (electrical and electronic)	29.4	44.8
Motor manufacturing	35.7	51.2
Shipbuilding, aerospace and railways	17.0	8.5
Consumer durables	21.4	50.5
Clothing, leather-footwear, miscellaneous industries	29.5	53.8
Publishing, printing, reproduction	0.0	69.1
Pharmaceuticals, cosmetics	36.0	63.0
Total	25.2	42.8

Origin of counterfeit products

	Percentage of firms suffering infringement	As a percentage of turnover lost
France	33	24
European Union	33	30
Non-EU Europe	3	3
Asia	23	24
America	5	14
Africa		5

Losses caused to firms which are victims of counterfeit products

NAF 40	As a percentage of turnover		Jobs destroyed (x 1 000)
	Annual average loss for costs of surveillance, legal action, etc.	Average annual loss due to loss of profits	
Basic metals and metal products	1.1	3.5	1.64
Chemicals, rubber and plastics	0.6	1.6	2.52
Minerals	0.8	4.9	2.75
Pulp and paper	1.1	7.2	0.58
Electrical and electronic components	0.9	3.5	2.66
Textiles	2.0	6.3	2.77
Capital goods (mechanical)	0.8	4.4	2.42
Capital goods (electrical & electronic)	0.8	2.3	1.63
Motor manufacturing	0.5	0.6	1.27
Shipbuilding, aerospace & railways	0.5	6.2	4.00
Consumer durables	0.9	2.7	1.52
Clothing, leather-footwear, misc. industries	1.5	6.5	3.64
Publishing, printing, reproduction	0.5	2.2	0.28
Pharmaceuticals, cosmetics	1.1	2.4	1.33
Total	0.8	2.6	28.99

Source: SESSI.

Forms of infringement affecting firms

Percentages

NAF 40	Copy of identical appearance				Copy not of identical appearance		Copy with and without identical appearance	All counterfeits: total
	Crude copy only	Intelligent copy only	Crude and intelligent only	Only	Intelligent copy only	Crude copy only		Total
	1	2	1 and 2	3	2 and 3	1 and 3	1, 2 & 3	
Basic metals and metal products	9.5	47.9	4.6	11.8	13.1	2.3	11.0	100.0
Chemicals, rubber and plastics	7.6	35.2	0.0	54.4	1.6	0.5	0.7	100.0
Minerals	4.7	79.0	1.1	14.2	0.0	0.0	0.9	100.0
Pulp and paper	42.8	43.3	0.0	9.3	4.6	0.0	0.0	100.0
Electrical and electronic components	9.0	37.0	5.8	44.0	1.1	3.1	0.0	100.0
Textiles	6.5	49.6	5.8	27.6	3.2	3.3	4.1	100.0
Capital goods (mechanical)	24.7	49.2	10.1	8.3	5.5	1.1	1.1	100.0
Capital goods (electrical and electronic)	12.0	11.3	23.4	45.6	7.8	0.0	0.0	100.0
Motor manufacturing	0.0	13.9	0.0	45.8	28.2	1.6	10.6	100.0
Shipbuilding, aerospace and railways	0.0	0.0	0.0	100.0	0.0	0.0	0.0	100.0
Consumer durables	20.5	38.9	4.9	30.2	1.3	0.0	4.3	100.0
Clothing, leather-footwear, miscellaneous industries	6.7	31.4	6.2	41.9	4.4	0.0	9.3	100.0
Publishing, printing, reproduction	38.3	48.5	0.0	13.2	0.0	0.0	0.0	100.0
Pharmaceuticals, cosmetics	16.9	17.3	3.7	34.8	4.8	9.2	13.4	100.0
Total	13.1	39.5	5.5	31.1	4.8	1.6	4.3	100.0

Source: SESSI.

Stage 4: the capabilities needed to protect know-how

A final study is in progress with the aim of clarifying firms' capabilities to manage technological appropriation and protect themselves against leakages of know-how. This should be concluded during the first half of 1997.

The survey questions are as follows:

CONTROLLING AND DEFENDING INTELLECTUAL PROPERTY

Patents, designs and patterns, brandnames and trade-marks

	Yes	No	Using special procedures		Using staff from outside the firm	
	Yes	No	Yes	No	Yes	No
1 – Do you continuously innovate and/or is the rate of innovation increasing?						
2 – Do you decide to file (or not to file) an industrial property title according to the overall benefit of the firm?						
3 – Do you take into account the risk of copying and imitation at the design stage of products or processes?						
4 – Do you keep the existence and dissemination of copies and imitations under surveillance?						
5 – Do you take legal action to counter copying and imitation?						
6 – Do you take action such as to degrade copies and imitations in the eyes of customers and the retail trade?						
7 – Do you identify your strategic knowledge and know-how?						
8 – Do you identify people holding strategic knowledge?						
9 – Do you make your staff aware of the strategic and confidential nature of this knowledge?						
10 – Do you monitor communications pertaining to this strategic knowledge?						
11 – Do you provide specific incentives to the persons holding strategic knowledge (by way of salary, career development, and so on) to prevent them from leaving?						
12 – When staff leave the firm do you ensure that the firm retains the maximum of strategic knowledge?						

Part VIII

Final Session

Chapter 23

LEARNING TO GOVERN IN THE KNOWLEDGE ECONOMY: POLICY CO-ORDINATION OR INSTITUTIONAL COMPETITION?

by

Peter J. Sheehan

Director, Centre for Strategic Economic Studies, Victoria University of Technology, Melbourne

Introduction

It is widely agreed that the global economy is in the early stages of an era of fundamental change, as the emerging information industries permeate all aspects of economic and social life. There is much emphasis on the necessity for improved methods of learning, as firms, individuals and institutions try to adjust to the new realities. But it is not so often realised that this is as much true of government as of any other group within society. Governments must learn – through a dynamic, iterative and often painful process – how to pursue the national interest effectively and efficiently in the new environment. This is likely to involve major changes in the attitudes, structures and relationships currently in place in developed countries, which have evolved over long periods to serve the needs of industrial societies.

This chapter briefly addresses some of these issues, and in this context touches on the question which is the title of this session: policy co-ordination or institutional competition? The paper is presented in five parts. In the first section I review briefly some of the characteristics of the knowledge economy and, in the second, explore some implications of these trends for the nature of the policy challenges faced by governments. The third section discusses the issue of policy co-ordination or institutional competition between the various relevant arms of government, a case being made for high level co-ordination and probably new structures to meet the challenges of the knowledge economy. The fourth section then comments on some mechanisms for intra-government co-ordination and the management of change, with particular reference to some Australian experience over the past decade or so. Conclusions are presented in the final section.

The knowledge economy: some characteristics

Different terms have been used in different sources to describe the quite new set of global economic activities emerging from the impact of the revolution in computing and communications technology. Here I follow OECD (1996) and the organisers of this conference in referring to this emerging set of activities as *the knowledge economy*. The defining technological fact leading to the knowledge economy is the ability to deliver codified knowledge, assembled on a global basis if necessary, very quickly and very cheaply to the area where it is needed, to transform such knowledge extensively as required and to make it effective in machines and other production and service delivery processes.

The fundamental changes underway concerning the production, storage and use of knowledge have, as has been widely recognised, major implications for the operation and control of national and international economies. Some of these implications are noted briefly below.

Goods industries

Some of the key trends in these industries include:

◊ continued dramatic improvements in the efficiency of production processes;

◊ increasing ability to customise goods for particular needs or individuals, including through the incorporation of "smart" capabilities into physical products;

◊ intensifying global competition in goods industries, and increasing pressures on firms in all countries; and

◊ the increasing importance of service activities within goods industries, reflecting the growing knowledge intensity of these industries and the progressive elimination of physical processes, such service activities often being deliverable across international borders.

Service industries

Within the services sector relevant trends include:

◊ growing ability to deliver codified knowledge, including images, to support the delivery of services;

◊ globalisation of service activities and industries, with rapid growth likely in the next two decades in the delivery of services across national and international broadband networks;

◊ increasing ability to meet the specific service needs of individuals, in areas such as health, education and entertainment, by remotely delivered services if necessary; and

◊ the continued importance of cultural, social and personal factors in the effective delivery of services.

General implications

Among the many general implications of these trends, the following may be particularly relevant to the present context:

◊   major adjustment processes in firms, community institutions and governments, as they search for effective responses to new pressures;

◊   rapidly increasing diversification of the range of goods and services available, with increasing resources being devoted to production of diverse products and to competition across global markets;

◊   signs of growing inequality in many communities, as the costs and benefits of the knowledge economy are unequally distributed; and

◊   pervasive uncertainty facing individuals and firms, as the nature of work and the basis of competitiveness change rapidly.

Aspects of these trends are explored in many recent sources, a central contribution being OECD, 1996; see also, *inter alia*, Dodgson and Rothwell, 1994; Freeman and Soete, 1994; National Research Council/World Bank, 1995; and, for a regional perspective, Sheehan *et al.*, 1995.

Implications for the nature of policy

As is well known, the standard neo-classical model on which so much of our policy and institutional structure is based is one which takes as given the existence of an adequate supply of firms with the necessary skills and capabilities; which assumes full information and complete markets, including in relation to future technological developments and the skill inputs to production; which assumes that technological change is external to the economic system, taking place as a result of the independent development of science rather than the intentional action of profit-seeking agents; which abstracts from increasing returns and feedback mechanisms, which otherwise might lead to increasing polarisation of economic outcomes for regions and countries, and so on. It is now clear that in these and other ways the basic neo-classical model falls far short of describing central features of modern economies – its application is restricted to a particular case, only to be seen in very special circumstances (Stiglitz, 1991).

This does not mean that the conclusions of that model should be automatically rejected. Recent economic history in many countries again demonstrates, for example, the importance of market mechanisms and the value of open economies and freer trade. But these are matters of experience and judgement, not absolute deliverances of theory, and should be interpreted in terms of their practical limitations and in the light of changing circumstances. In this pragmatic vein it is worth noting briefly some of the challenges for policy which seem to arise from the emerging knowledge economy, as a prelude to addressing some of the institutional issues. The nine points noted below are not put forward as a systematic or complete account, but simply as examples of the new policy challenges facing governments, many of which require integrated rather than portfolio-specific responses.

i) *Rapid changes in the competitiveness of firms, nations and regions.* In some industries, being internationally competitive is a matter of achieving competitive prices for relatively standard products in rapidly globalising markets, with the intensity of the competition increasingly daily, as new processes reduce costs and as new supplier countries enter the market. In many others it depends above all on the ability to access or create market-relevant knowledge, and to incorporate this knowledge in a timely manner in goods or services delivered to users. In either case the competitive position of firms and industries is changing rapidly, and the existence of a set of competitive firms able to secure the economic future of a given country or region cannot be taken for granted. Witness, for example, the rapid change in the position of Japan and the United States over the past five years; Japan's evident superiority in technology-based manufacturing processes giving way to the clear dominance of the United States in knowledge-based services. Another example is the growing doubts in many East Asian economies about whether they will be able to maintain rapid growth in the new era, as the global emphasis shifts from standard manufacturing products to knowledge-intensive goods and services. Thus the existence of firms, and indeed clusters of firms, with competitive capabilities sufficient to secure the economic position of a country or region becomes a central issue for policy. Dealing with global competition requires identifying and enhancing competitive knowledge strengths, firms and clusters of firms and other institutions in an open trading environment.

ii) *Distortions in the production and application of knowledge.* There are in many cases systematic distortions of the incentives facing those with the ability to produce and apply knowledge capable of generating social benefits; policy must address these distortions. There are many sources of these distortions, and most are well known. For example, much knowledge is created in not-for-profit research institutions, by individuals whose motivations are not linked to commercialisation; firms creating usable knowledge are not able to appropriate the full economic benefits of that knowledge, or to represent its value as an asset in financial markets; small firms creating knowledge often face heavy sunk costs, entry barriers and failures of capital markets which make it impossible for them to apply their knowledge effectively; in the services sector, much valuable knowledge is created in public-sector agencies, which lack mechanisms to support innovation and incentives to apply knowledge beyond the immediate environment. Many of these distortions have been the subject of discussion for decades, and governments have taken initiatives, with varying degrees of success. What is new is their increasingly systematic character, and their position at the heart of the knowledge economy.

iii) *Distortions in the use of the fruits of knowledge.* Equally important, but less widely noticed, is the often systematic imbalance between those new goods and services which will generate increased social welfare and those which will generate adequate returns in the market-place. This imbalance can arise because, for socially beneficial applications, producers cannot capture an adequate share of the benefits to provide a return on investment or because consumers are unable to pay, while applications which are profitable may return little social benefit. Take the global expansion of broadband telecommunication networks, for example. It is arguable that the advent of global optic-fibre networks reaching to the home or business site can have important economic and social benefits, particularly in areas such as businesses services, health and education. But it is difficult for private providers of network services to capture early returns from these applications. As a result communication carriers and others around the world are spending billions of dollars on the installation of fibre to the home, but with an emphasis on pay TV and home entertainment, often with an emphasis (as in Australia) on the highest income areas, most willing to pay for these services. These investments appear hard to justify, relative to others, on social cost/benefit terms; their specific character being driven by the market distortions. Certainly, in the presence of such distortions the standard response – that these are market-driven investments – does nothing to remove doubts about social inefficiency. This is just one example of what is likely to be an increasingly systematic issue; policy must also address these imbalances.

iv) *The knowledge economy is a service-activity economy.* Technology is leading to ever-increasing efficiency in the production of goods. This means that purchasing power and employment, but not to the same degree value added, is shifting to the services sectors. But it is a mistake to overemphasize the role of knowledge-intensive activities in the emerging economy, and in the emerging pattern of employment. Many jobs will not be skilled in traditional terms but may require different capabilities (*e.g.* interpersonal skills) to unskilled jobs in primary and secondary industries. Men, especially those whose employability has been based on physical characteristics such as strength and endurance, seem to be particularly at risk in this changing economic structure. Nevertheless, it remains true that the bulk of employment in the knowledge economy will be in the person-based services sector, and one explicit objective of policy should be to create a vibrant, efficient and growing services sector.

v) *Education and skill requirements are changing rapidly, in different ways in different industries, and are difficult to foresee.* This is related to the point above. While it is tempting to assume that, in the knowledge economy, skilled labour must be increasingly in demand, analysis of detailed occupational trends, for example in the United States and in Australia, suggests that the skill composition picture is much more complex. Many high-skill occupations are growing only slowly, while employment in some relatively low-skilled occupations is growing rapidly and in other relatively low-skilled occupations is falling quite sharply. The wage or skill level of an occupation is no guide to employment prospects. This is a powerful argument for strong generic education and training mechanisms. But, in addition, governments need agents and processes of change which are close to firms and industries, and which can influence educational and training institutions quickly.

vi) *Pressures for growing inequality in the knowledge economy.* There appear to be substantial pressures in the direction of increasing inequality in the knowledge economy, and there is an interplay between rising inequality and the distortions referred to above. For example, rising inequality means that the pattern of demand increasingly shifts to the highly diversified products preferred by higher income groups, reducing relative living standards for those on low incomes, and to applications of new technologies (for example, digital networks focused on home entertainment and personal services as noted above) which offer lower overall social returns than other applications (such as in health and education). Uncertainty, rapid change and global competition are placing a premium on the managerial, marketing and technological skills thought necessary for firm survival, relative to the more mundane skills provided by the bulk of the workforce. These and other factors are contributing to an increasing dispersion in the distribution of earned income in many countries. The various dimensions of policy must therefore address this apparent dynamic interlinking between technological change and rising inequality.

vii) *Balance in organisational adjustment processes – between flexible adjustment of factor use and emphasis on training and use of people as the central knowledge resource – is a critical issue.* The OECD *Jobs Strategy* report (OECD, 1996) valuably highlighted the different patterns of organisational adjustment observable across the OECD countries at present. In the Anglo-Saxon countries, rapid external adjustment is occurring in both public and private agencies, by the use of downsizing, restructuring, contracting out, and the use of consultants and short-term casual labour. In many cases this process seems to be proceeding without any regard for the need to retain key knowledge competencies and skills and to develop existing staff, or even of the value that committed staff can add to an organisation. In some European countries, by contrast, adjustment is focused mainly on internal adjustment, through retraining, reassignment and so on. While having great value, these processes alone may prove too slow to keep up with the rapid pace of global change. But the central point is that governments cannot stand aside from these changes, leaving them to the sole discretion of firms and agencies – their effectiveness is likely a key factor in the future position of national economies.

viii)*Expansionary macroeconomic policies and good growth rates remain essential if adjustment is to be achieved with acceptable levels of unemployment.* There is, at least as yet, no clear reason for believing that the technologies associated with the knowledge economy are responsible for rising aggregate unemployment rates in most OECD countries. Rates of growth of recorded labour productivity for virtually all of these countries have been lower, rather than higher, over the past two decades or so than in earlier decades. The most advanced economy, the United States, now has an unemployment rate comparable to that of the 1960s, although it is virtually unique in this regard. There are also reasons for thinking that there are strong anti-inflationary forces at work in the knowledge economy – notably the joint impact of technological change and global competition leading to falling prices for many traded goods and services – and perhaps to some overestimation of inflation. Thus, while specific policies to allow economies to adjust to the knowledge economy are necessary, these will be no substitute for balanced macroeconomic policies which permit rates of economic growth consistent with higher levels of employment.

There will, of course, be different constraints in different countries militating against such expansionary policies, constraints which in various ways may be made more severe by the present period of intense structural change. In Australia, for example, the dominant constraint is the current account deficit and the resulting high level of foreign debt, the deficit substantially reflecting the impact on Australia of the transition from resource-intensive to knowledge-intensive patterns of economic activity. In other countries the central constraint may be the budget deficit, itself exacerbated by slow economic growth and by the costs of declining industries and of high unemployment. In yet others inflation may be seen as the central issue, either because of wage pressures as employees try to maintain their position or because of the impact of uncertainty in generating continued adherence to low inflation targets.

ix) Both the level of revenue flowing to governments and the expenditure demands on governments will be heavily influenced by knowledge-economy trends. The endogenous character of both revenue and expenditure is a familiar theme of the theory and practice of public finance. Taxation receipts from companies and individuals depend directly on the level of economic activity, as do the cost of unemployment benefits and other economic and social programmes. But this endogeneity seems to be taking on a new intensity and developing a more profound structural dimension. Not only are the basic competitive structures of economies changing rapidly, in ways which may have major revenue implications, but whole components of revenue (*e.g.* many elements of capital taxation) are at risk as the on-line economy develops. On the expenditure side, both re-adjustment and new technologies may increase expenditure demands, but there are also major opportunities for the reduction of the costs of service delivery through judicious use of information technologies. It is no longer possible to manage the budget over the medium term in splendid isolation from technological change or from changing economic structures.

Policy co-ordination or institutional competition?

While there are many important differences between countries, the government institutional structure relevant to economic development in the OECD countries broadly revolves around five functions, and the various associated institutions, *viz*:

◊ a *Treasury/Finance function*, focused on the efficient operation of the national economy, the management of the budget and the oversight of fiscal and monetary policy;

◊ an *Industry/Science and Technology* function, often focused on the development of policies to assist individual industries, to help them to adjust to changes in the global economy, and to support the development and take-up of technology;

◊ a *Labour/Employment* function, placing emphasis on oversighting the terms and conditions of employment, on labour-market programmes for those on the margins of the labour force and for specific employment creation activities;

◊ an *Education and Training* function, with responsibility for national education systems at all levels and for major training programmes, such as apprenticeship programmes; and

◊ an *Environmental and Regulatory* function, monitoring the activities of firms and individuals and pursuing broader environmental goals.

Generally speaking, these functions are carried out by one or more departments reporting to a Minister, operating within a Cabinet system of government and decision making, but with very limited processes of co-ordination across government. While generalisations are dangerous and can be irresponsible, it is hard to resist the conclusion that in most countries the dominant feature is institutional competition rather than effective policy co-ordination.

This institutional structure has emerged not only from decades of experience but also from a widely shared commitment to what Stiglitz (1991) has called the *neo-classical synthesis*. This is the view that, while management of the economy over the short run requires intervention by way of monetary and fiscal polices, apart from this the economy should be treated as a self-adjusting market-based system on neo-classical lines. The separation of these five functions, and more importantly their management in relative isolation from one another, reflects belief in the assumptions of that neo-classical synthesis. As noted above, the standard neo-classical model assumes, *inter alia*, an adequate supply of competitive firms, full information and complete markets, exogenous technical change and skill formation, the absence of increasing returns and feedback mechanisms, and so on.

In short, this model validates an institutional structure in which the Treasury/Finance departments have the prime role of securing the efficient operation of the market economy, of controlling the revenue and expenditure flows of government, which arise predictably from that economy, and of managing cyclical fluctuations. The role of the other economic agencies is then to assist in improving the efficiency of firms and markets, to influence the exogenous development of technology and skills, to contribute to the take-up of those best-practice inputs by firms and to help to manage the adjustment processes forced on individuals and firms by market forces. The exogeneity of production inputs and the automaticity of market processes provides a rationale for discrete government functions, independently administered and co-ordinated only at the level of Cabinet decision making.

By the same token, the collapse of these assumptions – for example, the inherently endogenous processes of technology and skill formation, the need for continual re-creation of competitive strengths, the pervasive failures of full information and the existence of strong feedback mechanisms linked to the global economy – imply that this administrative model is no longer viable. While there is no apparent reason to call into question the five functions, none can any longer be administered in isolation. Each requires substantial and systematic input from the other areas if its objectives are to be achieved. Even more clearly, massive and effective co-ordination will be required if the overall objectives of government are to be achieved in the knowledge economy. New institutions are likely to be necessary to achieve this co-ordination.

Mechanisms for co-ordination and the management of change

My argument so far has been that quite new forms of policy co-ordination, involving both new structures and new initiatives, are likely to be necessary if governments are to serve their national interest effectively in the emerging knowledge economy. Evolution of these structures and initiatives will involve a substantial process of learning from diverse experiences, and of trial and error, before viable mechanisms effective for individual countries are developed.[1] In this section I make some initial comments on some of the mechanisms for co-ordination and for the management of change which may be worth considering, having specific regard to experience over the past decade at both the federal and state level in Australia. The Australian experience may be of some interest, given that the Australian economy has for some time been undergoing a process of structural change, now seen as a move from a resource-based economy with a protected manufacturing sector to one with a broader-based competitiveness arising from both resources and knowledge. Within Australia the case of the State of Victoria may also be of interest, since Victoria is the heart of both Australia's manufacturing sector and its knowledge base, and in the 1980s experimented with the most extensive methods of policy co-ordination so far tried in Australia. In respect of neither case do I claim to be an unbiased observer, having been involved to a significant degree in both cases,[2] and readers should interpret these remarks in the light of that caveat.

Australian Government economic policy 1983-90

Economic policy in Australia at the federal level has traditionally been dominated by the Australian Treasury, which has been a high-quality institution pursuing the common agenda of most Treasuries around the world, namely market-based efficiency, government frugality, fiscal balance and low inflation. Challenges to its power or to its agenda have been fiercely resisted, and bureaucratic war between Treasury and other agencies with economic responsibilities has been the norm. In 1965, for example, the Report of the Committee of Economic Enquiry (The Vernon Report) recommended, in a final section entitled "The Integration of Economic Policies", the establishment of an Advisory Council on Economic Growth. Treasury vehemently opposed the report and this particular recommendation, and Prime Minister Menzies eventually shelved the report after an extensive campaign orchestrated by Treasury.

The Hawke Labor Government was elected in March 1983, while the Australian economy was still in the midst of the 1982-83 recession. Its election policy had emphasized recovery from recession and job creation in a context of contained inflation, the proposed policy initiatives being primarily expansionary and mildly interventionist in nature. The centrepiece was the Prices and Incomes Accord, a centralised agreement between the government and the ACTU about the moderation of wages and the creation of jobs, and also involving some commitment to active industry policies. An early initiative was a National Economic Summit in April 1983, at which public consultation and debate took place between the government and a wide range of interested parties. The Summit was important both in stimulating confidence and in influencing some of the views of the government.

Under the influence of a range of diverse forces, from the Summit and its aftermath to the continuing impact of the Prices and Incomes Accord and of Treasury and its supporters, the structure of economic policy which emerged in Australia over the period 1983-93 was quite distinctive. Indeed, the distinctiveness of the policy mix is not widely understood. On the one hand, free-market principles were pursued aggressively in some areas, as evidenced in the deregulation of the financial system, the virtual abolition of tariffs, the introduction of competition into many hitherto monopoly sectors and the extensive programme of microeconomic reform which was put in train. Yet the linchpin of policy over the decade remained the Prices and Incomes Accord; a complex series of industry-specific policies were put in place, in areas ranging from motor vehicles and footwear, clothing and textiles to information technology products and pharmaceuticals – new science and technology policies implemented at that time have contributed to a fundamental change in the innovative activities of much of Australian industry. However, these "interventionist" policies were directed not at protecting inefficient or unproductive activities but at assisting firms and individuals to prepare for, and then to engage in, internationally competitive activities. Australia indeed developed its own unique blend of "plan and market" (for further documentation see Sheehan *et al.*, 1994, 1995).

The example of the science and technology policies is instructive. In 1983, following the identification of technology issues as of central importance at the National Economic Summit, a National Technology Conference was organised to give serious consideration to these matters. In the same year the Espie Committee of the Australian Academy of Technological Sciences published its important report, *Developing High Technology Enterprises in Australia* (Espie, 1983), and in 1984 a

National Technology Strategy was issued (DST, 1984), with a revised draft being issued in 1985 (DITC, 1985). The key initiatives arising from these activities provided the basis of the four-point programme progressively put in place over the decade, the key elements of which were:

◊ *the existence of powerful incentives for private businesses* to undertake R&D activities, in the form of the 150 per cent R&D allowance and particularly the Syndicated R&D Programme;

◊ *the strong focus on the commercialisation of public-sector research outcomes*, for example, through the encouragement of joint-venture or other collaborative research programmes and the setting of targets for external research revenue for key government agencies;

◊ *continuing support from the Commonwealth Budget for R&D activities*, as indicated in a 4.5 per cent per annum real growth in outlays and revenue foregone between 1984-85 and 1994-95; and

◊ *effective industry policies specifically encouraging R&D*, such as the Partnerships and Fixed-term Arrangements Programmes in the information technology and telecommunications areas and the Factor (f) Programme in pharmaceuticals.

There is little doubt that, taken as a whole, this amounted to the most powerful set of measures for the development and commercialisation of science and technology that Australia has yet seen. And the impact was equally striking. Business spending on R&D as a share of GDP increased four-fold between 1981-82 and 1995-96; the R&D intensity of manufacturing (the ratio of R&D to value added) also trebled, from 1.0 per cent in 1983 to 3.2 per cent in 1993, and many industries approached or exceeded OECD average levels; high-tech exports grew by 26 per cent per annum (in current US dollars) between 1986 and 1993, albeit from a low base.

In many respects the results of the broader mix of policies were impressive too, at least up until 1990. The orientation of Australian business changed dramatically over this time, there was a flowering of new technology-based businesses, employment grew strongly and inflation was relatively well contained, even in the late 1980's boom. But many of these benefits were swept away in the serious mismanagement of monetary policy over the period 1988-92, and the resulting deep recession of 1990-92. However, even from a broader perspective which is more relevant to this chapter, the distinctive set of policies was deeply flawed. In particular:

◊ they arose from the fortuitous outcome of strong, contending forces rather than from a shared vision of optimum economic policies;

◊ individual elements were always at risk, as the balance of power between contending forces changed;

◊ as a consequence, no structures were put in place for overall co-ordination of the policy set, or for assessing outcomes and planning future developments; and

◊ individual policies were often introduced in a crisis situation, when a particular development provided a political opportunity, and hence without proper planning or foresight.

In short there was no national or even government consensus about this set of policies, but rather competing views about free markets and intervention, and hence no systematic co-ordination mechanisms, but rather intense institutional competition. Given their relative success in this environment, one can only speculate on what might have been achieved if these policies had been implemented in the context of a shared view that both open free-market policies and judicious market-conforming interventions form an inevitable part of the optimum mix in the knowledge economy, and that appropriate institutions to co-ordinate such policies are required.

The Victorian Economic Strategy 1983-90

In April 1982 the Cain Labor Government was elected in the State of Victoria, a state which contains about 25 per cent of Australia's population, but accounts for about 35 per cent of national manufacturing output and R&D. Perceptions about Victoria's long-term future were depressed in the early 1980s, because of its dependence on manufacturing at a time when growth prospects in Australia were seen as being largely concentrated on resources and tourism. One element of this government's election policy was that it would introduce systematic, strategic initiatives to address Victoria's long-term economic growth and competitiveness. To give effect to this, it proposed to create, and in the event did create, a new department (the Department of Management of Budget – DMB) which would incorporate all the traditional Treasury and Finance functions but would also take a lead role in the formulation and implementation of a broadly based economic strategy to promote the state's economic development. This was explicitly an attempt to respond to the traditional Australian antagonism between the central finance agency and other economic departments.

DMB was established in November 1983, and in April 1984 the first strategy statement – *Victoria: The Next Steps* – was published, and for the next six years this strategy was the over-riding focus of government policy. Its basic objective was to promote long-term growth in income and employment by strengthening the international competitiveness of the economy. This was to be achieved by action on two fronts. Firstly, diverse reforms impinging on both the public and the private sector would be pursued (*e.g.* increased efficiency in public instruments, reform of taxes and charges, improved regulatory processes) to make the general environment more competitive. Secondly, nine areas of competitive strength were identified – areas where the State was seen as having the foundations of continuing international competitiveness – and plans of action were developed to enhance those strengths and to encourage greater economic development on the basis of them.

Over the six-year period dozens of strategy documents were produced and hundreds of initiatives were put in train. But the most distinctive feature of this experiment, from our present perspective, was that the co-ordination was primarily carried out through the central finance agency, and the primary means of co-ordination was the annual budget. Departmental budget submissions were assessed in part on the extent to which they contributed to strategy objectives, financial allocations in part reflected that assessment, and both departments and DMB reported on strategy outcomes at the time of the annual budget. Not surprisingly, departments responded actively in reshaping their programmes to some degree in a manner consistent with the government's economic objectives.

Another important feature of the Economic Strategy was action driven by the view that, especially in the knowledge-intensive sectors, Victoria lacked the competitive firms and other institutions to take full advantage of its competitive strengths. This led to a systematic attempt to create, in partnership with the private sector, firms and other institutions which were of a scale to compete effectively themselves or which would assist firms to become more competitive. Eleven such organisations are listed in the following box. The top five are companies and are focused on long-term competitive activities on the world scene. All are accepted as leading firms in their areas in Australia in 1997. With the exception of the Victorian Education Foundation, the other five research and facilitative institutions shown are still active and effective on a national basis in 1997. While not all initiatives were equally successful, this aspect of the experiment did suggest that carefully planned initiatives involving public/private co-operation can indeed augment the nation's competitive base.

It is perhaps worth dwelling a little on some of the objectives of three of these newly created companies, to illustrate the diverse reasons why government initiatives may be necessary:

◊ Australia is a leading country in the refining of alumina and smelting of aluminium, but the global plans of the multinational firms which dominate these activities in Australia preclude any substantial downstream activities in the country. *Aluvic* was established to manage the Victorian Government's 25 per cent interest in the Portland smelter and to develop from this base the light metals industry in Australia. It is acknowledged as highly successful in managing the diverse risks involved in the aluminium business, and has applied these skills to developing a position in the global aerospace fabrication industry.

◊ Two of Australia's key strengths in knowledge-intensive areas are in medical research and software development, although the position is quite different in the two areas. In medical research the strength lies in many world-leading academic research institutions, but there is virtually no national presence in the pharmaceuticals industry. *Amrad* is a company set up, initially in public ownership but with equity participation by the key research institutes, to build a major pharmaceutical company on the basis of this research capability. Ten year's on, and now in majority private ownership, it shows real promise of becoming a global force in this industry.

Selected public/private organisations established in Victoria, 1985-90

Aluminium Smelters of Victoria Ltd (Aluvic)
Australian Artificial Intelligence Institute (AAII)
Australian Computing and Communications Institute (ACCI)
Australian Medical Research and Development Corporation Ltd (AMRAD)
Ceramic Fuels Cells Ltd

Biomolecular Research Institute (BRI)
Centre for International Research on Communications and
Information Technologies (CIRCIT)
Industrial Supplies Office (OSI)
Overseas Projects Corporation of Victoria (OPCV)
Strategic Industry Research Foundation (SIRF)
Victorian Education Foundation (VEF)

◊ *ACCI* is a not-for-profit company, the members of which are both private firms (*e.g.* IBM, Computer Power) and public agencies, set up to create critical mass to link Australia's real but dissipated expertise in software and communications into global markets. It is in the process of spinning off two business into majority private ownership – Australian Business Access, an advanced technology Internet business, and Tentas, a telemedical products and services company – both of which are leaders in Australia and look poised to have a significant impact in South and East Asia

Like aspects of the Hawke Government programme, the Victorian Economic Strategy was a casualty of the monetary turmoil of 1988-90 and of the deep slump which began in 1990. The Department of Management and Budget was split into traditional Treasury and Finance Departments in April 1990, and some functions were transferred to other departments. By mid 1990 the attempt to co-ordinate Victorian policy through an overall strategy had been abandoned. It is difficult to separate the impact of the Economic Strategy from the turmoil of 1990 and the controversy to which it gave rise. On the one hand, the attempt to provide a coherent long-term vision was strongly supported by business and other economic agents; Victoria's performance relative to other states on the major economic indicators was much stronger over the 1983-90 period than either before or since; many institutions and structures were created which are central to the State's economy today. On the other hand, the experiment in co-ordination was abandoned in 1990 in an environment of great hostility and controversy, with accusations of uncontrolled debt levels and with an intense focus on initiatives which proved unsuccessful. Reflecting a collapse of confidence and other factors, the economic performance of Victoria since 1990 has been much weaker than that of the rest of Australia taken as a whole.

My own assessment of this experiment, on the issues relevant to this paper, is three-fold.

◊ The ambitious attempt to bring an overall economic co-ordinating function together with the budget and financial management function, so that government strategies can be implemented in an integrated way through the whole of the budgetary process rather than just through individual programmes, has much to recommend it. There are dangers, however, in concentrating such a workload in one agency, especially if it is not adequately resourced. In Victoria, DMB became increasingly unable to cope adequately, in part because of the perceived success of the strategy and the additional programmes which it generated.

◊ A broader consensus than prevailed in Victoria is necessary if such a long-term co-ordination process is to be successful, and if the institutions charged with co-ordination are to be able to do their work effectively. Successes and failures are inevitable in any such exercise, and progress will be made only if lessons can be learnt from both.

◊ Conscious and systematic co-operation with the private sector, both to change the behaviour of public sector institutions and to create new firms and institutions in areas of potential competitive strength, can be very effective and can contribute to increased competitiveness with only modest financial outlays.

Conclusions

My central argument is that quite new forms of policy co-ordination, involving both new structures and new initiatives, are likely to be necessary if governments are to be able to govern in the emerging knowledge economy. The evolution of these structures and initiatives will involve a substantial process of learning from diverse experiences, and of trial and error, before viable mechanisms effective for individual countries are developed. In this process of learning the lessons of past experience in many countries will be invaluable. The Australian experience is a salutary reminder both of the need for co-ordination of policy and of the intense difficulties of achieving such co-ordination in modern democratic societies with widely diversified views about appropriate economic strategies.

NOTES

1. Chalmers Johnson's seminal work, *MITI and the Japanese Miracle* (Johnson, 1982), documents in impressive detail the process of trial and error over more than 50 years in developing the institutions and policies which lay behind the rapid economic expansion in Japan over the 1950s to the 1970s. Similar large-scale institutional and policy experimentation is likely to be necessary in responding to the emergence of the knowledge economy.

2. As a contributor to the development of the Hawke Government's policies in the decade prior to its election in 1983, as special adviser to the Prime Minister and Treasurer in 1983 and as Director General of the Department of Management and Budget in Victoria 1982-90.

REFERENCES

DIST (Department of Industry, Science and Tourism) (1996), *Australian Business Innovation: A Strategic Analysis*, AGPS, Canberra.

DITC (Department of Industry, Technology and Commerce) and Department of Science (1985), "Technology Strategy – Revised Discussion Draft", Canberra.

DODGSON, M. and R. ROTHWELL (eds.) (1994), *The Handbook of Industrial Innovation*, Edward Elgar, Cheltenham.

DST (Department of Science and Technology) (1984), *National Technology Strategy*, Canberra.

ESPIE, N. (1983), *Developing High Technology Enterprises in Australia,* Australian Academy of Technological Sciences, Canberra.

FREEMAN, C. and L. SOETE (1994), *Work for All or Mass Unemployment?*, Pinter Publishers, London.

JOHNSON, C. (1982), *MITI and the Japanese Miracle,* Stanford University Press.

NATIONAL RESEARCH COUNCIL and THE WORLD BANK (1995), *Marshalling Technology for Development*, Washington.

OECD (1996), *Technology, Productivity and Job Creation*, Paris.

SHEEHAN, P.J., N. PAPPAS and E. CHENG (1994), *The Rebirth of Australian Industry: Australian Trade in Elaborately Transformed Manufactures 1979-1993,* Centre for Strategic Economic Studies, Victoria University, Melbourne.

SHEEHAN, P.J., N. PAPPAS, G. TIKHOMIROVA and P. SINCLAIR (1995), *Australia and the Knowledge Economy: An Assessment of Enhanced Economic Growth Through Science and Technology*, Centre for Strategic Economic Studies, Victoria University, Melbourne.

STIGLITZ, J.E. (1991), "Information and Economic Analysis: A Perspective", NBER Working Paper No. 3641, National Bureau of Economic Research, Cambridge, MA.

VICTORIAN GOVERNMENT (1984) *Victoria: The Next Steps*, Victorian Government Printing Office, Melbourne.

MAIN SALES OUTLETS OF OECD PUBLICATIONS
PRINCIPAUX POINTS DE VENTE DES PUBLICATIONS DE L'OCDE

AUSTRALIA – AUSTRALIE
D.A. Information Services
648 Whitehorse Road, P.O.B 163
Mitcham, Victoria 3132   Tel. (03) 9210.7777
    Fax: (03) 9210.7788

AUSTRIA – AUTRICHE
Gerold & Co.
Graben 31
Wien I   Tel. (0222) 533.50.14
    Fax: (0222) 512.47.31.29

BELGIUM – BELGIQUE
Jean De Lannoy
Avenue du Roi, Koningslaan 202
B-1060 Bruxelles   Tel. (02) 538.51.69/538.08.41
    Fax: (02) 538.08.41

CANADA
Renouf Publishing Company Ltd.
5369 Canotek Road
Unit 1
Ottawa, Ont. K1J 9J3   Tel. (613) 745.2665
    Fax: (613) 745.7660

Stores:
71 1/2 Sparks Street
Ottawa, Ont. K1P 5R1   Tel. (613) 238.8985
    Fax: (613) 238.6041

12 Adelaide Street West
Toronto, QN M5H 1L6   Tel. (416) 363.3171
    Fax: (416) 363.5963

Les Éditions La Liberté Inc.
3020 Chemin Sainte-Foy
Sainte-Foy, PQ G1X 3V6   Tel. (418) 658.3763
    Fax: (418) 658.3763

Federal Publications Inc.
165 University Avenue, Suite 701
Toronto, ON M5H 3B8   Tel. (416) 860.1611
    Fax: (416) 860.1608

Les Publications Fédérales
1185 Université
Montréal, QC H3B 3A7   Tel. (514) 954.1633
    Fax: (514) 954.1635

CHINA – CHINE
Book Dept., China National Publications
Import and Export Corporation (CNPIEC)
16 Gongti E. Road, Chaoyang District
Beijing 100020   Tel. (10) 6506-6688 Ext. 8402
    (10) 6506-3101

CHINESE TAIPEI – TAIPEI CHINOIS
Good Faith Worldwide Int'l. Co. Ltd.
9th Floor, No. 118, Sec. 2
Chung Hsiao E. Road
Taipei   Tel. (02) 391.7396/391.7397
    Fax: (02) 394.9176

**CZECH REPUBLIC –
RÉPUBLIQUE TCHÈQUE**
National Information Centre
NIS – prodejna
Konviktská 5
Praha 1 – 113 57   Tel. (02) 24.23.09.07
    Fax: (02) 24.22.94.33
E-mail: nkposp@dec.niz.cz
Internet: http://www.nis.cz

DENMARK – DANEMARK
Munksgaard Book and Subscription Service
35, Nørre Søgade, P.O. Box 2148
DK-1016 København K   Tel. (33) 12.85.70
    Fax: (33) 12.93.87

J. H. Schultz Information A/S,
Herstedvang 12,
DK – 2620 Albertslung   Tel. 43 63 23 00
    Fax: 43 63 19 69

Internet: s-info@inet.uni-c.dk

EGYPT – ÉGYPTE
The Middle East Observer
41 Sherif Street
Cairo   Tel. (2) 392.6919
    Fax: (2) 360.6804

FINLAND – FINLANDE
Akateeminen Kirjakauppa
Keskuskatu 1, P.O. Box 128
00100 Helsinki

Subscription Services/Agence d'abonnements :
P.O. Box 23
00100 Helsinki   Tel. (358) 9.121.4403
    Fax: (358) 9.121.4450

*FRANCE
OECD/OCDE
Mail Orders/Commandes par correspondance :
2, rue André-Pascal
75775 Paris Cedex 16   Tel. 33 (0)1.45.24.82.00
    Fax: 33 (0)1.49.10.42.76
    Telex: 640048 OCDE
Internet: Compte.PUBSINQ@oecd.org

Orders via Minitel, France only/
Commandes par Minitel, France exclusivement :
36 15 OCDE

OECD Bookshop/Librairie de l'OCDE :
33, rue Octave-Feuillet
75016 Paris   Tel. 33 (0)1.45.24.81.81
    33 (0)1.45.24.81.67

Dawson
B.P. 40
91121 Palaiseau Cedex   Tel. 01.89.10.47.00
    Fax: 01.64.54.83.26

Documentation Française
29, quai Voltaire
75007 Paris   Tel. 01.40.15.70.00

Economica
49, rue Héricart
75015 Paris   Tel. 01.45.78.12.92
    Fax: 01.45.75.05.67

Gibert Jeune (Droit-Économie)
6, place Saint-Michel
75006 Paris   Tel. 01.43.25.91.19

Librairie du Commerce International
10, avenue d'Iéna
75016 Paris   Tel. 01.40.73.34.60

Librairie Dunod
Université Paris-Dauphine
Place du Maréchal-de-Lattre-de-Tassigny
75016 Paris   Tel. 01.44.05.40.13

Librairie Lavoisier
11, rue Lavoisier
75008 Paris   Tel. 01.42.65.39.95

Librairie des Sciences Politiques
30, rue Saint-Guillaume
75007 Paris   Tel. 01.45.48.36.02

P.U.F.
49, boulevard Saint-Michel
75005 Paris   Tel. 01.43.25.83.40

Librairie de l'Université
12a, rue Nazareth
13100 Aix-en-Provence   Tel. 04.42.26.18.08

Documentation Française
165, rue Garibaldi
69003 Lyon   Tel. 04.78.63.32.23

Librairie Decitre
29, place Bellecour
69002 Lyon   Tel. 04.72.40.54.54

Librairie Sauramps
Le Triangle
34967 Montpellier Cedex 2   Tel. 04.67.58.85.15
    Fax: 04.67.58.27.36

A la Sorbonne Actual
23, rue de l'Hôtel-des-Postes
06000 Nice   Tel. 04.93.13.77.75
    Fax: 04.93.80.75.69

GERMANY – ALLEMAGNE
OECD Bonn Centre
August-Bebel-Allee 6
D-53175 Bonn   Tel. (0228) 959.120
    Fax: (0228) 959.12.17

GREECE – GRÈCE
Librairie Kauffmann
Stadiou 28
10564 Athens   Tel. (01) 32.55.321
    Fax: (01) 32.30.320

HONG-KONG
Swindon Book Co. Ltd.
Astoria Bldg. 3F
34 Ashley Road, Tsimshatsui
Kowloon, Hong Kong   Tel. 2376.2062
    Fax: 2376.0685

HUNGARY – HONGRIE
Euro Info Service
Margitsziget, Európa Ház
1138 Budapest   Tel. (1) 111.60.61
    Fax: (1) 302.50.35
E-mail: euroinfo@mail.matav.hu
Internet: http://www.euroinfo.hu//index.html

ICELAND – ISLANDE
Mál og Menning
Laugavegi 18, Pósthólf 392
121 Reykjavik   Tel. (1) 552.4240
    Fax: (1) 562.3523

INDIA – INDE
Oxford Book and Stationery Co.
Scindia House
New Delhi 110001   Tel. (11) 331.5896/5308
    Fax: (11) 332.2639
E-mail: oxford.publ@axcess.net.in

17 Park Street
Calcutta 700016   Tel. 240832

INDONESIA – INDONÉSIE
Pdii-Lipi
P.O. Box 4298
Jakarta 12042   Tel. (21) 573.34.67
    Fax: (21) 573.34.67

IRELAND – IRLANDE
Government Supplies Agency
Publications Section
4/5 Harcourt Road
Dublin 2   Tel. 661.31.11
    Fax: 475.27.60

ISRAEL – ISRAËL
Praedicta
5 Shatner Street
P.O. Box 34030
Jerusalem 91430   Tel. (2) 652.84.90/1/2
    Fax: (2) 652.84.93

R.O.Y. International
P.O. Box 13056
Tel Aviv 61130   Tel. (3) 546 1423
    Fax: (3) 546 1442
E-mail: royil@netvision.net.il

Palestinian Authority/Middle East:
INDEX Information Services
P.O.B. 19502
Jerusalem   Tel. (2) 627.16.34
    Fax: (2) 627.12.19

ITALY – ITALIE
Libreria Commissionaria Sansoni
Via Duca di Calabria, 1/1
50125 Firenze   Tel. (055) 64.54.15
    Fax: (055) 64.12.57
E-mail: licosa@ftbcc.it

Via Bartolini 29
20155 Milano   Tel. (02) 36.50.83

Editrice e Libreria Herder
Piazza Montecitorio 120
00186 Roma   Tel. 679.46.28
    Fax: 678.47.51

Libreria Hoepli
Via Hoepli 5
20121 Milano   Tel. (02) 86.54.46
    Fax: (02) 805.28.86

Libreria Scientifica
Dott. Lucio de Biasio 'Aeiou'
Via Coronelli, 6
20146 Milano
Tel. (02) 48.95.45.52
Fax: (02) 48.95.45.48

JAPAN – JAPON
OECD Tokyo Centre
Landic Akasaka Building
2-3-4 Akasaka, Minato-ku
Tokyo 107
Tel. (81.3) 3586.2016
Fax: (81.3) 3584.7929

KOREA – CORÉE
Kyobo Book Centre Co. Ltd.
P.O. Box 1658, Kwang Hwa Moon
Seoul
Tel. 730.78.91
Fax: 735.00.30

MALAYSIA – MALAISIE
University of Malaya Bookshop
University of Malaya
P.O. Box 1127, Jalan Pantai Baru
59700 Kuala Lumpur
Malaysia
Tel. 756.5000/756.5425
Fax: 756.3246

MEXICO – MEXIQUE
OECD Mexico Centre
Edificio INFOTEC
Av. San Fernando no. 37
Col. Toriello Guerra
Tlalpan C.P. 14050
Mexico D.F.
Tel. (525) 528.10.38
Fax: (525) 606.13.07
E-mail: ocde@rtn.net.mx

NETHERLANDS – PAYS-BAS
SDU Uitgeverij Plantijnstraat
Externe Fondsen
Postbus 20014
2500 EA's-Gravenhage
Tel. (070) 37.89.880
Voor bestellingen:
Fax: (070) 34.75.778

Subscription Agency/ Agence d'abonnements :
SWETS & ZEITLINGER BV
Heereweg 347B
P.O. Box 830
2160 SZ Lisse
Tel. 252.435.111
Fax: 252.415.888

NEW ZEALAND – NOUVELLE-ZÉLANDE
GPLegislation Services
P.O. Box 12418
Thorndon, Wellington
Tel. (04) 496.5655
Fax: (04) 496.5698

NORWAY – NORVÈGE
NIC INFO A/S
Ostensjoveien 18
P.O. Box 6512 Etterstad
0606 Oslo
Tel. (22) 97.45.00
Fax: (22) 97.45.45

PAKISTAN
Mirza Book Agency
65 Shahrah Quaid-E-Azam
Lahore 54000
Tel. (42) 735.36.01
Fax: (42) 576.37.14

PHILIPPINE – PHILIPPINES
International Booksource Center Inc.
Rm 179/920 Cityland 10 Condo Tower 2
HV dela Costa Ext cor Valero St.
Makati Metro Manila
Tel. (632) 817 9676
Fax: (632) 817 1741

POLAND – POLOGNE
Ars Polona
00-950 Warszawa
Krakowskie Prezdmiescie 7
Tel. (22) 264760
Fax: (22) 265334

PORTUGAL
Livraria Portugal
Rua do Carmo 70-74
Apart. 2681
1200 Lisboa
Tel. (01) 347.49.82/5
Fax: (01) 347.02.64

SINGAPORE – SINGAPOUR
Ashgate Publishing
Asia Pacific Pte. Ltd
Golden Wheel Building, 04-03
41, Kallang Pudding Road
Singapore 349316
Tel. 741.5166
Fax: 742.9356

SPAIN – ESPAGNE
Mundi-Prensa Libros S.A.
Castelló 37, Apartado 1223
Madrid 28001
Tel. (91) 431.33.99
Fax: (91) 575.39.98
E-mail: mundiprensa@tsai.es
Internet: http://www.mundiprensa.es

Mundi-Prensa Barcelona
Consell de Cent No. 391
08009 – Barcelona
Tel. (93) 488.34.92
Fax: (93) 487.76.59

Libreria de la Generalitat
Palau Moja
Rambla dels Estudis, 118
08002 – Barcelona
(Suscripciones) Tel. (93) 318.80.12
(Publicaciones) Tel. (93) 302.67.23
Fax: (93) 412.18.54

SRI LANKA
Centre for Policy Research
c/o Colombo Agencies Ltd.
No. 300-304, Galle Road
Colombo 3
Tel. (1) 574240, 573551-2
Fax: (1) 575394, 510711

SWEDEN – SUÈDE
CE Fritzes AB
S–106 47 Stockholm
Tel. (08) 690.90.90
Fax: (08) 20.50.21

For electronic publications only/
Publications électroniques seulement
STATISTICS SWEDEN
Informationsservice
S-115 81 Stockholm
Tel. 8 783 5066
Fax: 8 783 4045

Subscription Agency/Agence d'abonnements :
Wennergren-Williams Info AB
P.O. Box 1305
171 25 Solna
Tel. (08) 705.97.50
Fax: (08) 27.00.71

Liber distribution
Internatinal organizations
Fagerstagatan 21
S-163 52 Spanga

SWITZERLAND – SUISSE
Maditec S.A. (Books and Periodicals/Livres
et périodiques)
Chemin des Palettes 4
Case postale 266
1020 Renens VD 1
Tel. (021) 635.08.65
Fax: (021) 635.07.80

Librairie Payot S.A.
4, place Pépinet
CP 3212
1002 Lausanne
Tel. (021) 320.25.11
Fax: (021) 320.25.14

Librairie Unilivres
6, rue de Candolle
1205 Genève
Tel. (022) 320.26.23
Fax: (022) 329.73.18

Subscription Agency/Agence d'abonnements :
Dynapresse Marketing S.A.
38, avenue Vibert
1227 Carouge
Tel. (022) 308.08.70
Fax: (022) 308.07.99

See also – Voir aussi :
OECD Bonn Centre
August-Bebel-Allee 6
D-53175 Bonn (Germany)
Tel. (0228) 959.120
Fax: (0228) 959.12.17

THAILAND – THAÏLANDE
Suksit Siam Co. Ltd.
113, 115 Fuang Nakhon Rd.
Opp. Wat Rajbopith
Bangkok 10200
Tel. (662) 225.9531/2
Fax: (662) 222.5188

**TRINIDAD & TOBAGO, CARIBBEAN
TRINITÉ-ET-TOBAGO, CARAÏBES**
Systematics Studies Limited
9 Watts Street
Curepe
Trinidad & Tobago, W.I.
Tel. (1809) 645.3475
Fax: (1809) 662.5654
E-mail: tobe@trinidad.net

TUNISIA – TUNISIE
Grande Librairie Spécialisée
Fendri Ali
Avenue Haffouz Imm El-Intilaka
Bloc B 1 Sfax 3000
Tel. (216-4) 296 855
Fax: (216-4) 298.270

TURKEY – TURQUIE
Kültür Yayinlari Is-Türk Ltd.
Atatürk Bulvari No. 191/Kat 13
06684 Kavaklidere/Ankara
Tel. (312) 428.11.40 Ext. 2458
Fax : (312) 417.24.90

Dolmabahce Cad. No. 29
Besiktas/Istanbul
Tel. (212) 260 7188

UNITED KINGDOM – ROYAUME-UNI
The Stationery Office Ltd.
Postal orders only:
P.O. Box 276, London SW8 5DT
Gen. enquiries
Tel. (171) 873 0011
Fax: (171) 873 8463

The Stationery Office Ltd.
Postal orders only:
49 High Holborn, London WC1V 6HB

Branches at: Belfast, Birmingham, Bristol,
Edinburgh, Manchester

UNITED STATES – ÉTATS-UNIS
OECD Washington Center
2001 L Street N.W., Suite 650
Washington, D.C. 20036-4922 Tel. (202) 785.6323
Fax: (202) 785.0350
Internet: washcont@oecd.org

Subscriptions to OECD periodicals may also be
placed through main subscription agencies.

Les abonnements aux publications périodiques de
l'OCDE peuvent être souscrits auprès des
principales agences d'abonnement.

Orders and inquiries from countries where Distribu-
tors have not yet been appointed should be sent to:
OECD Publications, 2, rue André-Pascal, 75775
Paris Cedex 16, France.

Les commandes provenant de pays où l'OCDE n'a
pas encore désigné de distributeur peuvent être
adressées aux Éditions de l'OCDE, 2, rue André-
Pascal, 75775 Paris Cedex 16, France.

12-1996

OECD PUBLICATIONS, 2, rue André-Pascal, 75775 PARIS CEDEX 16
PRINTED IN FRANCE
(70 97 03 1 P) ISBN 92-64-15679-8 – No. 49803 1997